My GENTLE MUSINGS

One woman's journey
of self discovery

KAREN JOHANNSEN

ENDORSEMENTS

Karen's extensive knowledge, deep wisdom, and compassionate nature shine through in every one of her 'gentle musings.' Her open-hearted honesty reverberates as clearly as a tuning fork. Her words bring recognition, comfort, and inspiration. Kudos, Karen, and thank you.

—Marianne Streich, Reiki Master Teacher and Practitioner, and author of *Reiki, A Guide for the Practice of Levels I and II*, Lynnwood, Washington

In her book, *My Gentle Musings*, Karen speaks from the foundation of what it means to be human, to struggle with the reality of our desires, pain, dreams, and imaginings. Through her writing, we find a place to understand our own struggles around holding on, letting go, and navigating the prickly parts of inner and outer relationships.

—Therese Antony, Executive Director, *Soul Bridging*

In Karen Johannsen's enjoyable new book, she shares her quest for truth, and for personal growth and change as she addresses issues that we all face. She applies a spiritual lens to her life and is a mentor for all of us. She is a wise and loving teacher.

—Sharlyn Hidalgo, author of *The Healing Power of Trees,* and *Nazmy: Love is My Religion*

This book is truly a gem. Karen's wisdom, humor and honesty shine like a beacon of light for us all. On every page we receive insights and guidance for how to live a more authentic life. It is truly a toolkit for navigating the everyday ups and downs that we all face. A book to keep on your nightstand!

—Sheryl Guidera, retired business owner

Additional endorsements on the back cover.

MY

GENTLE
MUSINGS

*One woman's journey
of self discovery*

KAREN JOHANNSEN

Starseed Publications
an imprint of Lorian Press LLC
lorianpress.com

My Gentle Musings
One woman's journey of self discovery

Cover photograph and design by Coren Lindfield

Print ISBN: 978-1-939790-25-5

Johannsen, Karen
My Gentle Musings: One woman's journey of self discovery/ Karen Johannsen

First Edition: February 2019

Printed in the United States of America, the United Kingdom and Australia

Starseed Publications
an imprint of Lorian Press LLC
lorianpress.com

DEDICATION

To men and women everywhere who courageously stand up, speak
their truth and share their stories with the world.
Together we rise.

CONTENTS

INTRODUCTION 1

THE INCARNATION OF KAREN...1

CHAPTER 1: THE BOOK 9

    Spring Equinox and the Aries Festival of Spring   10

    Spring Cleaning – poem   11

    Moving Forward   13

    Anxiety and the Inner Critic   15

    Cargo – poem   17

    On the Road   18

CHAPTER 2: SELF-LOVE...21

    The Burning Ground New Moon in Aries   23

    The Mantram of the Disciple   24

    Magnificence   25

    More on Self Love   28

    I Know A Woman – poem   28

    I Am Enough   33

    Lovingkindness   34

    Humility   36

    Meditation on Humility   39

CHAPTER 3: JUDGING AND CRITICISM 41

    We Are All Trees   42

    We Are All Trees ... and more (Part II)   44

    Revisiting a Gremlin   46

    Lessons From the Gym... "Just Like Me"   49

CHAPTER 4: ANGER..51

    Anger is My Edge   52

    Anger is My Edge, Part II   54

    Anger is My Edge, Part III   57

    My Last Blog on Anger, I Promise   59

CHAPTER 5: HUMOR 61

    Just for Laughs   62

    Just for Fun   63

CHAPTER 6: JOY 65

Pain and the Open Heart 66

Movin' and Shaking 68

CHAPTER 7: CANCER MOON AND THE RHYTHMS OF LIFE 71

Belonging 72

In Between Times 73

My Grandson Has Finally Arrived 74

A Cancer Grammy 76

CHAPTER 8: DETACHMENT AND LETTING GO 79

Frustration Cure #1, and #2, and #3 81

She Let Go – poem 82

More Letting Go 84

Freedom 87

A Small Step for Karen, a Giant Leap for her Cancer Moon 89

Another Layer of Letting Go 92

CHAPTER 9: TRUST..97

Wise Effort 99

Lions and Tigers and Spiders, Oh My!! 101

A Bit of Philosophizing 102

Sitting With Ram Dass 104

Warrior Am I 107

Lazarus Blessing – poem 109

God Works in Mysterious Ways... Yes, She Does 111

Warrior, Warrior, Wherefore Art Thou, Warrior? 114

Did Curiosity Kill the Cat? I Don't Think So 116

CHAPTER 10: BOUNDARIES AND CODEPENDENCE 119

Taking People at Their Word 121

When Understanding is Not Enough 123

Every Day, in Every Way, I Just Keep Learning 125

Taking My Stand, For Others 127

Breathing In 129

Ouch (x3) 131

CHAPTER 11: INJURY 135

Mindful Attention 136

The Pity Pot 139

We All Need Somebody to Lean On   143
Resting in Each Step – poem   145
A Note I Sent Out to All My Friends and Family   146
Change Me Prayers   147
The Rhythm – poem   149
Listening to My Body   150
And My Life is Really Very Blessed   152
Sugar, and Caffeine and Popcorn, Oh My!!   154
Over the Funk, Part II   157
The In Between – poem   158
Honoring the Pause   160
Lessons From The Hermit   162
Claiming My Space   164

CHAPTER 12: ALL ABOUT SCORPIO 167
Scorpio and the Hydra   170
Scorpionic Revelations   172
The Aftermath   174
Acceptance, Loving Attention, and Clarity   177
What If Today We Were Grateful for Everything?   179

CHAPTER 13: HOLY DAYS 181
Pwetty Wites   184
Preparing for Wesak, An Invitation   185
Illuminating Hope   187
Stepping into Stillness   189
Welcoming Winter Solstice   192
Blessing in the Chaos – poem   192
Entering 2016, Gently and Lovingly   195
The Great Root on Which We Live: 198
Honoring the Summer Solstice   198
I Build a Lighted House and Therein Dwell   200
The Prayer Tree   201
A Sweet Easter Blessing   203
Signs and Synchronicities   204
LUGHNA… WHAT?   207
Care Of The Growing Crop – poem   208

CHAPTER 14: SHIT HAPPENS...211
A Five-Day Personal Retreat? Hmmmmm, Not So Much   212

CHAPTER 15: SURRENDER 217
A Little Act of Surrender   219
An "Aha" Moment in the Dentist's Chair   221
At War with Nighttime   223
Insomnia Blessing – poem   225

CHAPTER 16: OPENING THE HEART TO GREATER LOVE 227
Can I Love More?   228
I Want to Know What Love Is   231
Unconditional Loving   233

CHAPTER 17: MAGIC...237
Do You Believe in Magic?   238
Can it Really Be That Simple? The Magic of Asking   241

CHAPTER 18: SEX, ONLINE DATING, AND PARTNERSHIPS............245
Single on Purpose   260

CHAPTER 19: AGING AND DYING 265
What's So Funny About Getting Older?   267
On Turning Seventy-Four   269
On Being Mortal   274

ACKNOWLEDGMENTS 276

APPENDIX...277
The Ten Tenets of the Esoteric Philosophy   277
The Seven Rays   278
The Enneagram   280
Bibliography   290
Resources   293
Other Offerings By Karen Johannsen   296

INTRODUCTION
THE INCARNATION OF KAREN

What was going on before I was born? Sometimes I imagine walking into a celestial conference room in the heavens and sitting down with the teachers and guides that will help me plan out this particular incarnation. As I walk up to the table, I realize that I'm a bit afraid to be here, doing this. Do I really want to go back? I'm not sure I want to face another lifetime of struggle, starting my whole life over again. I know it's not a completely new beginning. I have learned things in all of my previous lifetimes, but there is still trepidation about what might be ahead in this incarnation of Karen.

In my imagination, I sit down, take few deep breaths and try to quiet myself. From this place of stillness, I realize that under the fear there is excitement. *Wow, I get another chance to experience life, to contribute to the overall human consciousness just by showing up. I wonder what it will be like? Who will I meet? What will I learn?*

One of the teachers at the table comments, "Do you not see how all of these lifetimes unfold, one after the other in a seamless pattern of intention and purpose?"

I am filled with awe and wonder at the truth of this perspective. It makes perfect sense to me, so I ask, *"Could we talk then about the purposes for me in this incarnation?*

"I know that I will struggle with trusting myself and my own inner process. I am prone to believing in other people's wisdom, rather than claiming my own. I will need to develop courage to show up and stand in the truth that is my own, leaving behind structures that no longer support my evolutionary purpose."

One of the Elders adds, "From what I have observed of you in previous lifetimes it appears you have learned to be afraid of your power. You will need to learn to trust in your own compassionate nature and realize that your strength, coupled with your compassion can be a great healing force in the world."

I agree.

"I know that I will have many fears that will have to be transformed, especially around being out in the world and being seen. Maybe we should set up some circumstances and experiences that will help me develop resilience and inner strength."

Another Elder nods thoughtfully. "Well, you have some karmic issues around sexuality that will have to be dealt with. Giving you a Scorpio sun will assist you as you look into any psychological patterns that may need to be transformed. Scorpio is the sign of the warrior, and that energy will support you as you dive into this deep work. With Mars and Pluto as the ruling signs of Scorpio you will be given the energy of fearlessness as you go into the underworld to face these challenges."

The astrology master adds, "Giving you a Scorpio Sun will certainly help you make sense of your psychological life, but if you are to fulfill your life purpose, you will have to climb the mountain of Capricorn. Step by determined step, you must strive for your highest spiritual attainment. So, I think we must make Capricorn your Ascendant. Then, a moon in Cancer will create the desire for children, and this will teach you about detachment and letting go. All of these elements will support you as you strive to fulfill your Soul's purpose."

We are all in agreement that this is plenty to put on my plate for a lifetime, and with that decision the blueprint is created.

• • • •

Of course, I didn't remember any of this when I arrived here, having crossed the River of Forgetfulness. Perhaps that's the only way to truly incarnate into life. If we have all of the answers wrapped up in advance, then what is the point of taking the journey at all?

The environment I was born into definitely set the stage for my memory to return, encounter by encounter, one poignant lesson at a time.

• • • •

My birth took place on an overcast Sunday morning in November 1941, one month before the bombing of Pearl Harbor. The energy of war was in the air; perfect timing for a Scorpio whose *mantram* is, "Warrior am I, and from the battle I emerge triumphant." I would need that warrior energy to break through the strictures of my family.

My father was a well-respected leader in our church. There were morning devotionals around the kitchen table, saying prayers before we went off for our day, two services on Sunday and a bible study on Wednesday night. Our whole family life was structured around the church and the social life it created. There was a lot of emphasis on having all the right answers. I was taught that anyone who did not believe as we did would suffer for eternity in hell.

The grace in all this dogmatism was that it gave me a safe structure in which to mature. There were answers to lean into and rest upon. I didn't struggle with any of the big questions. I was devoted and committed to the Christian life. Through this faith in God I had many experiences of the Divine, especially the Master Jesus. I never doubted that I was a child of God.

The other gift of this environment was that our home was filled with the energy of love which gave me a solid foundation for the rest of my life. But after I graduated from college, moved away, and began experiencing different ways of living in the world, I could no longer cling to the beliefs of my childhood. Were the gentle, loving people that I met, who were doing good work in the world, destined to spend eternity in hell, just because they couldn't say the words, "I take Jesus Christ as my personal Savior?"

In my mid-twenties I rejected the dogma of fundamental Christianity and the belief that there was only one way to God. I remember vividly the first time I heard the word, reincarnation. It was an epoch moment. I felt this amazing sense of relief fill my body. I no longer had to fear that if, in my moment of death, I was not "right with God" I would be lost for all eternity. I had time to figure it all out, and if I didn't get it right this time, I could work it out in my next incarnation.

Part of the purpose of reincarnation is to balance out our karma. What we have reaped we will eventually sow. There is no judgment with karma. It is simply a spiritual law. Everything depends on how I live my life and the choices I make. I may not escape the consequences of my choices, but I can learn to make better decisions if I'm committed to a life of integrity and authenticity.

This introduction to reincarnation opened my eyes and propelled me into a whole new perspective on life. I explored a lot of different spiritual paths to see what felt like a good fit for me.

I remember being fascinated with Eastern Religions and studied that for a few years. The Buddhist path made a lot of sense to me. It seemed psychologically sound as well as spiritually relevant. Even though I didn't consider myself a Buddhist, I related to many of its tenets.

By this time, I was married, had traveled around the world twice, and had my eyes opened to a greater physical reality. Being exposed to such a variety of human experiences shifted my awareness to a much wider perspective. I remember sitting on my deck one night, back in the States, looking across the water at the horizon. Suddenly I was aware of that expanded vision. People halfway around the world were spreading their loved ones ashes in the Ganges River in India. Bedouins were riding their camels through the Moroccan desert. People were laying their heads against the wailing wall in Jerusalem. It wasn't just about my little corner of the world anymore.

Even so, as a young mother I was settling down. After my second child I let go of all my questions about the meaning of life. I had come to a place of peace about reincarnation. Even if it wasn't true, I would still be living my life in the same way. My values were intact. My life was filled with ease, and I stopped searching for something to replace my earlier devotion. I was now devoted to being a full-time mother.

Fast forward twenty years. At forty-five, I entered graduate school to get my master's degree in Transpersonal Psychology. This was another opportunity to expand my consciousness, although I didn't see it that way at the time. I had given up my career when my children were born. This urge to explore my inner life had been building for some time. I felt a pull within to re-open the questions I had set aside in my twenties. Not only did I want to explore my spiritual life again, but I had an acute desire to figure myself out psychologically.

During those five years, I opened up again to a wider vision of myself, my family, and the spiritual world. I began meditating and following my interest in spirituality. I took a cold, hard look at my stuff: my dysfunctional patterns, my family of origin issues, my tendency toward codependence, my marriage.

A few years after obtaining my master's and opening my private practice, I ended my marriage. As I began to grow spiritually and mature psychologically, I realized that my husband and I were going in different directions. The relationship could no longer support the deeper me that was emerging. We had been together for over thirty years, so this was a life changing decision.

Expereiencing the expansion that occurred for me through my graduate years, I saw making this decision as a challenge that would test my newfound sense of inner strength. I had to face my fear of not being able to provide for my two teenaged children. Being alone never frightened me, but not being financially secure was terrifying. The alternative was to continue putting my energies into a dysfunctional relationship, into trying to hold the family together, versus devoting myself to the pursuit of my own spiritual path. The decision was difficult but clear. I could no longer wear myself out trying to hold together a system that was not healthy.

What supported me in that decision was that I was beginning to trust the deeper connection I was making with my Soul. And my Soul was guiding me to reclaim the lost feelings of my childhood when I felt so close to God. I wanted that connection again, but this time I would forge my own path. I would choose what felt right for me, what fit for who I was.

At that time, I was introduced to what are called the "Ancient Wisdom" teachings, or the "Perennial Philosophy". I was drawn to these teachings partly because they reinforced my belief in reincarnation as part of a deeper spiritual reality. From this perspective, we incarnate as a way to evolve and to be of service to our fellow humans. When the personality awakens to the presence of the Soul, our return to earth comes with a plan and purpose that is directed by our Soul. The purpose of evolution is to reach more expansive states of consciousness until we become fully enlightened.

These teachings also resonated because it was important for me to believe in a philosophy that encouraged me to experiment with the ideas presented and make sure they fitted what was true for me.

Now, I am in my late seventies, and for the last twenty years I have been immersed in these teachings. They have provided me with a framework in which to view my life and my place in the cosmos. I feel at home here. I claim it as my personal path knowing that, as the poet Rumi says, "There are a thousand ways to kneel and kiss the earth."

• • • •

The Incarnation of Karen-as-Writer came about as a direct result of a deep connection with my Soul. As part of the Ancient Wisdom teachings, I adopted a regular meditation practice. Meditation, in this system, is a means by which we continually reach toward a deeper connection with our higher selves. This practice allowed me to recognize the inner voice of my Soul.

Let me take you back to the year 2010, when I began to feel my Soul prompting me to write my first book, *Full Moon Magic.*

It all started with a set of cards. I created meditation cards for myself after reading about a spiritual practice of honoring the full moon. In his book, *Signs of Christ*, author Harold Balyoz speaks about how we can connect more deeply with the spiritual realms at the time of the full moon. Because there is an astrological alignment taking place, a portal or doorway is opened to allow the energies of a particular constellation to pour down onto the earth like a golden, electromagnetic beam of light.

Since this is such a potent opportunity for spiritual connection, the author suggests a five-day period of reflection, preparation, and mindfulness. So I decided to create a deck of cards that would remind me of the focus and intention of each of those five days.

On one particular day, after using the cards for a few years, I realized just how worn out they had become. They looked sad, coffee stained, smudged, tattered around the edges. I thought, *I need to make a new deck for myself.*

Then, as I entered meditation, the nudge from my Soul came:

Soul: Nudge.

Me: What?

Soul: You know those cards you've been using for many years now, that are frayed, and coffee stained?

Me: Yes.

Soul: I think you should make another card deck that is similar but more explicit.

Me: What do you mean?

Soul: Well, it's important for more people to be educated about the five-day period of the full moon, and I think you could make a beautiful set to distribute to people.

Me: You've got to be kidding!?

Soul: I don't usually joke about things like this.

Me: Oh, okay.

Soul: And while you're at it, maybe it would be helpful to write a book to accompany the card deck. Sort of a manual about astrology, the rays, and why the full moon is important.

Me: But I've never written anything in my whole life, well, with the exception of that article I submitted to the Reader's Digest back in the sixties. But they rejected it. See, I'm not really a writer.

Soul: That was then; this is now.

Me: Right. Well, let me think about it.

Soul: (sigh)… Here we go again.

It took me a few years and many more nudges before I actually took any concrete steps. I had so much resistance. But that Soul of mine just wouldn't let me go. I would sit in meditation and hear, "The book, the book, the book." Finally, I surrendered and began.

It took another three years to actually complete it, find a publisher, print it, and figure out how to distribute it. But through the long struggle - and it was a struggle - I felt a sort of grace. Like I was doing something very important that could potentially educate and help a lot of people. So, I persevered, in spite of all of the resistant voices that needed to be dealt with. I could see the Soul at work as doors opened. The right people appeared at just the right time, and I even began planning a book tour that would take me across the United States. Friends invited me to their cities and organized venues for me, so I could present my book and card deck. It was an amazing experience.

As the publication of the book and card deck, *Full Moon Magic*, became a reality, I realized that I needed to generate some interest. The idea of writing a blog seemed a natural way to begin putting my voice out into the world. I soon realized that I loved the writing of it. It felt organic and real as I began just chronicling my journey, the challenges, and the lessons.

Those blog posts comprise the essence of this second book, *My Gentle Musings*. They follow my journey from the ages of seventy to seventy-six. As you read, I hope you will see how the Soul has directed my life in a way that brought me face-to-face with challenges that needed to be met mindfully and opportunities that graced my life through synchronicities and magic.

My hope is that through my words you, too, may recognize the promptings of your own Soul, and find the courage to follow it wherever it leads you.

CHAPTER 1
THE BOOK

The entries in this chapter were all written in 2013, just as I was preparing to launch my first book. You will begin to see how the Soul is preparing me to take on this monumental task. I needed to believe in my own strength and power. I had to find my true voice, and my courage to send it out into the world.

March 2013
Spring Equinox and the Aries Festival of Spring

So, today, on this first day of Spring, I am lucky enough to be in San Diego with my sister and husband enjoying the sunshine and the warmth. I am grateful.

The long winter has ended, and I ponder: What has been lying dormant in me all these months and is now ready to burst forth into new life?

A few weeks ago, at the Pisces new moon, when the energy of compassion was filling the ethers, I breathed that compassion into myself. I breathed in balance and I leaned into the strength and clarity that was in my body. My intention emerged out of that place of alignment.

"I release the old worn out mind stuff that keeps me accommodating and self-sacrificing and welcome in the new vibrant energy of aliveness, power, and strength."

Well, certainly with this release, a space was created for something new to emerge. But what form would it take?

I have inklings. Often the Soul nudges me in this way, just little pieces of intuition, little sparks of excitement about a picture I see or something I read. Just hints, if I'm paying attention.

And often I wait, and ponder, and ruminate; but finally the urge becomes too strong to ignore.

I think this time the nudging has to do with my being more visible in the world. I am reminded of a card that sits on my altar, given to me by my sister-in-law for my birthday one year. It says, "I came to live out loud." I love that. What would that mean for me, to live out loud?

Certainly, living from that place of strength and clarity would give me a stronger sense of where I was headed.

I think I will be making much more noise this year. My sense is that this new beginning is also connected to the book and card deck that is finally in print and ready to be distributed.

I will be doing book signings and traveling to promote my project, and I realize that my years of semi-anonymity are coming to an end. I have treasured my anonymity for years, feeling very comfortable in this place. Partly out of an ancient fear of being seen, and noticed, and persecuted for speaking my truth, but that isn't all of the story. There has also been this part of me that believed I needed to be perfect and do everything perfectly and not be seen as a flake. I know exactly who to thank for planting those seeds in me. But the point is, I'm not in any danger these days, and no one is telling me I have to be perfect, except myself. So that can go "bye-bye in the car, car," as we say in my house.

A very dear friend once gave me a wonderful piece of advice about this very dilemma. She said, "Your love of humanity has to be greater than your fear." And isn't one definition of courage that you feel the fear and do it anyway?

So, I'm stepping out, in spite of my fears and doubts. I'm doing it, because that Aries energy has me on fire and I'm ready and I do love humanity, hugely.

A poem for spring:

Spring Cleaning

Time for tulips, worms, resurrection
the tulips open and close, open and close
like breathing wings
testing the possibility of spring.

Time for dawn to lick out the last
of that rich dark bowl of night
and bleed her own colors into the world.
Branches that were bare just last week
shoot volleys of blossoms in the sun
and green wood on the apple tree takes off
Like an arrow into the sky.
Even old beams in the house begin to softly sing
of leaves and the fresh arc of wind.

Time to take a spade and shove sharply
with your heel in its old rubber boot---
TURN OVER YOUR LIFE
see what survived, shake out the bugs
get some air in the roots.
Throw out piles of papers,

unfinished projects
like layers of old mulch.

In the morning your heart is still
A cupped leaf holding dew
If you can match that stillness
And look into the sweet water of your own heart
You may catch the wild promise, a goddess just waking
The magic of your own rebirth.
—Miriam Dyak, 1996

June 2013
Moving Forward

Last week I was in a car accident. The other driver was cited for negligence. No one was seriously injured. We were both insured. My car was a total loss, but still I am mostly grateful.

Today, five days later I am just in from a glorious thirty minutes on the deck, arm wrapped in ice, soaking in the Vitamin D and the light. Just sitting … still … doing nothing.

This accident was unlike my other two when I was dead-still and a car crashed into me from behind… *forcing* me forward.

On this day I was clearly moving forward, of my own volition. Well, of course I was driving a car, but that was my choice that morning. Then the impact. Crash!!! Stopped me in my tracks.

I know there is symbolism here. I am moving forward, in my life, in my work, in the environment I have created for myself. No one is forcing me; no one violently pushing.

I am hardwired to move forward, and I welcome the move. Okay, there are still some small little "ancient fires" (as my teacher calls them) burning away in my head.

Wait, it's too soon. We're not ready. We like it here, they say.

But truth be told they are merely embers by now, not capable of stopping anyone in their tracks.

Still, being the ponderer that I am I notice the symbols and I do ponder. Joan Jerman, my gifted healing friend said to me at her workshop yesterday, "Are you comfortable moving forward in your life? What do you think you will gain and what will you lose by moving forward?"

I see my next step as being out in the world promoting my book and card deck. Well, as I said, I am mostly comfortable, but I do love the life I have. Will I lose that? Will I get caught up in busyness, someone else's schedule? How will I handle being more exposed, more seen? And what about my solitude, the precious hours spent in stillness and quiet? Those are the embers.

I'm pretty sure of what I will gain: a deeper honoring of the gifts I have to offer, a stronger knowing of my value. I think my voice will change. I think I will speak with more authority with fewer apologies for taking up space, perhaps less permission asked and no more, "Alright? Okay?" I can sense there will be a deeper timber in the tone of my words. I think I will gain immense satisfaction knowing I have made a valuable contribution to the world. Probably, I will experience more ease with myself, a self-assuredness that is based on the knowing that I am capable of handling whatever life throws at me. I guess all that is worth the little I have to lose.

While attending Joan's workshop that day we were asked to meditate on the questions we have asked and to write down the guidance we receive. So, I ask about my concerns and my inner voice responds:

You are being prepared for your next step. There are some hindrances, stuck places, in the body that will need to be aligned. All of the body work you are doing will assist with that. Know that you don't take this next step alone. Always you have the love and support of your guides, teachers, and angels. Don't forget that we are working in a partnership with you. Moving forward with ease is the goal. Your life is being re-structured. Your body is being re-structured, so new pathways need to be created. As your life unfolds, move with grace and trust.... This will fill you. This will guide you. Now is the time for radical trust. Even with your misgivings you will move forward. You can trust the flow and grace of life moving through you. Relax, and know that you are not alone. All you need will be provided. Just follow what is presented... in your own time... in your own way. Listen to the wisdom of the body. It will also guide you. No worry, no concerns, no anxieties. Let it all go. Just sink into the ground of your being and rest there.

I think I'll try that. ☺

August 2013
Anxiety and the Inner Critic

Last week I facilitated a women's group that I belong to. In thinking of what I would create as a ceremony, I had an inspirational thought. It stayed with me for a few weeks and then I let it slip away in the rush and tumble of my daily life.

A few days before the circle, I began to feel anxious about having no time to prepare. I decided, at the last minute, to use the same ceremony that I was using for the full moon meditation which was taking place the night before the women's circle.

The inspiring thought was swallowed in the anxiety and rush. The full moon ceremony was wonderful... uplifting, inspiring, and affirming; going into the women's circle I felt at ease.

We opened the circle. We drummed, we shared, and I felt us go deep into the dream time... soft, flowy, sweet energy. Taking out my notes to talk about the astrological aspects that were happening at the time didn't seem to fit the atmosphere that had been created. But I couldn't let go of my "plan". I couldn't release the notes I had prepared to just *be* with the energy of the moment and ask for inspiration to continue in a different way.

My "talk" felt stilted and unfocused. I couldn't follow my notes, and the poetry felt flat and uninspiring. I have no idea how it was received, but this was my perception.

On the way home, my niggly little inner critic started in on me. Now, I have mostly made friends with the little guy, so he doesn't stick around long. But nevertheless, I could feel the old, "not enough" whisper in my ear.

How would I ever be able to talk and inspire a room full of people on my book tour if I couldn't even get it together for five of my women friends?

Sometime during the night, the thought occurred to me that at the full moon ceremony, the night before, I had opened myself and invited into my life the awareness of what was needed to be released in me. I had talked about how big changes are coming, for us as a planet and also personally. I could certainly feel that in my own life, and as I sat in meditation that night, I said, *I am ready. Show me what no longer serves my higher good.*

So, my little friend the critic emerged, and it was time to have another conversation. We know each other so well by now that the conversation doesn't last long. We will mostly just sit together in the silence holding each other gently with love and compassion and acceptance. Hopefully, one of these days he will grow up.

Later in the night more realizations came. Anxiety blocks my access to creativity; I want to learn to be more present in the moment. No, not big news. But I wondered, *how would it have been different if I had just sat with the energy in the circle the way it was? What if I had quieted myself and asked, "How can I proceed here to support the field that has been created,* and then just waited?

Perhaps my original inspiration would have come to mind. Maybe I could have just asked that we sit and acknowledge the felt sense in the room.

I think the bigger learning here for me is, as I'm stepping out into more public speaking, I want to be more aware of the interaction of the subtle energies between me and my audience.

What am I feeling within myself? What am I picking up from them? How can I adjust my talk to accommodate what is happening in the moment?

This means that I let go of too rigid a reliance on my notes, that I take the time to create the atmosphere that will support me before anyone arrives, and that I stay attuned to that energy as I proceed. It means trusting in my inspirations and not letting busyness or anxiety block me from that channel of creativity. It means more trust, more presence, and more willingness to risk.

I guess if big changes are coming my way these are good tools to have in my toolbox.

I am grateful for the awareness.

Then I came across this poem that reminded me that the purpose of all of this is to humbly offer my gifts to the world, as uncomfortable as that may feel.

Cargo

(*For Malidoma Somé, Loon Lake 2000*)

You enter life a ship laden with meaning, purpose and gifts
sent to be delivered to this hungry world,
and as much as the world needs your cargo,
you need to give it away.
Everything depends on this.

But the world forgets its needs,
and you forget your mission, and
the ancestral maps used to guide you
have become faded scrawls on the parchment of dead Pharaohs.
The cargo weighs you heavy the longer it is held.
Spoilage becomes a risk.
The ship sputters from port to port and at each you ask:
"Is this the way?"
But the way cannot be found without knowing your cargo,
and the cargo cannot be known without recognizing there is a way.
It is simply this:
You have gifts.
The world needs your gifts.
You must deliver them.

The world may not know it is starving,
but the hungry know,
and they will find you
when you discover your cargo
—Greg Kimura

October 2013
On the Road

Even before I set foot onto the plane to launch my book tour, the learning had begun.

It started with the women's circle a few weeks before I left, where I realized that part of being a presenter involves being willing to give up your agenda and go with the energy of the moment. I took that in as an assignment to go deeper into trusting of myself, trusting the energy would carry me, even if that meant shifting gears in mid-stream.

The next revelation came as I received an email from a friend. She is part of my spiritual community. She wrote that even though she lives in North Carolina, she and her immediate group there would hold me in their meditations each morning from 7:30-9:00am while I was on tour. Wow, that struck me so powerfully. I guess I had never really understood what support I *could* tap into.

This prompted a Facebook entry where I asked my friends to also hold me in their thoughts as I was traveling. Many responded with commitments and reassurance.

Then something very profound began to occur in my meditations. I would open myself up, as I do when meditating, and I would feel throughout my whole body this downpouring of strength, love, and support. Just as if someone had said in my ear, *You are not alone in this. We are always here to hold you.*

I noticed the visible effect of all these happenings one morning a week or so before I left. I began thinking about the tour and instead of the ever-present anxiety and fear, I felt a surge of excitement. What a revelation. Underneath fear and anxiety lives excitement and enthusiasm.

The final "aha moment" came about just a few days before I left when two people asked me, out of the blue, to explain what my book was about. I heard myself launch into a very articulate, clear and precise explanation. The next thought was, *Hey, I know this stuff. I don't need my stack of 3x5 cards that are underlined and highlighted. I think I can just work from a general outline.*

I immediately went home and condensed my talks into working outlines. A BIG step for me. I have to admit, I kept the detailed notes, just in case, but mostly the outline worked just fine. It was a tremendous boost to my confidence.

So, a note of encouragement and perhaps caution: If your calling is to be a teacher or a public presenter, get ready for the powerful lessons that will help you on your way.

PS I wrote these reminders in my "book tour" folder and read them every day:

And we do not fear.
—Nicholas Roerich, written on the back of a painting I have in my kitchen

I choose the way of the interpreter, and therefore ask for Light.
I choose the way of loving guidance, and therefore ask for lifting power.
I choose the way of inspiration, and therefore ask for flowing life.
I choose the way of integrating, and therefore ask for the Seal of Silence
—Alice Bailey, *Discipleship in the New Age, Vol. II*

I am a servant of the Greater Life, an agent on behalf of its creative intention.
—William Meader,

CHAPTER 2
SELF-LOVE

I was in graduate school in the mid-eighties when I met Dr. Laura Fraser. Little did I know at the time what an impact she would have on my life's direction.

It was serendipitous how it all came about. I was a few weeks into my internship as a soon-to-be psychotherapist, when I began having symptoms of extreme fatigue and lethargy. I brought this situation into my meditation time to see if I could get some clarity or guidance about what was behind it all. Almost immediately, I got a strong intuitive hit. I needed to quit school and take a quarter off if I wanted to remain healthy. What??? That was so unlike me, to quit anything once I had started. I sat with it for a few days and finally decided to risk just going with what had come to me. I was reassured by the university that I could resume after one quarter's absence with no dire consequences, so I quit.

A few weeks later I got a call from my friend, Marie. She had come across an interesting class that she wanted to take and asked if I would be interested in joining her. I don't remember the name of the class, but it had to do with spirituality. It was taught by Laura Fraser. It was also held on one of the nights that I would have been in school if I had not quit. It felt like this might be the reason I was guided to take some time off.

Laura was the first female in the state of Washington to take on the robes of an Episcopalian priest. When she began teaching her understandings about reincarnation, karma, and past lives, she was given the ultimatum by the church to either stop talking about those subjects or give up her robes. She gave up her robes and founded her own organization called the Foundation for Inner Enlightenment and Spiritual Freedom, taking many of her former church members with her.

It was at this point that she came into my life. I attended her classes and services for many years until her passing. She was the one who introduced me to the writings of Alice Bailey. Bailey's books are based on the Ancient Wisdom teachings, sometimes called the Perennially Philosophy. They have their roots in Theosophy. It's a daunting study. Bailey wrote over twenty books that were dictated to her by the Tibetan Master Djwhal Kuhl. The information is abstract and not easily understood, but Laura had a gift of explaining these ideas in an understandable way and I began to think of this path as my own.

After her death I attempted to continue the study on my own but soon gave up. It seemed impossible to go on without a knowledgeable teacher to decipher them.

Then I came across the University of the Seven Rays, a school that taught this ancient wisdom. I immediately signed up to be on their mailing list. Every year the brochure would come inviting us to the yearly conference, and every year I looked at it longingly, but never went.

In 2001 the brochure appeared again, and I immediately felt compelled to go, even though it was held in New York. It was such a strong urge that I barely questioned it. I just made my reservation and went. I didn't know anyone but felt fearless in my decision. It was there that I met the man that was to become my next spiritual teacher, William Meader. I heard him speak at one of the workshops and I thought, "I need to get this man in Seattle. I want a teacher like him who can explain these teachings in a way I can understand." I was also interested in establishing a community of seekers that could share this journey with me. Two years later it all came together, and we have been a group of students studying with William since 2004.

This philosophy has enriched my life in so many ways. One of the things that was most appealing to me was its inclusivity and non-dogmatic approach to the spiritual life. It is not a mandate to believe in a certain way. We are always encouraged to seek our own inner knowing and not put our faith in what any spiritual teacher tells us.

I love it when I can look back at one single soul-inspired decision and watch how it weaves itself into a whole new pattern of life changing events.

The original University of the Rays has now morphed into the Seven Ray Institute, and we meet every year in Arizona for our annual conference. You will see me refer to this conference several times in this book. The conference draws students and speakers from around the world who are interested in these Ancient Wisdom teachings.

I have been attending this conference every year, as I always have found it so inspiring and uplifting as well as an opportunity to practice thinking in a more abstract way. It doesn't hurt that it is now held in Arizona every year in the month of April or May, a perfect time to be away from Seattle.

It was at one of these conferences that I crossed a personal "burning ground." One step of many that has led me to a stronger sense of my own power and a deeper self-love.

Have you ever known anyone who didn't struggle with loving themselves?

April 2013
The Burning Ground New Moon in Aries

At the Seven Ray Conference here in Arizona we are focusing on the Sixth Ray of Devotion and Idealism. This ray is found most prominently in the planets Mars and Neptune.

So, our meditation this day has to do with how we cross the burning ground to reach a new state of consciousness. Before any great expansion can occur, there are conflicts, tests, and trials. The fiery burning ground.

In this meditation we imagined a doorway that we wished to pass through. But to pass through we had to be willing to walk through the fire. We were asked to consider what our own personal burning ground is right now.

Are we looking at the fire, or feeling it in our body and through fear remaining immobilized unable to continue on?

Are we cautiously taking baby steps as we draw near?

Are we rushing through the fire only focused on the other side, without considering what the fire represents to us?

Where are we on this burning ground?

Well I felt the heat, felt the fear, and identified it as my fear of inhabiting my own power.

When we studied the planets Mars and Neptune, I learned that Mars holds the energy of courage and fearlessness. It charges forward unafraid. Part of Neptune's job is to dissolve barriers, to see the ideal and hold the vision.

So, I called upon Mars for courage to go forward, and I asked Neptune to help me hold the vision of what this expansion would mean to me. I saw myself in the middle of the fire, holding strong the image of standing in my own strength while still including another.

I asked for courage to stand there, embodying and balancing the joining of the masculine and feminine energies.

I asked for the will to confront all the obstacles in the way of that joining. I could clearly identify those barriers that stand in the way of my authentic power: my need to be loved, my feelings of unworthiness, my believing I am somehow separate, my lack of trust in myself. All the dross that's in the way of my fully becoming my own inner authority.

So, I call again upon Neptune to dissolve the dross, and I invoke the Mars energy to give me courage and the "will to persist."

I want to not be afraid of my power. I want to know that I can trust myself enough to be strong *and* compassionate. I don't have to choose one over the other.

Finally, we are asked to step through the doorway and experience what it feels like to embody our ideal, our vision.

I feel the freedom and the liberation in my body.

I breathe with my whole body, deeply and profoundly.

I feel strength and purpose and love flow through me.

There is no fear.

And there I take my stand.

The Mantram of the Disciple

I am a point of light, within a greater light.

I am a strand of loving energy within the stream of love divine

I am a point of sacrificial fire,

Focused within the fiery will of God

AND THUS, I STAND

I am a way by which men may achieve

I am a source of strength enabling them to stand

I am a beam of light

Shining upon their way

AND THUS, I STAND

And standing thus, revolve,

And tread this way,

The ways of men

And know the ways of God

AND THUS, I STAND.

—Alice Bailey, *Discipleship in a New Age, Vol. 11*

April 2013
Magnificence

I'm reading a book called, *Dying to Be Me, My Journey from Cancer, to Near Death, to True Healing*, by Anita Moorjani.

It's a remarkable story of courage and miracles.

Anita was diagnosed with an aggressive stage four cancer and was on her deathbed and in a coma when she was admitted to the hospital. The doctors did not expect her to make it through the night because her organs had already started shutting down.

At one point Anita leaves her body and travels to a realm of light. She can still hear everything that is said in her room in the hospital, and everything the doctors are saying down the hall.

While in this out-of-body state, she meets her deceased father and a close friend who had passed a few years earlier. They are in a realm she describes as one of pure light and unconditional love. She feels herself a part of the universe and knows there is no separation between her and everything else. She recognizes her own magnificence as a divine being and realizes nothing she ever did in her life *made* her worthy of this love. She didn't have to earn it, she *was* it. Her whole being became love and she recognized that love was the very fabric of the universe.

At one point she has to decide whether to return and at first, she says, "No, why would I want to return to that sick body?" But then the understanding came that she was healed. It was the unconditional love she now held toward herself that had healed her, her acceptance of her own magnificence. She realized she now had an important purpose to fulfill. So, she returned. And miraculously, the doctors could find NO trace of cancer anywhere in her body. Her father's last communication to her was, "Now that you know the truth of who you really are, go back and live your life fearlessly."

These words stuck a strong chord in me, especially after having stood in the middle of my burning ground and feeling my fear. I wondered how it would feel to have NO fear.

On a walk with my daughter and granddaughter a few days later, I was sharing Anita's story and how I had been struggling with this fear issue for quite a while. My daughter's comment to me was something like, "Are you sure you're not just rehashing old stuff, because I haven't seen you living from your fear in a long time."

It got me to thinking. *Is this just an old story I've told myself so long that I really believe it?*

I realized that the reality of my life doesn't bear witness to living in fear. I survived abuse, divorce, loss of two significant relationships, loss of my parents and stepmother, and still I went on to travel the world, to teach, to get a master's degree, to establish my private practice, to write a book, to organize a spiritual community here in Seattle, and to hold full moon meditations in my home.

I *had* walked through the fire of my burning ground.

So, I guess I have seen myself very differently than I actually am. I know I have felt fear, I'm not saying that I haven't, but I also see that I have acted in spite of it. It hasn't stopped me from doing what I felt I needed to do. It's an old story that I have still held onto but that has definitely outlived its usefulness.

It occurred to me as I was making these mental observations that we were in the midst of the full moon period and three eclipse periods, astrologically. While reading up on the significance of this, imagine my surprise to discover that the theme of these upcoming events is resolving or releasing long standing patterns, usually karmic patterns. That made a lot of sense. So wherever this pattern originated, I now declare that I am through with letting it have any kind of hold on me, mentally or psychologically.

When Anita talked about the healing that occurred for her when she accepted that she was a divine creation, loved unconditionally and magnificent just because she was born, it resonated with me in a deep way. *What if the years of naval-gazing, striving so hard to become better, seriously and arduously trying to figure out all my stuff, are over? What if the rest of my life is about seeing myself as magnificent, just as I am?*

Not that I shouldn't have done my psychological work, but being too intensely focused on myself and my "issues" has taken some of the joy out of life and where is there room then, for the appreciation of who I *essentially* am…the core of me?

I want to change what I identify with. I don't want to close my eyes and not see where change has to occur. I want to gaze at that part of myself softly, in compassion. Noticing, honoring, accepting, and then with intention, I want to turn my focus to the fullness and wonder of who I *really* am and feel the joy of *that* fill my being.

Anita describes it this way, "I realized that all those years, all I *ever had* to do was be *myself,* without judgment or feeling I was flawed. At the same time, I understood that at the core, our essence is made of pure love. *We are pure love*---every single one of us. How can we not be, if we come from the Whole and return to it? I knew that realizing this meant never being afraid of who we are. Therefore, being love and being our true self is one and the same thing!!"

AMEN.

April 2013
More on Self Love

After I wrote the last blog, I came across a blog from a woman named Claire Zimmer. She spoke so eloquently to the theme I was trying to express. I'd like to quote her here:

Unconditional self-love has to do with a fundamental awareness of the inherent value of your being---your very existence is enough to be worthy of partaking in the goodness of life and receiving love and support of the universe and others.

However, there is an additional step that's necessary to complete the process of true self love that many of us skip over, which is unconditional commitment to ourselves—not just loving yourself for your inherent value but standing for the potential of who you can become, which requires us to challenge and mentor ourselves through our growing edges and be honest with ourselves about where we're missing the mark.

Self-love creates the container. Ferocious commitment, the positive, creative tension that enables our full becoming.

Crossing the burning ground, walking through the door, standing in my full power was my ferocious commitment, made at the Seven Ray Conference in April.

And if we need even more permission to be our radiant selves, here is the powerful poem by Heidi Rose Robbins. Reprinted with permission.

I Know A Woman

I know a woman
who is exhausted.
She works midnight hours,
carving out the time she needs
from days given twice over
to all who require her care.

She forgets to put herself
into her own arms,
neglects to feed

the very woman who feeds
all other need.

I know a woman
who is climbing Kilimanjaro,
19,000 feet of unstoppable courage,
but does not fully know
her own majestic light.

I know a woman
who is wrenched with
too many
good-byes
in too short a time
whose heart
burns daily for
all who are in pain.

I know a woman
who is banishing fear,
ushering it
out of her house.
It held sway
one too many years.
Now she is done.

I know a woman
who has found
an empty room.
She is scrawling on the walls.
She is splashing paint.
She is making noise.
She is dancing a fiery dance.
She is willing to fail.

I know a woman
who quit her job,

and every day
makes friends
with her unknown.

I know a woman
who holds us
with prayer.
I mean prayer that can change your life.

I know a woman who is enraged,
pain stitched in her pockets,
tears carried too long,
who now must
open her mouth
and sing
or shout or
speak her truth.

I know a woman,
a warrior queen
whose
little girl
heart
needs a lullaby.

I know a woman who
cracks herself
open
open
open
to be boundless love,
a priestess of raw devotion.

I know a woman
who lost her son
and gained her voice
to let loose a fury of light

upon the world.

You know a woman.

We know a woman,
struggling
to grow her radiance,
the flame of her heart
burning away
who she is not.

Our stories together
hold back the darkness.
Our struggles together
wrestle fear into light.
Our bodies together listening,
breathe a breath
that forges the new.

So yes.
And yes.
And yes.

Let's rally to birth the light.
Buoy one another,
Stand fully alive.
Let us breathe upon the flame.

There is no longer time
to sit alone at the kitchen table
and weep
for a fractured world.

The doors of our hearts
are swinging open.
We are calling to one another
arms outstretched.

We are joining hands.

The birth cry of the new world
is a song sung by women
silenced for centuries
heard again
now
when we gather
in the name of light.

Oh women,
Blind me with your radiance.
Bear witness to one another.
The time has come.
We have everything to give
to a world that
needs nothing more
than
our
fierce
present
love.
—Heidi Rose Robbins

September 2017
I Am Enough

So many people I know or have seen in my practice believe at their core that they are somehow deficient, that they aren't good enough. I ask, *Good enough for whom? Our parents, our society, our friends?*

In the Christian faith we have been conditioned to believe that we are born in sin and in need of redemption, that a Savior must absolve us from this sinful nature. Hogwash, I say. *We are born with the seed of Divinity within us. How can that seed, who is a part of God, (the Mystery, Universal Intelligence, whatever you name it.) How can our divinity be sinful? Our Divinity is our true essence.*

To use a metaphor, Spirit is a hand and our ego, or personality, is merely the glove that covers up that Divine nature. Our job is to recognize that and realize more fully that all we need to do, really, is connect more and more deeply with that hand and less and less with that glove. Our personalities are in need of integration and refinement, that is true, but that doesn't change the fact that we are Divine human beings at our core.

In fact, I believe that it is part of our job while we are in a body to let the hand determine what the glove does. Let the Soul of us be in charge.

That is a work in progress for all but the most enlightened of us, but it does not mean that we are deficient.

Let us look at our personality foibles, warts, I call them, with the compassion of our Divine Nature. We're all in this together, learning how to live from our highest selves (our Soul). Can't we have compassion for our humanness without thinking that the core of us is sinful, or lacking, or not enough?

I love the *mantram*, "I have enough. I do enough. I am enough." And it's true.

We are all enough.

March 2015
Lovingkindness

A few years ago, while reading a Buddhist-type book I came across some statements that jumped out at me as if they were labeled, "Priority Mail."

The author, whose name I wish I could remember, was suggesting that several times during the day we stop, pause, and mindfully send ourselves gentleness, kindness, and love.

I immediately thought to myself, *How many times a day do I do that?* The answer was, *Like, never.*

And it stunned me how I can so easily think of doing that for the people in my life that I love, or for the world, or for the disempowered, but that the voice I most often hear in reference to myself is anything but kind or gentle.

Now, I have evolved some. I don't castrate myself with loathing or abuse, but the subtle messages are usually around the theme of "not enough", "not perfect", "could have done that better."

I'm not suggesting here that we don't ponder our actions or spend time contemplating our behavior. When I began to be mindful of the nature of my self-talk, I resolved to retrain my brain. And I think really that's all it involves. After we have done our major healing work, I think the job becomes one of just re-education. We must teach our thoughts how to come up to speed with who we really are. I think we do this by mindfulness, noticing first what the dialogue is up there, then making a commitment to change the conversation.

It takes time and patience, but since I began that practice I have noticed a softening, a subtle shift in the sharpness with which I held myself.

And I have found that this practice spreads to other parts of me that need this same re-education, like some of my habitual emotional responses. When I catch myself beginning to react in not-very-helpful ways, I find that if I immediately send this sweetness and tenderness to myself, the intensity of the emotions subside.

I know it's still important for me to feel whatever I'm feeling, but if I can contain it within the compassionate heart, it shifts and dissipates and becomes more manageable. It doesn't sweep me away.

My intention in this practice is to help myself remember who I truly am. I can't do that if I'm always feeling "less than."

The Buddhists say a prayer that includes this phrase, "May I remember the beauty of my own true nature." I revised it somewhat to read, *May I remember the beauty and JOY and STRENGTH of my own true nature.*

In the esoteric philosophy that I study there is a *mantram* that I also find healing.

More radiant than the sun
Subtle than the ethers
Is the Self,
The Spirit within me
I am that Self
That Self am I.
—Alice Bailey, *From Intellect to Intuition*

I aspire to that knowing.

August 2017
Humility

Last week I attended a workshop on Orcas Island on the "Soul of the Enneagram" facilitated by the wonderful teacher N'Shama Sterling.

I was so looking forward to the peaceful hour-long ferry ride and the beautiful still waters of Puget Sound. I was mindful of a bit of anxiety. It was a long ride to Anacortes... *Will I make the ferry? Can I find my way to Indralaya? How will it be in a room full of strangers?* I knew there would be deep process going on. Nevertheless, I was mostly peaceful.

Finding the perfect spot on the ferry, I settled in. Not three minutes later, two women sat down in the booth next to me and they were having a jolly time - a loud, lots-of-laughter, voices raised in joy time. I tried to ignore the niggly irritation, aware that some of it was envy. *When was the last time I laughed with that much abandon?*

I tried changing my perspective. They were having a good time. Could I just open to that? Not easily, as it turned out.

I put in my ever-present ear plugs. I could still hear them.

Finally, fully exasperated I moved my seat to a not-so-perfect location. Oh well, I thought, so it goes.

Getting off the ferry I realized I would have to drive slowly if I were not to miss the Indralaya sign, so several times I had to pull over and let the ferry traffic behind me pass. Finally, I pulled into the retreat center, found my cabin, registered, and went to settle in.

When I walked into the cabin there were signs everywhere about making sure the cabin was cleaned before I left ... bathrooms, vacuuming, bedding removed, rooms cleaned. *Crap!!! I have to do housework??* Going into the kitchen I saw a chalk board with everyone's name next to a chore. Of course I was on pots and pans... double crap.

So, at this point my petulant, spoiled, little child was in quite a snit. Don't get me wrong, philosophically I totally believe in the idea of everyone doing their share. I just wasn't in the mood (another one of those "moods").

Walking down to the water before the first session began, I wandered upon a beautiful bench overlooking the still water. The breeze was gentle, the sun was peeking through and my body could not take any of it in. I was still stuck in the old pattern of negativity that comes to visit when I am a bit anxious.

Finally, a chant came to me and I began to sing, wishing I had my drum with me. *Oh, Great Spirit, I'm calling on you, Oh, Earth Mother, what else can I do. Open me up so I can receive, open me up so I can believe, oh oh oh oh Great Spirit I'm calling on you.*

Over and over I sang until the tension in my body and my mind began to lift. Feeling somewhat refreshed and a bit more open, I walked into the first session. And, of course, you can guess what happens next. The two laughing women are sitting in the circle and the first exercise we do where we pair up??? …I'm paired with the two of them.

Now tell me this isn't the big Kahuna in the sky saying, "Pay attention here, this is important." So, I paid attention and what I learned is that once I am eye-to-eye with anyone, and open just enough to hear their story, my humanity overrides my negativity. Now this is nothing particularly new to me, but I think the important thing was to recognize the pattern of negativity and how it kicks in within me.

When I posted this we were in the midst of three powerful eclipses and part of their message to us was to notice where we were stuck in habitual responses and reactivity, and to be *willing* to create that new groove in our brain. Just as in my hanging on to my internal story about fear, this is another inner response whose time has come: delete, delete, erase, erase.

The rest of the weekend was spent discussing the "passion" of each enneatype. Passion here means the way that we lose our center and become distorted in our thinking, feeling, and doing. Well, I'm a Type Two, the type described as the "helper," and the way I lose my center is in pride. So, as I help others it's easy to slip into a pride in my own virtue. *See what a good person I am?*

I know I have a deep, sincere, compassionate nature that is not trapped in that mindset, but when I lose my sense of that true self, I can feel that prideful part emerge. It's a way of being separative in my consciousness and placing myself above other people.

It's the same if I continually try to gauge and compare where I am in relation to others. I am creating a division. What I *truly* believe is that, "there is no other."

So, the antidote to pride is humility.

Remembering my entry on magnificence, I asked the question, "*How do you join magnificence with humility?*"

N'Shama replied, "How do you see it.?"

I realized that when I truly acknowledge my own magnificence - just as I am, just because I'm here - then I must acknowledge everyone's magnificence.

We are all cells in the body of the One Life.

We are all brothers and sisters belonging to the same family.

We are all magnificent just because we were born, and that doesn't mean just the people who make me happy or comfortable, or who think like me. It means *everyone*.

If I can *see* how we are all connected and *feel* the magnificence within myself and inside another, I can *open* to them in love and acceptance.

It feels like another layer of awareness to the whole "magnificence" revelation. A clearer understanding of how I can love more deeply.

Another veil has lifted.

Our job is to love others without stopping to inquire whether or not they are worthy.

—Thomas Merton

October 2013
Meditation on Humility

It's an interesting phenomenon that during my every day, waking life I sometimes struggle for a few minutes to retrieve a name or a word but when I'm deep into meditation I often hear songs (usually hymns from my church days) or chants (from my drumming circle days) and every word comes through loud and clear, sometimes several verses at a time.

Occasionally, as part of my meditation practice I will choose a meaningful word and just sit with it and open myself to impressions. After my experience at Indralaya and my work with the issue of pride and humility, I decided to contemplate the word *humility* during my meditation time. To my surprise, this familiar chant came into my awareness. It was an old chant that I used to drum and sing in a drumming circle I belonged to:

Open my heart
Let holy love pour through me.
Center my Soul
Upon the path of peace.
Make of my life
A melody of Love
Singing Alleluia, Oh Spirit, Alleluia
The following words are what came to me in relationship to this chant:
I think when love flows through me like that there is no room for pride....
only gratitude and a feeling of immense grace.
A melody of love. What if I could sing love, dance love, live love... like a
melody that gets stuck in my head?
Could I live love like that?
Stuck on love? Never able to move away from that melody?
Love can trump anything, negativity, judgment, pride.
I want to fill myself up with this kind of love.
Open my heart... fill up all the closed off places, all the tightness and
constriction.
Drown out all the fear.... just wash over it until there is no air left to
breathe in fear.
Open every closed door, every latched window, every sealed off place.
Let the love in.

Let the light in.
Oh Yeah!!!!

You know quite well, deep within you, that there is only a single, magic, single power, a single salvation, and that is called loving.
—Herman Hesse

CHAPTER 3
JUDGING AND CRITICISM

I know where I began to criticize and judge other people. It began with the constant comparing of myself to others that is inherent in the fundamentalist religion in which I was raised. We were so sure we were on the right side of God and that everyone else was living in sin. "I'm okay and you're probably going to hell."

There was the constant awareness that God was watching you and judging your behavior. Really? Did God really care that I was hungry and took an apple from the neighbor's tree on my walk home from school?

My sweet and gentle father tried so hard to model being a good Christian dad, but he never let an opportunity pass to verbally judge the bad behavior of another.

Then I happened to marry a man who had an amazing sense of humor that I only later realized was usually at someone else's expense. Making fun of the flaws he saw in another. He was funny, and I laughed along with him, but later I became sensitive to his sarcasm. Maybe because eventually it was aimed at me.

In any case I have a natural tendency to judge that has been one of my most active gremlins. It is only through the practice of mindfulness that I have been able to get a handle on it.

Also, I've had a little help from my friends, Ram Dass, Sylvia Boorstein, Heidi Robbins, and Pema Chodron.

July 2014
We Are All Trees

A while back I was in a new group of people. My pattern in these situations is to get a bit critical and judgmental. I know this about myself, and I understand why I do it. I feel a bit shy, a bit uncertain of my place, and in my anxiety around this I start to judge.

In this particular situation, I noticed fairly quickly what I was doing, so I was *sort of* observing my behavior rather than getting totally absorbed in the feelings. But then I began another old pattern of brooding about *why* I was still reliving this old response.

God, I thought I was so done with that.

That triggered the old imprint of, "I'm flawed somehow. I must be the only person in the universe who is this slow at learning to transform old habits." I've written previously when I was awash in the beauty of seeing the magnificence in everyone, the knowing that all of us are perfect, divine expressions of the One Life, just as we are. Where was *that* awareness hiding?

I asked for clarity in my meditation and I began to remember. Whenever I judge, it is ego doing the judging. Personality feels threatened in some way and thinks it needs to defend itself. I remembered the prayer that I have by my bedside, "May I generate a kind heart toward myself. May I see what I do without turning it against myself."

I guess it's not so much about never judging again - and holding myself to that impossible standard. I think it's more about accepting myself in spite of the fact that I'm not always acting from my highest self.

I know I've written about this before, so I'm pretty sure it's another one of those "themes" of my life that keeps popping up.

I ran across an article as I was pondering all this, one of those sweet co-inky-dinks. Someone was interviewing Ram Dass, and asked the question, "How can I judge myself less harshly and appreciate myself more?"

He answers,

I think that part of it is observing oneself more impersonally. I often use this image, that when you go out into the woods and you look at trees, you see all these different trees. And some of them are bent, and some of them are straight, and some of them are evergreens, and some of them are whatever. And you look at the tree and you allow it. You appreciate it. You see why it is the way it is. You sort of understand that it didn't get enough light, and so it turned that way. And you don't get all emotional about it. You just allow it. You appreciate the tree. The minute you get near humans, you lose all that. And you are constantly saying, 'You're too this, or I'm too this.' That judging mind comes in. And so, I practice turning people into trees.

Isn't that great?!!!!

He goes on to say that we should do the same with ourselves. "See ourselves as just a story line, unfolding and that we are just sort of watching this story unfold."

In other words, I'm not the storyline, and I don't want to be so identified with my personality reactions that I forget who I really am.

Who I really am is this essence of Love, a radiant, magnificent, unique being that is here to shine her light on her little corner of the world.

And in this month of Leo, where the Sun plays such an important role, I want to shine brilliantly.

August 2014
We Are All Trees ... and more (Part II)

You probably could have guessed that once I had the awareness of people as trees (my last entry) that I would get a chance to see if I was ready to put it into practice.

So, of course, the very next week I was in a confined space, for over an hour, with a talker. Now this particular situation is something that I always find difficult, someone who just *yadda yadda yaddas*, without any awareness of whether the person they are talking to is interested.

I felt my muscles tighten, my chest constrict, my old judging mind start to kick in, but this time I remembered. "Okay," I said to myself, "he's a tree. He probably didn't get enough water and I'm sure he must have been deep in the woods where there was no sunshine."

My heart stayed open. I felt compassion and understanding. I was clear I would not voluntarily choose to spend more time with him, but still I did not shut down. Yay, for me.

A few days later I was preparing for the Leo full moon ceremony and I came across a quote from my astrology teacher, Heidi Robbins, a brilliant light of wisdom. She said in reference to the Leo month,

Imagine there is a sun at the center of your chest. Wherever you go, imagine it is shining 360 degrees from that center. Include all those that you see and interact within that light. Imagine then that the light that is within you is the same light within another...and grow your experience of Self. Let the boundaries blur. Feel the I-ness that can expand beyond your isolated personality. Practice including more in the warmth of your heart, the light of your body and the eternal You that cannot be contained by the boundaries of the body.

I was impressed with this idea and decided it might be a good practice for me to try this month. Sure enough, the next day as I was in my Zumba class there were two women in the back who always talk through the whole class. I felt myself start in with the critical inner voice. Then again, I remembered, *Imagine your heart as the sun, radiate it out 360 degrees.* I did that. *Then imagine the same sun within them.* Wow, major shift in me. Not *just* compassion and understanding but acknowledgment of the essence of who they really were. That changed everything. Now we were three suns dancing our buns off, lighting up the whole room.

There is no way of telling people that they are all walking around shining like the sun.

—Thomas Merton

July 2015
Revisiting a Gremlin

A few weeks ago, I got to spend a few days with a dear friend who was visiting from out of state. We had a wonderful time of catching up and just being together.

She is a woman who has worked her whole adult life outside the home and has risen to the top of her chosen profession. She could literally choose to work anywhere and be assured of a six-figure income.

After she left, I woke up in a funk. With my moon in Cancer I'm aware that my moods change with the tides, so it could have been just that, a temporary funk. But as a Scorpio I always want to dig deeper to see what else might be lurking in my underworld.

The previous two weeks of over-the-top heat here had seeped all the juice out of me, and I hadn't exercised, or done my physical therapy, or had much social contact.

My "not good enough" gremlin reared its head and my thinking process went something like this:

Why aren't I motivated to do anything right now? I feel like the slug that my ex-husband once called me. I can't access my confidence, my feelings of worth, my belief in my magnificence. *Maybe my whole life has been a wrong turn.* (Notice how the gremlin so sneakily gets global?) *Should I have stayed working longer at my profession?*

This is when my friend came to mind. I noticed I was feeling a bit envious. Not of her stature or her income, but of her mastery of her profession. There was a confidence in her of how to operate in the world that seemed to translate into how she felt about her place. She knew how to negotiate, she knew how to work with a team, she knew how to be a leader. For God's sake, she was even competent on the computer, the iPad, the iPhone and every other electronic device one could think of. And if she didn't know, she was sure she could figure it out. She was self-assured. I think that's what I envied, and I was not feeling anything like that on this day.

It occurred to me then to check the astrology for the week to see if I could get a clue as to what was happening with the planets. It's always helpful if you can blame the planets for your lousy mood.☺

Sure enough, Saturn (the ruler of my chart) had just re-entered the sign of Scorpio, (my Sun sign). This is a configuration that will impact everyone until this fall, but since those two signs are so prominent in my chart, they will impact me more powerfully. Basically, this means that it's time to look deeply again at what is still operating within me that is in need of transformation. Here's another perspective:

As we swing back into Saturn in Scorpio, we are given the opportunity to revisit the Victim Archetype and break out of its suffering. The intensity of this retrograde (re-evaluation) brings our Shadow to the surface to face what we have tried to bury in the past. Saturn calls this "being responsible … depression, grief, fear, and doubt are the feelings that may accompany a descent back into the rabbit hole that the Victim must face.

Walking through this Saturn in Scorpio time is a sort of death. We are being asked to let go of what must die so that something new can be formed, restructured and incorporated."

— Teresa Campos and Corey Gilbert

So, I was revisiting the rabbit hole and being reminded that my old familiar gremlin, named, "not good enough," had once again reared its head.

I went into meditation then to see if I could gain some clarity about how to once again work with this ancient belief. I began practicing *tonglen*, the Buddhist practice of breathing in the world's despair and depression and breathing out compassion and lovingkindness to all who suffer. This helped create within me a compassion for that gnarly gremlin. Then still in the quiet, I remembered a Tom Kenyon workshop I had attended last November on the shadow. He suggested that we don't need to **work** at transforming the darkness, we only need to bring the light of our awareness to those parts of us in need of healing and then just allow the healing to take place.

So, I invoked the light of my Soul and visualized it irradiating that dark place and bringing it to the light. I believe that once we expose the gremlins to the light, the underlying energy (which is always benevolent) becomes available to us to be used in a more positive way.

So, I imagined this happening to, "not good enough." There was some relief that I felt in my body, but the transformative shift came with this realization:

I have lived a life filled with extraordinary experiences and I have woven those experiences into the fabric of my life in such a way that now, at age 73 I have some degree of wisdom. That wisdom is to be used in service to my world. I have, in a sense, mastered my life and have learned how to glean the most important learnings from whatever comes my way.

Whew!!! Take that, sweet gremlin.

I am under no illusions that this gremlin has disappeared forever. I believe that complete transformation only rarely occurs with one aha moment. More realistically, it is a slow climb up the mountain meeting each gremlin as it presents itself, and hopefully learning to greet it with love and compassion.

Slowly its voice subsides to a whisper and we are left free to make wiser use of this energy.

May I meet each moment fully. May I meet it as a friend.
—Sylvia Boorstein

May 2016
Lessons From the Gym... "Just Like Me"

Recently I was reading an article by Pema Chodron, one of my favorite people, in which she talked about how she deals with her judgmental mind - not her discerning mind, which is different than the critical/judgmental mind. Discerning, as I interpret it, means to see clearly the differences, the truth, the objective reality. The critical mind, (as in criticizing) is the part of us that then jumps in and gives it an emotional tone.

For instance, I see a person being obnoxious and rude. My discerning mind makes an observation. "This is a person I would rather not associate with." My critical mind could then take it a step farther. "I really don't like this person. He/she is a real creep/jerk/or some other expletive." See how the emotional body can react to a simple observation? That's judgment, criticism - not discernment.

At any rate, Pema was saying that she has made a habit of being mindful of her critical thoughts and then to pause and repeat to herself, "Hmmm, just like me." So, just like me... I can get obnoxious and rude too sometimes. I thought this might be a good exercise to practice, to use this phrase as a *mantram* to carry though the day.

So, on the first day of holding this intention, I was off to the gym. I sat in the steam room trying to rid my body of any germs I may have picked up from my two grandchildren who are both sick. I was alone. The steam came on and it increased in intensity the longer I was there until an automatic shut off stopped it for a while. I had been enjoying the break when another person walked in and immediately turned it on again. My judgmental mind kicked in without a second's hesitation. "How rude is that, to come into the steam room and not even ask if the other person wants the steam back on." I could feel myself getting irritated. Then I remembered, "Just like me." Just like me I sometimes forget to consider other people's needs. My body unclenched, and my mind regained its balance.

A few days later I was in my water aerobics class. I'm not sure why this seems to always trigger me, but people who talk, talk, talk when I'm trying to exercise really annoy me. There was this one woman in the pool who every day goes to her friend and they talk the entire time, never doing anything. My mind started in again, "Why do they even bother coming to class? Why not just go to a coffee shop and gab?" Then I remembered... "Just like me." Now

I know that I don't have that particular habit, so that part is not just like me, but there are times when I can get carried away in conversations and lose track of other people… so, "just like me."

With this practice you do have to sometimes look a little deeper to see the connection or the underlying motive, but it has made such a difference in my ability to not only stay neutral in my observations, but also to relate more deeply to the ways in which we are connected. It has increased my compassion and understanding and made me more tolerant.

Another incident, on a different day, happened just outside the steam room. A woman had shared the room with me and I hadn't even noticed her because the steam was so thick. Coming out we sat down on the benches to dry off. I realized she was a woman from my Zumba class that I had tried on a few occasions to engage. She always was aloof and standoffish. I had sort of labeled her in my mind as "snobbish."

This particular time I tried again to interest her in conversation and to my surprise she opened up and shared a lot about her life. I realized she was a very sweet, nice person. So, my, "just like me" was about acknowledging that I too have days where I don't feel like engaging or being social.

The other realization came as a reminder of something I have known for a long time, that almost always when I hear another person's story, my heart opens and that judgmental mind goes right to sleep.

The last example I will share occurred in the women's locker room at the gym. There is a machine there that wrings out our wet suits when we get out of the pool. I was second in line and the woman using the machine is using it over and over, even though one rotation works really well. I start getting impatient. I have places to go, things to do, people to see, dontcha know? Suddenly she looks up, and sort of shakes herself and says, "OMG I'm so sorry, my mind just drifted off." This one was a no brainer (so to speak): JUST LIKE ME!!!

The reason we don't want to judge someone is that then we're inviting the least evolved part of them to dance with the least evolved part of us and it's just never pretty.
—Caroline Casey

CHAPTER 4
ANGER

I think this chapter should more accurately be called, "My Sensitive Emotional Nature, and How I Deal With Other People's Anger", but that is too long a title so I'm just naming it Anger.

I've never been very good at expressing my anger. It was never encouraged in my childhood. Usually it was stuffed and swallowed like a bitter pill. It certainly was not supported by the model of a good Christian girl that I was shown. I grew up feeling like it was un-Christian to even feel anger, let alone express it. So-called "negative emotions" were not supported.

When frustrated, I would sometimes explode with what I considered an expletive, "GEEZ." I was told that was swearing because it was just an abbreviation of the word Jesus. So, more swallowing and stuffing. The truth is, there was not a whole lot to be angry about in our family. It was mostly loving and gentle, but there was also a palpable undercurrent when someone was upset, and it was rarely discussed or talked about openly. I had no tools for how to negotiate difficult feelings.

It's been interesting to watch myself as an adult, early twenties and thirties mostly. But when I got angry, I began swearing like a trooper and it felt *so* freeing. I felt liberated just saying those "nasty" words.

One time when my parents were visiting us in California, where we lived, they took my daughter out to their RV to play. During the course of some game they were playing my daughter became frustrated and yelled out, "JEEE SUS CEEE RIST." She was two years old. My mother, flustered and upset, ran into the house and said, "Karen, where did she hear such language?" I don't remember what I said, but I realized then that we needed to monitor our language a bit since we now had a toddler with very big ears.

The point of all of this is that it has taken me many years to try to come to terms with my own anger and especially other people's anger, when it is directed toward me.

As you will read in the following entries this is not something that happens to me very often. So, when it occurred over and over again in a short period of time, I realized that this was something I needed to look at carefully.

July 2016
Anger is My Edge

It's not often that people get angry at me. My "accommodating" nature doesn't usually ruffle people's feathers.

So, when it happened twice in one week, I paid attention. The first event happened at a gathering at a friend's house. This particular friend and I don't see eye-to-eye on some things, and I thought we had sort of reached a truce with that. We each accepted that we would probably not change the other's mind and resolved to co-exist peacefully despite our differences. So, I was unprepared for her outburst at me while we were gathered around the table with friends, having a bite to eat. Not thinking, I sort of fired back, but in a defensive mode and with no more rational thought than she had given to her outburst. The table went silent and then someone thankfully changed the subject.

As the gathering ended and we prepared to leave, my friend came over and apologized. I demurred and acted like it was nothing and, "No worries, I'm fine." But I wasn't really. I kept regurgitating the conversation, over and over, in my mind. I was mad at myself for reacting on the same level as she had. Why hadn't I just named what was happening, like I do with my grandkids when they get upset? "Wow, you sound really angry. What's going on?" But I reacted and then tamped it all down.

I didn't sleep well that night, pondering how I might have handled it differently. It felt abusive and part of me wishes I had just called it that, "You are being rude and disrespectful." But this was a fairly new groove that I was trying to etch into my brain. -how to appropriately deal with anger, especially when it is directed at me.

I grew up with my father's way of dealing, "It's not worth getting angry about," so I didn't see many outbursts in my family of origin. Occasionally my mom would emerge out of the bathroom with puffy eyes and we knew she was upset, but she would never cop to it. It all went underground.

On the surface, one big happy family. And to be honest about it, we mostly were. But there were no models for what to do when things weren't so rosy.

Then I went on to marry a person who had known too much rage in his family and only knew that way to deal with frustration and anxiety. It was a good schoolroom for me in that I learned that there needed to be a mediating way between complete denial/repression and out of control, abusive rage. Unfortunately, there was no way to mediate the differences within our marriage and we divorced.

The situation with my friend had an unusual component in that the group was disbanding so I probably would not see her again. We hadn't ever socialized outside the group, so I had nothing invested in maintaining a relationship. Because of that, or maybe just out of cowardice, I decided not to confront my friend with my feelings.

However, I did begin the practice I wrote about in the entry, Just Like Me. I began to see how sometimes I am also unaware of how I come out and can be unintentionally rude or disrespectful. And after all, she did apologize. Case closed.

The second event was resolved amicably. Nevertheless, because it was the second time within a week that I had been confronted I decided I needed to take a good long look at what these outbursts had aroused in me. I saw my discomfort, my tendency to freeze and not be present to the moment, my hesitancy to speak from my authentic voice, my desire to have harmony no matter what the situation. I remembered these old patterns, my old friends, so I tried to just notice them and not judge myself because they had come to visit me again. Telling myself, *It's alright, I'm still learning.* And I have learned a lot since those early childhood days.

In my close, intimate relationships I've pretty much learned to be okay with my vulnerability. To speak when I'm hurt or upset and to try to examine and admit to my part in a disagreement. And after all, this happened in a Gemini month where we were being asked to lovingly communicate what we really feel and accept responsibility for our part. So, I guess it's absolutely appropriate that this issue came up for me at this time.

But anger is still my edge. What is most difficult for me, so I make a deeper commitment to being more mindful, aware and present.

Never forget that conversation is a form of activism and what you allow in is as much a revolutionary act as what you speak

—Chani Nicholas

August 2016
Anger is My Edge, Part II

Here's how my life seems to work sometimes:

I have an aha moment, there is a new clarity, and something seems to shift, then a challenge occurs relating to the new awareness. If I can hold the clarity I received through the challenge, then the new insight becomes embodied… more easily accessible… overriding the old instinctual pattern.

And there seems to be a synchronicity to it all. When the challenge occurs there is almost always help available to help me make sense of it, like a passage in a book, or a conversation with someone. And if I can recognize the underlying purpose of the challenge, (I call them FGOs, another "f*cking growth opportunity") then I can more easily detach from the emotional reaction.

So, as I wrote about in my last entry, when two times in one week people became angry at me, it caused me some distress, some worry, and I had sleepless nights after each encounter.

Now, I'm participating in a webinar called, "Glamour, a World problem." Glamour is loosely defined as any response that triggers your emotional body. Well, certainly my emotional body was triggered as I struggled with how to deal with my feelings about people being mad at me.

In this webinar we are asked to name a particular glamour we are aware of. Immediately I thought, "My sensitive emotional nature." It's a glamour, you see, because it is not my True Self. It is not my essence. It is my ego's response to a perceived threat.

There is a lot that I like about my sensitive nature. I care deeply, I can easily perceive another's pain, I have empathy and compassion. But when it takes me over, when I lose myself in it, then it's a distortion of that pure energy of the Soul.

So, the next step in the seminar was to do a meditation to help dispel that particular glamour. After we had finished, I went to open the book called, *Glamour a World Problem*, by Alice Bailey. I happened to open it to the page where it defines "indifference". Here's what it says,

Indifference means, in reality, the achieving of a neutral attitude towards that which is regarded as the Not-self. It signifies a refusal to be identified with anything save the spiritual reality as far as that is sensed and known at any given point in time and space. It is active repudiation without any concentration upon that which is repudiated.

I took this to mean that the antidote to my "sensitive nature glamour" was to practice indifference. To attempt, in a situation where I feel entrapped in my emotions, to try to become neutral to my feelings. To not give them so much attention. To focus on the spiritual reality as far as I can access it.

It doesn't mean denial or repression, it just means don't get lost in the emotional field, scattering and dissipating your energy.

Next, I came to this passage in which the Tibetan Master who dictated the words to Alice Bailey tells us not to identify with all of the obstructions, all of the difficulties we struggle with in our personality nature, but to constantly remember the truth that we are the Self (the Soul, as I translate that).

To me, that was helpful because I could see that by identifying with my higher self when trapped in my emotions, I would be able to more clearly see the truth, that this emotional reactiveness/sensitivity was just an ego response.

Shortly after taking in that understanding I began listening to a podcast by Sounds True. It's an amazing site, by the way, where you can get free downloads of Tami Simon's interviews with spiritual teachers around the world. In my opinion she is one the best interviewers I have ever heard. She asks in depth questions that always seem relevant to what I am thinking. These interviews are available at soundstrue.com.

In any event, this particular day she was interviewing, Matt Kahn, the author of *Whatever Arises, Love That*. Kahn suggested that a wonderful practice for living a life that is love filled is to begin with ourselves. He suggested that several times a day we pause and just say to ourselves, "I love you."

I began using this practice as I noticed feelings come up around the anger issue. I would begin to feel angst, and I would silently just say, "I love you," directing it at the angst. I would feel hurt, "I love you, hurt." Whatever feeling arose, I would just pause and send it my love.

Buddhism has a similar practice where you hold everything that comes up in your compassionate heart, but for some reason saying the words, "I love you" felt more powerful. When I could love all of the feelings around people being angry at me the intensity diminished, the anxiety fell away, and my own level of self-acceptance grew.

If I want to consciously participate in my own evolutionary process, in a healthy way, I need to look at everything that comes my way as an opportunity to grow.

I'm sure there are more revelations to come around this deeply held issue, but until they come, I'm resting in the love for myself

August 2016
Anger Is My Edge, Part III

Well, as predicted in my last entry, the learnings around anger continue to come my way. After the first two incidents, three more appeared. So now I'm really focused on what all of this means to me and how I operate in the world. So far this is what I've gleaned:

The new attitude of "indifference", the practice of loving whatever comes and the readjustment of my focus on my higher self, I discussed in my last entry. Since then:

A re-commitment to courageously speaking up about how someone's behavior affected me. In two of the cases where friends were angry with me, I spoke about how I felt and asked if there was something we needed to work out between us that might be causing the outburst. I felt resolved once we had processed the interaction.

I believe the above approach is helpful because I always want to be aware of how my actions affect other people. But when I examined why I was habitually questioning if they were upset *with me* over something, I realized that once again I was more concerned with their feelings about me than I was in just stating, "I don't want to be treated that way by my friends," and then stating clearly what is acceptable behavior. As someone once said to me, "We train people how to treat us by what we accept and what we expect."

A strong determination to be much more mindful about boundaries. I totally overstepped my bounds with two people I love very much. I really need to get this lesson because it keeps coming up and I want so much to be aware of what is appropriate and what is not and not hurt the people I love. There are all kinds of reasons why this is such a big issue for me, but nevertheless I need to pull up my big girl pants and get on with it.

Remembering that I always get a deeper understanding of things when I sit in silence, align to my Soul and ask for clarity. In one case I realized I still had some angst about one of the people who was angry with me even though she apologized and offered to process whatever I needed to in order to get clear with me. In meditation I could feel my *appreciation* for her willingness to work this out and her ability to take ownership of her part in the interaction. When I could connect with that, the angst disappeared.

After the month of outbursts, I read the astrology post from Chani Nicholas that described the energies that were going on at the time of these incidents.

I'm always amazed to see how accurate astrology can be, and of course, it's always convenient to blame our moods, etc. on the planets, but in any case, this post was particularly relevant to what I had just gone through.

Your journey might get a little rocky this week. Your need to "speak up and tell it like it is" might become too tense to tame. You might have to risk some of your security in order to reclaim some freedom. But this could help you break new ground. This could help you see your path more clearly. This could help you to harness your energy and move it in the direction that you most wish to go.

Take the risk. Revealing ourselves can be a spiritual experience. Telling the world who we really are requires that we have enough faith in ourselves to get through any response we might hear.

This week starts and ends with abrupt squares to Uranus, the planet of upheaval and change. **The first is between Mercury and Uranus on Monday. These two aren't at terrible odds with one another thematically – they both speak to ways of receiving and transmitting information. But squares cause friction. This one is about being able to speak about and to allow discord.** Mercury, the messenger, is still in Cancer, the sign that deals with home, family, needs and nourishment. Uranus, the planet of rebellion, upheaval and revolution is in Aries, the sign of the courage it takes to become an individual.

Still working on it!!!!

We cannot live in a world that is not our own,
In a world that is interpreted for us by others.
An interpreted world is not home.
Part of the terror
Is to take back our own listening,
To use our own voice,
To see our own light.
—Hildegard of Bingen

September 2016
My Last Blog on Anger, I Promise

Okay, this is it on the anger subject, but during my ruminations this past month I came across several truths that it seems are important for me to remember.

1.Whenever a brother/sister attacks you, hear it as a cry for more love. (A Course in Miracles, paraphrased). In other words, "don't take it personally."

2.When someone is angry or defensive toward you, recognize it as the parts of themselves that they haven't loved enough. (Matt Kahn, Whatever Arises, Love That: A Love Revolution That Begins With You) In other words, "Don't take it personally"

3.Right before a walk last week I had just read from Tosha Silver's book, Outrageous Openness, this story:

A person in an airport line got frustrated with her and lashed out. Instead of reacting defensively Tosha paused and considered what the other person might be going through. She saw the woman's anger as a manifestation of someone who had never been listened to, whose own voice had never been acknowledged, so no wonder she was angry. Tosha realized it had nothing to do with her. She also saw that this must be the way the woman talked to herself, that this must be how she was treated and because of Tosha's own childhood she could understand that feeling. This brought her to a place of deep compassion for this woman's pain and suffering and she decided she would respond by sending her good thoughts.

So, the learning for me is this: Instead of constricting in hurt, or defensiveness, or shutting down, when someone is upset with me, I can open my heart wider. I can allow the feeling and then *choose* to expand so that I see with clarity the other's pain and acknowledge their suffering. I can remember to not take it personally, which helps my heart to open.

This doesn't preclude expressing what my needs are or sharing how the outburst affected me, this is important to remember, but it does mean that when I do take action it will come from a more compassionate place.

It also doesn't hurt to take a few moments to gently examine my part in the interaction. Not taking it personally doesn't mean I don't own whatever part I played.

Iyanla Vanzant is a well-known author and teacher who hosts a reality show on the Own network called "Iyanla, Fix my Life". When asked in an interview how she dealt with attacks from others she explained that she felt we should always speak up, but to do it with a loving and compassionate heart. Here are two ways that she herself responds to an attack:

"Beloved, I did not give you permission to speak to me in that way."

"Please forgive me for anything I've done that made you think you had permission to speak to me in that way. Please tell me what it was."

I think one would need to be careful in saying these phrases to not put a sarcastic spin on the words. But the idea is still valid. We can speak our truth while our heart remains open and compassionate.

One of the tools that I have used for many years when I'm dealing with any personal conflict with someone is to sit in silence, open my heart, and send them a lovingkindness blessing. "May they be at peace. May they be free from suffering. May they remember the beauty of their own true nature. May they live their life with ease." It's very hard to hold onto any angst toward someone when you are blessing them.

Another quote from Tosha Silver in her book, *Outrageous Openness*, says this,

Sometimes the people with the most anger need the most help. You never know what sending them blessings can do. You might be the only one on the planet winging good their way.

CHAPTER 5
HUMOR

Whenever I think of humor and belly laughs, my sister always comes to mind. Being two years older than me, I grew up idolizing her. She was my heroine. Plus, I loved that I got to date all the boys she discarded.

With Saturn as the ruling planet of my chart I have a tendency to be fairly serious, and when you combine that with a Scorpio sun you have a lot of intensity. My sister, on the other hand, is mostly upbeat, funny, and light-hearted. I mean, her name is Joybelle, after all, so how could she not be? We make a good pair and have had a close connection since our childhood.

We always got lightly admonished, when we were young, for getting the giggles at the dinner table. What was not so funny was when we would get an attack of giggles at church services, especially communion services which were very somber and serious. Once, when we noticed how everyone threw their heads back at the same moment as they were drinking down the grape juice, we were thrown into gales of laughter that I'm sure embarrassed everyone but us.

So, you see we have this history of humor between us. We find the same things funny and usually we are the only ones who see it. It's that warped.

Since the last chapter focused on Anger, I thought it might be fun to insert my entries on laughter here. Of course, I shared them with my sis and we had many jolly laughs over them.

Hopefully they will tickle your funny bone like they did ours.

July 2013
Just for Laughs

Okay, I'm the first to admit I have a warped sense of humor, but truly, it's not my fault, it's genetic. My sis and I share that gene, and, in the past, we have been known to pee our pants from uncontrolled laughter. Wait... that was just last week.

Anyway, at this intense time of solstice, full moon, and all kinds of challenging vibrations bombarding us from the cosmos, I decided a little lightening up would be good for my soul. So here it is, my compilation of funnies, totally plagiarized from some catalogue selling tee shirts.

Never piss off someone who bleeds for a week every month and doesn't die.

This next one wasn't on a tee shirt, but I thought it profoundly funny as well as most likely true:

We are all a little weird and life's a little weird and when we find someone whose weirdness is compatible with ours, we join up with them and then fall in mutual weirdness and call it love. -Dr. Seuss

Remember as far as anyone knows we're a normal family.

(It's too late for my family. We've known for years we are anything but normal.)

Don't grow up ... it's a trick.

(Yeah, why didn't someone tell me this about 60 years ago?)

If it walks out of the refrigerator, for God's sake, LET IT GO.

(We tried to tell this to my dad on his last days, but he would have none of it.)

This last one may not be entirely politically correct, and I don't usually like name calling but this was funny

I'm not saying you are stupid. I'm just saying you've got bad luck when it comes to thinking."

That's it. Hope it brought a smile if not a mess on the floor.

November 2014
Just for Fun

Would you like a few giggles this day to lighten up the darkness of the approaching winter and the intensity of Scorpio energies?

Every now and then it is very uplifting for me to stop pondering, analyzing, and philosophizing. So, you won't find any words of wisdom in this blog unless you can somehow extract a metaphysical message from the tidbits below.

I occasionally get a catalogue advertising coffee mugs, tee shirts, and posters with clever sayings on them. Yesterday one of those magazines appeared and I spent the next ½ hour chuckling and sometimes laughing out loud at their humor.

I think I have admitted in a previous blog that my humor is a bit warped so don't feel badly if the sayings below leave you with a feeling of "what?" It's just my weirdness coming out.

Below are some of my favorites:

I childproofed the house, but they keep getting in.

I thought about being a stay at home mom until I realized the kids would be there too.

Dear Karma, I have a list of people you missed.

If you are alone in the forest and you spill your glass of wine can you suck it out of your shirt?

Who the hell would throw shit at a fan?

Children are often spoiled because no one will spank grandma.

We'll be friends until we're old and senile, then we'll be new friends. (Actually, not too funny, these days.)

I'm so old I remember when water was free, and you had to pay for porn.

I thought growing older would take longer.

A lack of planning on your part does not constitute and emergency on my part.

I will not yell in class. I will not throw things. I will not tease the other kids. I'm the teacher. I'm the teacher.

So, I just found out I'm awesome. You might want to get yourself tested.

Changing the toilet paper will not cause brain damage.

I hate being bipolar. It's awesome.

Three Wise Women, would have asked directions, arrived on time, helped deliver the baby, cleaned the stables, made a casserole, brought practical gifts. And there would be Peace on Earth.

I think this might be my favorite:

Side effects include weight gain, depression, and loss of sex drive. Ask your doctor if marriage is right for you.

Until next time, hope your day just got a bit cheerier.

CHAPTER 6
JOY

The idea that I could choose the way I wanted to feel was totally new to me until a few years ago. Maybe it was reading Danielle LaPorte, maybe it was the "Awakening Joy" class, but it dawned on me that I didn't have to be a victim of my sensitive nature. For much of my life I walked in the world with a heart that felt everything and for many years I had no way to filter it all out. I would succumb to whatever the feeling was that I was holding. I would *become* that feeling and couldn't see beyond it. All of me, totally identified with the sorrow, the grief, the sadness, the whatever.

Later I learned tools for how to be with the feeling without becoming overwhelmed by them, but the idea that I could choose to see *beyond* the feeling to something new was a revelation. It wasn't about saying, "Oh I don't like this feeling. I will just ignore it and try to feel something more pleasant." No, it was more like, "Oh, here is this pain. I will feel it fully and in the midst of it I will open my eyes a bit wider to see if there is anything else that I can feel."

As long as we are in this human body, we will encounter the duality of human existence. The this-and-that, the yes-and-no, the light and the darkness. The challenge I think we face is to find the midpoint. To be able to choose where we put our attention and to strive to hold the common thread rather than identify totally with one side or the other.

> The place where the this and the that,
> Are not opposed to each other,
> Is called the 'pivot of the Tao.'
> When we find this pivot,
> We find ourselves,
> At the center of the circle.
> And here we sit, serene,
> While yes and no keep chasing each other around the circumference,
> Endlessly.
> —Chuang-Tzu

January 2014
Pain and the Open Heart

The question that is facing me today is: *How do I be with pain and still keep my heart open?*

There is so much suffering going around these days, like a contagious virus that is infecting everyone in some capacity. Young people dying needlessly. Old people giving up, waking up one morning to find a loved one has passed on in his sleep. And that's just on my home turf.

How do we be with it? That is the question. Shutting down, going numb? That's usually my default position, but I'm finding it too painful to do that anymore because it shuts out the joy as well as the pain.

And I *choose* to feel.

But how to feel fully without drowning in the sorrow, without sinking into despair, that is the larger issue.

Sometimes I discover what might work for me by paying attention to what doesn't work. So, here's what I know doesn't work for me when it comes to pain:

Look how good your life is, it could be so much worse. There are a lot of people who are suffering more than you.

This I know, but in the process of skimming over my pain to focus on how bad everyone else has it I somehow trivialize my own feelings and truth be told isn't there just a bit of arrogance in this stance? Like I'm saying to myself, *I'm so glad I'm not in their shoes.* Is that compassion?

Having said that, let me add that I am a great believer in the practice of gratitude, being thankful for the blessings in our lives.

A practice that helped me resolve some of these questions came through my daughter. A few years ago, she was moving to India for a year and she suggested we take an online class together called, "Awakening Joy", as a way to stay connected while she was gone. Well, as it turned out there was no Wi-Fi connection in Auroville where she was living, but I decided to go ahead and take the class anyway. One of the practices that was emphasized over and over again was that of mindfulness. Just paying attention.

I have found this is especially helpful when it comes to difficult emotions, grief, hurt, negativity, self judgement, etc. This concept is based on the premise that everything changes, all the time. Just remembering that in the midst of pain, "This too shall pass," is comforting. Not as a way of avoiding what is, but allowing for the possibility that something else can also be present. While we are in the pain, we learn to see that joy is also always available to us.

One of the constant intentions we were invited to use in the class was the phrase, "Incline the mind toward joy." That meant to me that we don't have to pretend to be joyful when we're not and that joy is not always about running around with a smile on our face. I can be in pain and if I remember to "incline my mind toward joy." I can begin to look around, to open my eyes wider, to see where joy might be possible. It can be as small as noticing the birds that come to my bird feeder while I sit in my chair. If I am inclining my mind toward joy I can pause, take that in, and stay with it, even if just for a few seconds. And in those few seconds, I bring joy into my being to sit with the pain.

Choosing joy is an intention that we can hold regardless of whatever our experience is bringing us. Again, it doesn't mean we ignore the pain, or try to replace it with a feeling of superficial joy, it just means we understand that joy is everywhere, available at any time, if we choose to see it.

This is the understanding that the book, *Awakening Joy*, by James Baraz and Shoshana Alexander, presents: It's easy to do all these joy practices when all is well in your life, but not so easy when the difficulties arise, however that's when you need this practice the most. It's not about ignoring the pain but noticing if there are moments of lightness or joy, in the midst of the pain.

They go on to tell the story of a woman who lost all of her material possessions - and she had accumulated a lot. But she didn't sink into despair. Instead she learned how to keep going by taking one step at a time. She would hold in her awareness the intention to incline her mind toward joy and try to remain conscious when the hard stuff happened. She also became determined to hold onto whatever good she could see in her life… and hold onto it for as long as she could. Being in a state of appreciation, and being kind toward herself, then getting up each day and doing it all over again. This was her practice.

This is my commitment to myself this new year: I CHOOSE JOY!!!!!

If you would like to explore taking the online class go to the website: http://www.awakeningjoy.info.

July 2014
Movin' and Shaking

"It was a teenage wedding and all the old folks wished them well."

The music is blasting, and it's got a great beat. I'm at my line dancing class at the gym when I suddenly become aware that I am grinning from ear to ear for no apparent reason, and there is so much joy in my body.

I'm not really surprised, dancing to the music I love (mostly rock and roll) always makes me feel almost ecstatic.

Perhaps in response to not being allowed to dance as a young person, ("I'm sorry, I can't. It's against my religion") I have gotten crazy joy out of it since I left home. I am always aware that I don't do enough of it.

When the housework calls, I put on the dance CD my son Ryan made for me one birthday, with all my favorite dance tunes. That usually gives me enough of a lift to do chores I rather not be doing.

But by and large I know that I could use more of that expansive, over the top feeling of exuberance in my life.

One of my goddess gurus, Danielle LaPorte, challenges us to ask the question, "What are your *core desired* feelings?" She goes on to say that instead of setting goals of trying to "accomplish", of trying to "do better", we could just notice what it is we really desire to *feel* in our life and then, "Do whatever it takes to feel the way you most want to feel."

I want more of that feeling of the dance, of moving rhythmically to sounds that resonate in my body. It's a type of freedom to me, to just close my eyes and let my body respond to the sounds that I hear, to move, unencumbered by worry, burden, or anything heavy. It's exactly the *opposite* of "heavy," and it seems that my whole life is moving toward that freedom, that release, that "untanglement" (Is that a word?).

I want to wake up each morning with that "zippity doo da" excitement.

Maybe I should try twenty minutes of morning dancing instead of my meditation practice☺☺. Or better yet, do both.

It is well known that when you tune into your body it quiets the mind so maybe dancing could *be* a meditation. Wouldn't that frost the old Free Methodists?

Someone told me a joke once that might offend some of you, but I'll tell it anyway, too old to care.

"Do you know why the fundamentalists are against sex? They're afraid it might lead to dancing." I was led to believe that who knew what could happen once you started *dancing*? Yikes, maybe I would actually begin to love my body, love moving my body to music.

Anyway, I am grateful to have my knees back working again, after tearing my meniscus, so I can rejoin the other sinners in my dance class.

CHAPTER 7
CANCER MOON AND THE RHYTHMS OF LIFE

It began as a deep longing, in my forties. As I've mentioned before, I had been on a sabbatical from anything spiritual since my late twenties. Suddenly I wanted a deeper connection to something. I was missing a feeling of purpose and meaning.

Then in 1990 I stumbled upon the works of Machaelle Wright, the founder of the Perelandra research center in Virginia. In her books she talks about the relationship between humans and the nature kingdom (angels or devas), and how we are meant to have a co-creative relationship with them. We can invoke their wisdom to assist us in our healing, in our relationships, in our gardens.

This was a new idea to me and I immediately resonated with it. I began thinking of nature as a living intelligence and became much more mindful of my footprint on the sacred earth. But to have a real relationship with that kingdom of nature meant that I needed to be more aware of her cycles, the in-breath, the out-breath, the pauses. It's what started me on my journey of honoring the full moon each month and offering full moon ceremonies in my home.

But along with that I began to see how all life moves in cycles, from the micro- to the macrocosm. When I began to view my own life in that way it became easier to accept the ups and downs and the in-between times.

In this chapter I introduce you to the "belonging" and the "resting" cycle that preceded the very active and engaged cycle of a new grandbaby and the beginning of my book tour in 2013.

May 2013
Belonging

This is a good moment, this very moment of 2:04pm on a Monday.

I feel content. I feel at home. I feel like I belong. To this very house. To my life. And to myself.

As most of you who read this blog know, this isn't a constant thing. I spiral. I waffle. I peak. I descend. I circle around. But today I am grateful for belonging fully to this moment.

Something has shifted and loosened.

The shackles feel not so tight.

The veils not so obscure, the constrictions and rigidity are breathing in openness and fluidity.

Surely, it is connected to the astrological energies of the recent eclipses and the full moon, but I'm not in the mood to analyze.

I'm just sitting in gratitude and feeling the lightness in my body.

Blessed be.

July 2013
In Between Times

I'm in an in-between-time. It's sort of like a pause. I know something big is coming and so there is this anticipation that is part excitement, part anxiety. But at this moment it is quiet.

A month ago, I was in the thick of busyness, a car accident, insurance details, getting a new car, pending surgery, my teacher William coming with two other house guests to stay for a week, and my spiritual community gathering at my home for a weekend intensive. Definitely not a pause.

Now two weeks later things have calmed down and I'm still adjusting to the new rhythm. It's nice, this easier pace, sleeping later in the morning, more flexibility with my time, more ability to be mindful because I am slowing down, more time to ponder and mull (two of my favorite activities).

One of the "bigs" that is coming is my second grandchild. I never go anywhere now without my phone, waiting for "the call" as we've dubbed it.

The second "big" is my upcoming book tour in September (2013). So, walking through this in-between-time feels not completely relaxing, but there's lots more room in my head. Maybe not such a good thing.

I love lying in bed in the morning just letting my mind wander, enjoying the peace, nowhere I must be, no time crunch pushing me out of that other in- between-time between full wakefulness and drowsy eyelids. I'm starting to settle in and I will bet money that just about the time I'm really comfortable here in this new place I will get "the call" and I'll be off to another rhythm.

I doubt that will be a "pause."

Blessed be!!

July 2013
My Grandson Has Finally Arrived

It was a royal birth of sorts, the birth of my second grandchild, a miracle of love, connection and karma.

He chose us, and we are already blessed by his presence. He didn't come softly, or quickly, into the night. It was more like a journey of slowly emerging, of fits and starts and many pit stops along the way.

"I'm ready, really. Oh wait, I have to catch my breath."

"Okay, now let's have a go at it again. Wait, I'm tired. Can we just rest a bit?"

"Alright, ready again. I'm moving. Phew, that was hard. Maybe just a little breather here."

And so it went for endless hours. My daughter, who has now been renamed "Amazon woman," was amazing, as was her wonderful husband. He was by her side the entire time, lifting, supporting, breathing, and whispering loving, encouraging words.

To actually go through those hours and not be screaming for meds??? That's courage and determination.

As for me? Well it wasn't exactly the transcendental, mystical experience that some have described. There were moments when I could feel the connection to something really big that was happening, and I would raise my hands to send that energy down the hall to my daughter, but mostly it was just many hours of trying to contain my anxiety and keep my mind from imagining the struggle going on in the room down the hall.

Finally, not being able to stand it any longer I snuck down the hall and waited outside the door. I won't go into detail about what I heard except to say there were a lot of expletives filling the air as baby J made his final push to the finish line.

I heard papa laugh, heard the numerous nurses and doctors cheer and then the most beautiful sound. A loud lusty cry from baby J, weighing in at 9lbs. 9 oz.

That's a big OUCH.

He and I have gotten acquainted over the last few days as I hold him and sing to him the lullaby passed down from my grandmother.

There is something magical and sacred about sitting in a rocking chair with a sweet-smelling bundle of life in my arms and his, not so tiny fingers, wrapped around mine.

What could be more "royal" than that?

Plus, he was born 4 days before the truly royal birth of Prince George.

August 2013
A Cancer Grammy

Is there anything more seductive to a person with their moon in Cancer than a new grandbaby?? I think not.

Cancerians, in case you are new to astrology, live to nurture, cuddle, soothe, and take care of, and up until a few years ago the pickings were pretty slim around my house.

My two adult children were out in the world, independent and enjoying their lives with their partners, but so far, no talk of grandbabies. Now, I'm not complaining. I fully believe in bringing little or big souls into the world only when you are ready, and I am mostly content with my single life. But *my* biological clock was ticking and as I hit 70 I began to wonder if I would be in diapers before I had a chance to change any grandbaby diapers.

Well, my kids finally came through and just last week my second grandchild was born, a sweet big healthy boy to accompany his 19-month-old female cousin.

All my Cancer molecules kicked into first gear. This was heaven. My schedule had been cleared for the entire month to be available for any needed help. And somehow there is something so freeing in being this focused. To just be clear that this is absolutely the most important thing I can do right now. And as long as the "right now" stays clear in my mind I will be alright.

The tendency, for me, is to continue to think that I should *always* be this available. Don't get me wrong, I love being available to my kids and of course, this will continue to be my priority, BUT, I watched my mother devote her LIFE to her kids. Always putting her needs, gifts, talents to the side to be there for us. When we all left home I saw her sink into depression and grief. What was her life to be about then?

Luckily for her, grandchildren soon came along and pulled her out of it. But I wanted to pull myself out of this tendency. I determined, as I watched her suffer, that I would always have a life separate from my kids. I know that sounds pretty elementary, but for a Cancer moon, that was raised in the 1950s, that is a tough road.

I was a stay-at-home-mom while my kids were growing up, so I got lots of time to be fully in my Cancer self. But as they neared adolescence I could see the end in sight. It is partly what propelled me into graduate school at age 45 to start a new career as a psychotherapist. I wanted to continue being curious about life, about learning, about growing, about myself as I aged. So, I am proud of having done that. I did carve out my own life and it is immensely satisfying.

When my first grandchild was born I, without any hesitation, volunteered to take care of her two days a week. After four months I could feel the toll on my body and I realized I had little time to devote to my life. As hard as it was for me I told my son and daughter-in-law that I would have to cut back. That was a big step for me and I am grateful for their graciousness and understanding

Now this new little life has come into my world and I can feel the pull again.

This time, I gave it a bit more consideration before I offered to help. I really thought about what I imagined I could handle and still maintain my life. I decided that devoting six weeks to helping out would be what I could give. Just checking in each day to see what was needed and what I could do.

My book tour starts at the end of the six weeks, so I will be forced to re-focus and re-direct my energies.

Make no mistake, I plan to ALWAYS be there for my kids, but I also pledge to ALWAYS be there for myself.

CHAPTER 8
DETACHMENT AND LETTING GO

What does detachment mean to you? How do you "let go?" These have been questions I have struggled with my whole life.

You know by now that I have a Cancer moon in my astrological chart. What this means for me is that the nurturing, care-taking, mothering part of me has had its way with me in previous lives. I have lived into it fully.

The moon is always about the past. So, this time around I am not supposed to let it rule my life. I'd like to say that I learned that early on, but truth be told it's only been in the last several years that I have really recognized its hold on me and have struggled mightily to subdue it's influence on my life.

Any Cancer influence will always affect your relationship to family and loved ones since that is where most of our nurturing energy goes.

The spiritual imperative for a Cancer person is to learn detachment or impersonality. Most spiritual traditions espouse this as a way to attain more freedom. Entanglements that bind up our emotional bodies are a limitation. This is not to say we should limit our love. Quite the contrary. In Cancer, we are invited to open our hearts to the entire world. To expand our capacity to love more than just our family and friends.

The problems come when we become controlled by our attachments to our loved ones. If we nurture too much, caretake too much or mother too much we are in danger of losing our way, losing our own sense of who we are and what we came to do in this lifetime. Of course, when our children are young and in need of a lot of attention we do what we have to do to be good parents, but often as our children grow up and leave home we find those patterns still operating in us and that is not helpful to either parent or child.

The other part of detachment that I struggled with was the tendency to want to control the outcome of whatever situation I was facing. I saw things unfolding in a certain way and life just didn't always work out that way. It's not always about my agenda and my wishes. The more attached I become to trying to control how things work out, the more pain and frustration I cause myself.

So, my intention these last several years has been to hold strong to my intention. Envision the outcome that I wish, then let it go. Leave it to Spirit to determine how it will unfold and what form it may take.

We are in this together, Spirit and I, and after I do what is mine to do, I leave the rest in the hands of Spirit.

March 2014
Frustration Cure #1, and #2, and #3

After an amazing Pisces full moon ceremony and feeling the joy of just sort of floating along with that mystical energy, I came back down to earth today.

The bank informed me of an unusual charge to my bank card. After checking it out pretty thoroughly I discovered that a recent "free trial" supplement that I had signed up for actually enrolled me in their "automatic payment plan." They would send me this supplement for only $87.91 each month.

It was my fault. I didn't read the fine print. So, I spent the morning trying to cancel. Twenty minutes on hold at their customer service number then a busy signal. Two emails to their "support" address, unanswered. Several minutes on the phone to the bank card center exploring my options.

I had promised myself, for Lent, that I would not open my computer before my usual morning spiritual practice, but for some reason I didn't follow that this morning. So here I was, frustrated, angry at myself, and off-center. Finally, my wiser self whispered in my ear, *Go outside and do your usual 15 minutes standing on the earth, barefoot.*

Tea in hand, I breathed into my body. Yes, definitely constriction at the solar plexus, also tightening of the throat. Yes, a lot of self-recrimination spinning around the head. Kept breathing. I followed my own advice for once and just sat with it until it had peaked. Then held it in my heart and talked to myself, as a friend.

Nothing fatal, my dear. All will be well. Put this into perspective. Everyone in the world feels this at some time or another. Everyone makes mistakes. This is just what it means to be human.

Kept breathing.

When I opened my eyes, I realized I did not feel like going back into the house.

I felt at peace and deeply connected to the earth.

I wanted to plant pansies.

I laid aside my immediate plans and dug into the earth. Bringing a little more beauty into the day I was able to let go and bring myself back to my Self.

So, frustration cure #1, do your spiritual practice, whatever that is for you.

Cure #2, plant pansies… get your hands into the earth.

Frustration cure #3 is the poem that follows.

She Let Go

She let go.

Without a thought or a word, she let go.

She let go of the fear.

She let go of the judgments.

She let go of the confluence of opinions swarming around her head.

She let go of the committee of indecision within her.

She let go of all the 'right' reasons.

Wholly and completely, without hesitation or worry, she just let go.

She didn't ask anyone for advice.

She didn't read a book on how to let go.

She just let go.

She let go of all of the memories that held her back.

She let go of all of the anxiety that kept her from moving forward.

She let go of the planning and all of the calculations about how to do it just right.

She didn't promise to let go.

She didn't journal about it.

She didn't write the projected date in her Day-Timer.

She made no public announcement and put no ad in the paper.

She didn't check the weather report or read her daily horoscope.

She just let go.

She didn't analyze whether she should let go.

She didn't call her friends to discuss the matter.

She didn't call the prayer line.

She didn't utter one word.

She just let go.

No one was around when it happened.

There was no applause or congratulations.

No one thanked her or praised her.

No one noticed a thing.

Like a leaf falling from a tree, she just let go.

There was no effort.
There was no struggle.
It wasn't good, and it wasn't bad,
it was what it was, and it is just that.
In the space of letting go,
she let it all be.
A small smile came over her face.
A light breeze blew through her.
And the sun and the moon shone forevermore.
—Rev. Safire Rose

March 2014
More Letting Go

I think there is a deep and subtle letting go that faces us when our children become adults and no longer need us to "parent" them in the same way.

The "not-so-subtle" letting go seems easy: no more complete financial responsibility, no more taxi cab service, no more waiting up at night to see if they get home safely.

But I'm talking about the deeper, more difficult letting go.

I think it may just boil down to one sentence that we believe with our *whole being*:

I don't know what's best for them, and besides I'm not in charge of that.

That's very hard after so many years of being the one responsible for their safety and physical and emotional wellbeing.

So, what does it mean for us when they no longer need the type of attention we've been habituated to give? How do we dis-identify with our role as a parent?

For me, it means attempting to be constantly mindful of those patterns of caretaking that are no longer necessary. And that practice has been quite a process, coming very slowly over many years and many stages.

But even more subtly, I think the letting go means asking how much do I ***trust*** that they can guide their own lives? How much do I really believe that their life has its own purpose, its own trajectory? And how do I accept being an adjunct to their lives? Can I watch the waves toss and turn in their lives and remind myself that I am not the primary lighthouse for them anymore?

In reality my kids have never given me any reason to believe they couldn't manage their own lives. They have almost always made good choices, at least the ones I know about. So I think I must now turn my worry, concern, and my own personal agenda for them over to *their* higher self.

I am slowly, very slowly, embodying this truth, and this is where my beliefs help me. I really do believe that they are on their own path, with their own lessons to learn, their own suffering to go through, so they can gain the wisdom and strength from those experiences that will help them grow. But oh, my, it is so painful to stand by and watch and not jump in there with solutions and advise when I see them in pain.

Eckhart Tolle describes this as their pain body activating mine, and that's exactly what it feels like. But if this is true, then it's my job to take care of my own pain body so I can stand by, with love and support, but not try to fix it or make it better.

If I have expectations for how they should live their lives, or if I don't show them the faith that I have in them, then I am doing them a disservice. It's as if I'm not really seeing *them* or being present to who they are.

Of course, I do have hopes and wishes for them, but I think that is different than expectations. Expectations imply that I am invested in the outcome. And why am I invested? Sometimes I forget, and I think my children are a reflection of myself. If they screw up I am worried about how people might judge me as a parent.

I do take responsibility for how I parented. I made plenty of mistakes, but sometimes kids make choices that have very little to do with how they were parented.

More often my attachment has been about me not being able to tolerate seeing them in pain. Again, the necessary action is for me to do the work to heal this part of myself. I wonder if I know how to tolerate my own pain?

What makes it equally difficult is that I almost always think I know how it *should* be for them, and if they just did this or that it would be better. But that does not honor them or who they are. It's just imposing my agenda onto them, and that is so not helpful. Besides which, it creates a feeling of separation between us that doesn't feel good.

I think this deeper level of letting go, this detachment with love, is one of my life's biggest lesson, especially when it involves my family.

As long as I think I know how things should be, how people should be, I am not present to who they really are or what is really happening right now. Byron Katie calls this "arguing with reality." This is what is, right now, right here in the midst of pain, or suffering or disappointment; this just is what it is. Can I trust that it has meaning and purpose that I may know nothing about? Can I just *be* with it?

It's definitely an inside job, this coming to terms with what triggers my over protectiveness. Okay, I know all this intellectually, but to be honest I very rarely can access those higher beliefs when it is most needed.

So, I am here, writing this in an attempt to remind myself of what I already know and to help me embody and integrate these truths more deeply into myself.

Thanks for listening. I plan to take this page out and re-read it frequently.

Your happiness and suffering depend on your actions and not on my wishes for you.
—Jack Kornfield

Staying in my own business is a full-time job.
—Byron Katie

May 2014
Freedom

I love it when life's accumulated moments of awareness morph into a major shift in my consciousness.

The Seven Rays Conference I attended a few weeks ago in Arizona facilitated that expansion experience for me. If you have been reading this blog you know that I have been encountering the dark side of my Cancer moon, attaching, over protecting, thinking everyone needs my help, etc. etc. etc. Moments of clarity have come as I realize this need to see differently and my intentions have been set. The signposts were there, and I noticed.

The astrological year was ending.

What needed to end within me?

The cardinal grand cross, the Pluto/Uranus squares … all asking, *What am I willing to release? Where does freedom lie, for me?*

And the new Aries energy wanting to birth something new and initiatory.

What is wanting to burst forth within me?

I was paying attention, so I did take it in and I did ponder, as we Ray Two souls have a tendency to do, but somehow it all came together in Arizona. It felt like a moment of embodiment, like I could really *feel* the shift.

It started with the first meditation during the pre-conference Astrology class.

We were asked to consider what virtues of the Soul we thought we had embodied (at least partially). I came up with compassion, love, and wisdom.

Then of course the next obvious question: What remains to be built into our being?

Two words came: detachment and humility.

The final question was, "How would that look, if it were truly a part of your nature?"

Wow, the word FREEDOM, in capital letters came pounding into my awareness. I could really feel how that would be in my body. Not free of connection, but free of the tendrils of *attachment,* of burdened energy, of heavy responsibility, of worry and anxiety.

FREE, to just be the joy that I long for and that I know is a part of my essence.

I think it's the feeling of an awareness taking up residence in my body that creates the final shift. Up until then the understanding is mostly mental. And perhaps this is just the way we grow. Maybe we just have to understand something fully, in our heads, before we can experience it fully in our bodies. At least that seems to be the way I process.

After that initial embodying experience, the rest of the Astrology class was spent looking at our charts to see where we might be supported in bringing this quality more fully into our lives.

I was delighted to see that much of what shows up in my chart right now (transits/progressions) is completely supportive of this shift into more impersonal love and detachment.

That tells me I can call upon these energies for help when I feel like I'm sinking back into old patterns. I can call in the will energy of Aries when I feel waffle-y. I can ask for the energy of Aquarius/Uranus to give me that more objective perspective. And as one of the astrologers pointed out to me, I can ask the question, "What am I moving toward?" rather than, "What am I letting go of?"

I want to remember that what I am moving toward is a freedom that allows the joy that is me to manifest as a lightness of being, as an automatic and spontaneous "yes" to life, as a feeling of gentleness and ease in my body.

Immersing myself in that stream makes the letting go a bit easier.

An old drumming chant:
Freedom, won't cha give me freedom
Freedom, won't cha give me freedom
Freedom comes from not hanging on
Ya gotta let go, let go.

Freedom won't cha give me freedom
Freedom, won't cha give me freedom
Freedom comes from not hanging on
Ya gotta let go, let go.

This chant just keeps repeating until one is almost tranced into releasing. However, it does sound much better with a drum

November 2014

A Small Step for Karen, and a Giant Leap for her Cancer Moon

So, on a scale from one to ten, this event probably rates about a two in comparison to other steps I've taken, but from a feeling perspective it's an 11+.

The date had been chosen, confirmed, planned for, for over a month. Saturday, November15th was the date that Jasper's other grandma and I had agreed to babysit so our adult children could celebrate their seventh wedding anniversary. Everyone was looking forward to it, the parents no less than the other grandma and I since we have become good friends in this cooperative effort to help our children.

Monday evening of that week I received an Evite from the daughter of my long-time (fifty years) friend in California, to come and surprise her mom with a retirement party.

Her mom and I began our teaching careers in the same school in San Jose in 1964. She had gone from her teaching career to starting her own business in a small town south of Santa Cruz, California. The business thrived as she created a resource for teachers and parents, called The Parent/Teacher Store. It carried everything in it that we wish we had had when we started teaching. She poured her heart and soul into that store and quickly made it a huge success. By her immense talent, the determination of her Taurus sun sign, and her charismatic personality she kept it successfully operating for over forty years.

Retirement was no small letting go process for her. She had come to my book signing in Santa Cruz in October where I held a Fall Equinox ceremony. It was all about letting go and opening to the new cycle. I quoted the wonderful poem, "She Let Go" referenced in my previous entry.

She told me that that ceremony had given her just what she needed to make peace with her decision to close the store. She read and re-read it during the closing up process.

When the Evite came, I was in "old Cancerian habitual response" mode. I had made a commitment to my children, for God's sake. I couldn't break *that.* I told her daughter how sorry I was but there was just no way I could make it. I spent the next few days telling myself all the reasons that it wouldn't work out for me to go, not the least of which were all the questions buzzing around my head - what to do with the car, how to get to the airport, how to get from San Jose to Santa Cruz - ad nauseum. It dawned on me somewhere in the midst of all this busy mind stuff that I was caught in a negative loop. Wow, look at how that mind tries to convince you that you can't tackle the details.

This was also my birthday week and I had given myself the gift of a lovely facial, amazing by the way, by my friend, Laura Bailey at samaraskincare. com.

Lying there peacefully absorbing her healing hands she asked me to set an intention. I immediately said, "balance", not really knowing exactly what I meant by that, but during the course of the facial I *felt* how much I wanted to be there for my friend, and for myself. How fun to be there when the surprise took place and share some time with her. Once I recognized that feeling, the intention of balance took on a more focused meaning, balancing my life over my desire to always be there for my children. This again. What to do?

I decided I would call my daughter, tell her how I felt and see if it would be possible to work something out. Well, bless her heart, she said, of course you have to go. I'm not sure it would have been as easy a decision had she disagreed, but I'm proud of the fact that my kids always seem to support me in taking care of myself, even when *I'm* not sure it's okay and even when it might inconvenience them.

There was an interesting insight that came to me after I got in touch with my deepest desire to go. I suddenly had access to the stronger part of myself that countered all that negative thinking with the reality. That voice reminded me that I had traveled the world twice in my twenties handling an immense amount of details. I was strong, healthy, somewhat astute, "What's the problem?"

So, I went, with bells on, and reveled in the look in her eyes when she saw me. So surprised and totally blown away by the fact that I had chosen her over my commitment to my kids (she knows me very well).

I came back feeling renewed and rejuvenated and also pretty proud of myself for taking this tiny step toward my own wellbeing.

If it was possible for me to share the video of she and I dancing the night away to Credence Clearwater, Janis Joplin and Aretha, you would see me glowing like a light bulb.

Fun, I tell you, pure fun is one way to feel a bucket full of joy.!!!

I awakened a few nights later with these words in my head:

It no longer serves me to see myself as small,
I claim my BIGNESS

I let go of obstacles and
Claim my FREEDOM.

I release the darkness and
Welcome in the LIGHT.

December 2014
Another Layer of Letting Go

Last week I experienced a 3.5 on the Richter Scale of disappointment. It was fairly short lived, only three or four days, but it's been a while since I have felt that particular emotion and it sort of threw me.

Of course, I immediately tried to figure out *why* it threw me, not always a helpful thing to do when in the midst of an emotional reaction. When I realized what I was doing I began practicing my own advice. Sometimes it takes me awhile to realize I can actually fall back on my own wisdom.

In this case it meant trying to just stay with it, not telling myself a story about it, analyzing it, or talking myself out of it. Not comfortable, true. Not able to do it fully, true, but well worth the effort. It did involve some crying, some tearing up, some surprise at the strength of it, after all it was really only a 3.5, but then trying to not diminish it, either. It just was what it was at that moment.

Later, after I regained my equilibrium and the peak of it had passed, as it always does, I got some clarity. It somehow tied into all the awareness's I've been receiving lately about detachment, impersonality, and letting go.

It also felt sort of like a test. My new resolve of the past few months being tested out in the messy arena of personal relationships. I find that often happens with me. I reach a new perspective or a broader awareness and then something happens, and I am forced to put it into the context of my daily life, just to see if I've really gotten it.

So, I sat through the disappointment, shared my feelings with a few close friends and my family. I'm absolutely no good any more at pretending that I'm okay when I'm feeling shitty. I then began to see the situation with more depth and understanding.

One of the tools I use a lot, when my emotions get the better of me, is to go to my stack of inspirational quotes that I've collected over the years as a way of reminding me of what I really believe.

We're told, in the philosophy that I study, that we need to learn to shine the light of the Soul onto our personalities to illumine our thinking. My thinking always feels more illumined when I read these inspirational quotes.

One of the quotes I came across was, "Look for a way to frame a difficult situation/experience in a context large enough to maintain equanimity in the mind." Unfortunately, I didn't record the author.

In my experience, equanimity of the mind only comes after fully feeling what I am feeling but looking for that larger perspective helped me reach a quieter emotional place.

Part of the larger picture for me was the reminder that no matter how much I may desire something, I really don't want it if it is not what is for my highest good and if it is for my higher good it will somehow work out.

So, when I am disappointed because I didn't get what I wanted I rest on that.

I also remembered that wanting something for a personality desire is not where I want to get entangled. I want to aspire to the highest that is in me, and that is Soul consciousness. It doesn't mean I can't *want* something, it just means that I want to keep that want subservient to the higher aspirations of my Soul, and I don't want it to disturb my emotional stability, the "acquiescent calm" as it is called in the books that I study, by Alice Bailey.

So here are some of the other quotes that helped me through those few days of upset:

May I meet this moment fully. May I meet it as a friend.
— Sylvia Boorstein

…instead of turning that moment against myself, as in, *somehow, I am to blame.*

Am I swept up by a sensitive emotional response to circumstance or by an intelligent reaction to life as it is?
— Alice Bailey

Here I understand that I wish to meet life with a steadiness, so I am not always buffeted to and fro by circumstances.

This is the attitude of the integrated thinking personality towards the emotional body.

Assume the position that not one single thing which produces any reaction of pain or distress in the emotional body matters in the very least. These reactions are simply recognized, lived through, tolerated and not permitted to produce any limitation.
—Alice Bailey

This is not telling me to ignore, repress, or disown these feelings, but to put them in their proper perspective. They are, after all, only feelings. They don't always tell me the truth of what is happening they just tell me how I am reacting in that moment. They should not be absorbed by me to the extent that I am constantly at the mercy of my emotional reactions, tossed every which way and always losing my center.

Spiritual Indifference:
Accepts what is offered
Uses what is serviceable
Learns what can be learned
But is not held back by personality reactions.
—Alice Bailey

So, I am here, back on track and feeling a renewed sense of energy that another old pattern of identifying too strongly with my sensitive emotional nature has been recognized, lived through, tolerated and only permitted to produce a few days of apparent limitation.

The following paper was not included on my blog, but it speaks eloquently to the theme of letting go:

To let go does not mean to stop caring, it means I can't do it for someone else.

To let go is not a cut myself off, it's the realization I can't control another.

To let go is not to enable, but to allow learning from natural consequences.

To let go is to admit powerlessness, which means the outcome is not in my hands.

To let go is not to try to change or blame another, it's to make the most of myself.

To let go is not to care for, but to care about.

To let go is not to fix, but to be supportive.

To let go is not to judge, but to allow another to be a human being.

To let go is not to be in the middle arranging all the outcomes but to allow others to affect their destinies.

To let go is not to be protective, it's to permit another to face reality.

To let go is not to deny, but to accept.

To let go is not to nag, scold or argue, but instead to search out my own shortcomings and correct them.

To let go is not to adjust everything to my desires but to take each day as it comes and cherish myself in it.

To let go is not to criticize and regulate anybody but to try to become what I dream I can be.

To let go is not to regret the past, but to grow and live in the present and plan for the future.

To let go is to fear less, and love more.

—Care Unit of Kirkland and Shoreline, Washington, Substance Abuse Coalition.

CHAPTER 9
TRUST

The word "trust" has over ten definitions in the dictionary. Only a few of them apply to the entries in this chapter. "Faith in, confidence in, belief in." And they apply to me, personally.

Faith in *me*.

Confidence in *me*.

Belief in *me*.

These are the issues I grapple with.

When I reflect, I can easily see how the pattern started, this not believing in myself. Believing in God so completely, so wholeheartedly meant that He was in charge of my life. I was to trust him. I did not yet see that I was part of that divinity and that trusting myself, my inner wisdom, was God's way of speaking to me. The authority was outside of myself.

Then there was my gentle, loving father whose way of disciplining his four children was to sit us down, calmly explain the situation and what he would prefer us to do and then he would say, "But it's up to you." It worked beautifully with the first two, they were compliant and submissive and wanted to please. Then I came along. I think my Scorpio energy scared them, because I had a rebelliousness to me that they had not encountered before.

One of the images I have of my childhood is this big thumb that is coming down to squash me. Tone it down, be quiet, be good, which I translated, "Don't be yourself. Don't trust your energy, because we don't."

In later years we would joke about it. My dad's favorite saying about me was, "One word from me and she did as she pleased." I thought that doing what I wanted to do was selfish.

In the 50's the big question about dating was whether you should let a boy kiss you on the first date. So unlike these days. I spent countless hours before a date agonizing over this dilemma, trying to decide what I should do. Geez… what a waste of energy. Why didn't someone say to me, "Wait and see how you feel. If it feels right, then go ahead and kiss him." But what was implied was that I couldn't trust my body or my feelings to make the decision, and I was told that it was up to me to set the limits. And for goodness sake, never lead a boy on because once aroused there could be dire consequences for him if he couldn't find "relief." Heaven forbid we should expect the boy to take responsibility for any of this.

Regardless of all of this, the message I took away was that the body was not to be trusted.

My one big defying act during those years was going to the Senior Prom against the wishes and the beliefs of my parents. No dancing was one of the rules. I now realize the courage it took for me to do that, but at the time I was accused of not caring about my parent's wishes. Well, I was in love, what can I say? Maybe I was being a bit selfish, but I refused to submit to a rule that I thought was stupid in spite of the Bible verses that were pointed out to me by my dad.

My mom took me aside and said, "Karen, this is really not such a big deal. I'll help you find a dress." One of the few times I remember her ever going against my father's wishes. In spite of her feelings however they left town the weekend of the Prom. I'm sure my dad was humiliated that his daughter would defy him in this way.

I remember having a really good time.

Today I ponder whether I would have felt freer somehow if I had always been encouraged to move my body organically in response to music and rhythm?

Would the cells in my body have come alive in a new way if I had been allowed the natural, physical expression of joy?

These are the issues I have struggled with and that I explore in these next several pages.

How do I learn to trust the wisdom of my body?

Can I trust the wisdom of my Soul, which is my own higher self?

Do I trust in the flow of life to carry me where I need to go?

Can I trust that I will not misuse my power?

What I continue to learn is that the more I trust in all those things the more I open myself to possibilities that I would not see or consider were I stuck in worry, or fear, or the need for comfort and safety.

It's a risk to trust, but I ask you, "What is the alternative?"

November 2013
Wise Effort

My daughter recently gave a dharma talk at the weekly Insight Meditation meeting here in Seattle. When I asked her what she spoke about she told me the topic was the Buddhist concept of "wise effort." She compared her recent labor and birth experience to this idea and explained that there were different *aspects* of wise effort.

In the early stages of labor, she said, she was focused on being totally present to what her body was experiencing, just allowing and flowing with the contractions as they came. This was one aspect of wise effort, just being with whatever was happening, no resistance, no struggle, just being carried by the moment.

Then at the last stage, a different energy was required. A *huge* effort was needed to actually birth this being. A focused, determined, commitment to do whatever it took to actually bring this baby into the world.

Both of these energies embody wise effort but have a far different quality to them. And, according to her, "Both aspects are fed by the discerning wisdom that knows what is needed in a given situation."

I've been thinking a lot about this idea since she shared her talk with me. Often when I'm pondering an idea, life gives me an opportunity to apply it. So, a few days ago, I was having a "tune up" session with my therapist and she shared with me her perception that I seem to have a belief that I must work very hard to become a better person. That somehow being a good person required a big effort and usually a great deal of struggle. She wondered aloud how it would be for me to see my essence as already perfect, divine even, and made in the image of that divinity.

Now this was not a new thought for me but somehow as I considered her words in the context of my daughter's speech, I began to sense how that might look. *What if, instead of committing to the next self-improvement class, for instance, I just **trusted** that I would be shown if something needed improving?*

Could I just allow life to bring it to me, instead of always, "pushing the river" as another friend described me?

Could "wise effort" be just meeting whatever came my way with an attitude of acceptance and flow, trusting wholly in the process? Then when the energy for a new birth was needed and it felt like a more focused commitment was being called for could I trust, again, that the right effort would be made?

As these thoughts sort of morphed into a deeper understanding my body immediately relaxed. I could feel the strain I have lived under with that old belief. It had a driven quality to it and that's not how I want to live my life.

Being a Scorpio I know that I am hardwired to go deep, to look for the essence. That blueprint will always be a part of me, and I sort of like that about myself.

What I think is now beginning to emerge is a deep trust in the *organic* process, the *easy* understanding, the *soft* awareness, without any *driving force*. No rivers to push, no struggle to be more, do more, no *need* to achieve, just a flowing forth in perfect timing and of its own volition.

I'm pretty sure I could rest easily in that flow.

October 2014
Lions and Tigers and Spiders, Oh My!!

Today on my walk through Woodway, the beautiful little town between my place and Edmonds, there was an amazing array of intricate spider webs. Between three trees I counted sixteen webs with their spiders seemingly floating in midair. These were not ordinary Halloween spider webs in beautiful circular patterns. These little guys were strung between two or three trees that were several feet apart.

Hanging by mere threads, it appeared.

It got me to pondering(which means a blog is on its way).

Now I'm no expert on the technicalities of spider web production, but it seems to me that little arachnid must have a lot of faith. It has to spew out its sticky stuff from the rear, (I'm guessing here) then trust that it will hold as it gets ready to spew more stuff, sort of like leaning into the abyss. But as it builds, a foundation is made that will hold it and support a larger web where it can catch some unsuspecting insect.

Isn't our journey somewhat like that? We have the stuff it takes to move us forward, but we must spew it out to start building our foundation and that takes faith. We don't always know if our strand of goo is going to hold us and we can't see a bridge ahead to walk on.

I think we must build that bridge ourselves, one gooey step at a time, trusting that when we reach that other tree, we can take a deep breath and then burst forth in all our glory and watch the miracles fly into our web.

July 2015
A Bit of Philosophizing

I recently attended a weekend retreat with my teacher, William Meader. The focus of the weekend was on learning about the steps we must take if we wish to become enlightened, or as this philosophy calls it, soul infused. This means that our higher selves, our Soul, irradiates our personality (ego), infusing it with the qualities of love, compassion, inclusiveness, unity, and selflessness, thus expanding our consciousness.

In order to reach this enlightened state, we must commit ourselves to the journey. We must be *willing* to grow and expand into our higher selves.

William talked about how in our lives each expansion of consciousness is preceded by a crisis of some sort. If we look at our struggles and suffering from this perspective, it gives some meaning and purpose to the chaos that we experience.

I'm experiencing the truth of this in my own life. When I'm in pain, or confused or struggling with some circumstance I try to remember to ask, *what is the learning here for me?* Curiosity about the situation and my feelings help me move away from any blaming self-talk or victim mentality.

Do I recognize this feeling?

Where do I feel it in my body?

Can I discern the roots of this discomfort?"

When I can do this, I find that almost without exception there is some edge that I'm coming up against within myself that I need to pay attention to, some area of stuck-ness that needs to open up and release.

It's difficult for me to find answers while I'm in the midst of the pain, but if I am patient and wait, just allowing the discomfort to be there, holding it in compassion, eventually I will get clarity.

Part of the clarity that comes is often a realization that I was forced, through that circumstance, to dig deep within to find a strength I didn't know I had. If I handled the situation with openness, and did not shut down, then I came out of it with more of a sense of my own inner power and a deeper compassion for other people's pain. Step by agonizing step I have begun to trust more deeply and question less about, "Why *me*? Why *this*? Why *now*?"

Each time we meet with William (once a year), he gives us a meditation to use in whatever way works for us. In this particular meditation he led us to a deep connection with our own Soul and from that alignment asked us to step forward and be willing to walk this journey, open and committed to our own evolution. He then invited us to trust that we are guided, that we are led, by this Higher Power called the Soul. We could ask that the Soul to arrange the circumstances of our lives to present us with the necessary opportunities and challenges that we need to transform our personalities into purified vehicles for the energy of the Soul.

I want to remember this.

I want to remember the next time the tsunami hits that I have *asked* to expand and grow and that if I am mindful and remain open during the storm, I can come out of it transformed in some way.

I want to remember that every crisis can lead me to greater expansion.

I also want to be clear. I don't believe anyone *asks* for cancer or *asks* to be abused. I believe that sometimes life just throws us major curveballs that may have nothing to do with our Soul, and, I think it's possible to *hold* both these perspectives. Sometimes sh*t just happens and sometimes our Soul is clearly operating, but when I remember my intention to learn and grow, I can better take *any* circumstance and use it as an opportunity for transformation.

We are continually challenged to learn how to ask for what we need, only to practice accepting what we're given. This is our journey on earth.

—Mark Nepo

November 2016
Sitting With Ram Dass

It seems that every five years or so I need to give myself a challenge. Maybe it's a way of trying to disprove that I am ageing, who knows?

When I turned seventy, I decided I wanted to prove to myself that I could travel alone. I had gone around the world twice in my twenties, but I had never attempted to travel very far without a companion. It seemed a bit scary at seventy to go to Europe alone, but that was my goal. I wanted to know that I could still navigate trains, buses, hotels, and connections without a partner.

I went for two weeks and came back feeling a sense of empowerment and very aware that lugging baggage and making countless arrangements wasn't quite the adventure that it was in my twenties.

So, in January 2016, I started thinking about my seventy-fifth birthday, coming in November. It was just a little niggle in the back of my mind, nothing momentous. Then across my email came an announcement of a five-day retreat on Maui with Ram Dass and friends. It was happening in my birthday month, November, so I was intrigued. Actually, I felt a strong pull that I needed to go so I wrote the date that registration opened, in my day timer. (Still don't know how to use the calendar on my iPhone)

Usually I'm not that punctual about making arrangements but the day came, in June, when we could sign up. I immediately put my name in. Registration closed right behind my application and within three days they had a waiting list that outnumbered the people that signed up. I didn't need any more signs, but as a bonus I realized I could use my miles to fly first class. Wow, now I was really excited.

I decided to give myself some R&R time while there, so I went three days early and stayed three days after the retreat ended. I had a beautiful room, with an ocean view and a full kitchen. I was in heaven. I sank into the beauty and the stillness. The feeling of warmth and connection to the land became stronger each day.

We meditated, some did yoga or Qi Gong on the beach, and we listened to all the wonderful teachers: Jack Kornfield and his wife Trudy, Sharon Salzburg, and of course Ram Dass himself, in his wheelchair speaking slowly and carefully as he has to measure each word since his stroke seventeen years ago.

They all talked about love, about compassion, about opening our hearts.

The name of the retreat was "Finding the Beloved, Touching the Compassionate Heart." In the evening we chanted with Krishna Das. There was something magical about singing with 350 people, drums beating, guitars and violin playing and Krishna's amazing voice.

The funny thing was that I have several of Krishna Das' CDs at home that I rarely play because they can be quite raucous, but surrounded by so many people joining together I was totally energized and uplifted, my heart opening to take it all in. One song that got me up out of my chair and dancing in the aisles was called "Jesus On the Main Line". Be sure to take a listen on YouTube.

The fact that I knew no one at this retreat didn't seem to inhibit me at all. Perhaps I am caring less about needing to surround myself with the familiar. I unabashedly walked up to tables with complete strangers, sat down, connected and made some wonderful friends. What a gift.

Of course, in a retreat where the opportunity to open our hearts is so available, it would be hard to feel disconnected or separate, but nevertheless I was proud of myself for taking these risks. I won't go into my snorkeling adventure, but I'm proud that I did it, again, alone.

Besides the evenings of chanting with Krishna Das and the wonderful speakers, the highlight for me was actually meeting Ram Dass face to face. I have heard him speak many times, read his books, but being in his presence was something I had never experienced. I'm working, in my life, on not pushing through, not plotting or manipulating situations. My *mantram* for a long time has been, "May I live my life with ease." I really want to learn to "go with the flow."

When the thought came into my mind that I would like a picture with Ram Dass, I could feel the old tendency to try to make it happen. Then another thought, "I'm not going to try to force this. If it happens, it happens."

So, one day as I was sitting in the back of the room, chanting to myself, I finished and looked up, and there was Ram Dass not five feet away with only one person next to him. Usually there is a line up. I jumped up, handed my phone to the person standing there and asked if she would take my picture. She did a beautiful job, snapping three photos.

The moment that was so powerful was when he actually looked into my eyes. I could feel unconditional love just pouring out of him. I wasn't expecting that. Wow, what an impact. It wasn't like a moment of complete enlightenment, like some people have described when they meet an enlightened being, but it was palpable, and it entered me. Something shifted.

I'm not a devotee, or a guru follower, but I have a lot of respect, admiration, and even reverence for those whose consciousness radiates that love that we label "unconditional." I think it is a vibration. I think it is a high level of consciousness, and I think we are all capable of reaching that state of being. It may be lifetimes before it manifests fully in us, but I do believe we will all reach this state at some moment in time (as unlikely as that seems at this particular moment in our history).

So, everything about this experience taught me to trust more deeply in life's flow, down to the most mundane experience of my flight home arriving an hour early which allowed me to make it home ahead of the snowstorm.

Opening my heart to possibilities, trusting in the unfolding, and learning to live with more comfort in uncertainty, these were the benefits of "Finding the Beloved."

February 2017
Warrior Am I

I am a Scorpio, with a birthday in November. I also study esoteric astrology which assigns *mantrams* to each astrological sign. One of the *mantrams* for Scorpio is, "Warrior am I, and from the battle I emerge triumphant." I have always resonated with those words, but the embodiment of them has been a lifelong challenge.

Flash back to 1964, or thereabouts. My ex and I were involved in the Human Potential Movement back then and one of the vehicles for this movement was the "Encounter Groups." We would come together and do a lot of role playing, acting out different parts of ourselves in an attempt to raise our consciousness.

One particular evening, we were divided into two groups. One group held power and control over the other group. I was assigned to the power group. I don't remember the exact scenario we were asked to play but I do remember the rush that came over me as I felt my power. I got totally into it, so much so that I lost my feeling of connection to the people we were controlling. One of them was even my very best friend, but after some time, I didn't even see her. She was just an object to subdue and control.

Later, as we processed the "game", it struck me with such force that I was speechless. I had completely lost touch with my own humanity and the humanity of the people in this group. I no longer saw them as a part of the human family, I saw them as objects only to be controlled and manipulated. It literally scared the sh*t out of me.

From that moment on I became afraid of my power and vowed to keep it under wraps.

Fast forward to the mid-1980s. Studying for my master's degree in psychology, I had taken a class in psychosynthesis. We practiced a lot of guided imagery in this class and one time we were asked to imagine our "ideal image." Could we see a picture of how we would most like to be in the world? I immediately saw a fierce Native American warrior standing tall and powerful with a long spear in his right hand. Then I noticed his left hand in which there was a soft, furry baby kitten.

What I took from this image is that somehow, I needed to join my warrior masculine energy with the softness and receptivity of the feminine. I understood this mentally, but it didn't translate into a *trust* in that power.

Fast forward again to 2015. In November of that year, I took a weekend workshop with the renowned sound healer, Tom Kenyon. We participated in several meditations involving sound and healing.

Sometimes, when I'm in a meditation where the energy is very powerful, I reach a point where I choose to shut down. I say to myself, *I can't take in anymore*. I think it's that old fear of too much and not trusting it.

This time, as I felt the energy reach a very high point, I just said to myself, *Welcome, please come into my body. You are welcome here.* I experienced such gratitude and appreciation as I said these words to myself. Then something really big opened up within me and I felt a surge of strength, power and will energy. I fully opened to it and felt it become a part of me.

Another insight I got during this meditation was that it was fear that stops me and that the antidote to that fear was a belief in my own resilience. When I truly believe I can handle whatever comes my way I am propelled out of the inertia that fear creates.

Tom works with a group of beings called the Hathors. They live in a high dimension of consciousness and work through Tom and his voice as he sings. It's a very powerful experience.

We did a meditation in which they were to gift us with energy from Sirius and Venus. I have long resonated with Sirius as it is the energy that pours through Scorpio. So, in this meditation I felt my heart and chest open and felt another surge of POWER course through me. I saw myself embody the warrior energy, strong and pure and unafraid. I trusted this power, because it was accompanied with a strong energy of compassion. I knew I would not misuse this gift. I had strengthened the compassionate energy within me to the point where I knew it would always balance any tendency to abuse my power. Now I was free to fully express my power in the world.

I have seen this blending of energies play out in my everyday life as a stronger feeling of confidence, as a willingness to take my work out into the world in a more active way without the accompanying fear and trepidation. There is now an excitement about giving what gifts I may possess, instead of the anxiety that I may not do it right, or may not know enough, or somehow, I will make a fool of myself.

Then, amazingly, new opportunities opened up for me to present my work and after meditating on the new possibilities I sensed no resistance, just a resounding inner, "Yes."

Lazarus Blessing

The secret
Of this blessing
Is that it is written
On the back
Of what binds you.
To read
This blessing,
You must take hold
Of the end
Of what
Confines you,
Must begin to tug
At the edge
Of what wraps
You round.
It may take long
For its length
To fall away,
For the words
Of this blessing
To unwind
In folds
About your feet.
By then
You will no longer
Need them.
By then this blessing
Will have pressed itself
Into your waking flesh,
Will have passed
Into your bones,
Will have traveled
Every vein
Until it comes to rest
Inside the chambers

Of your heart
That beats to
The rhythm
Of benediction
And the cadence of release.

Wanton Gospeller, *Circle of Grace*, Press, Orlando, Florida, 2015, Used by permission, janrichardson.com

March 2017
God Works in Mysterious Ways... Yes, She Does

My intention for some time now has been to try to trust more deeply in the ebb and flow of life. To be willing to be guided and led by my deeper knowing, instead of doggedly and perhaps, unconsciously, pursuing my own agenda. Then to wait, knowing that the next step will reveal itself. I don't have to go looking for it. My prayer has been, "I am willing to do what the Soul requires as soon as I register and recognize it as my next duty."

When one of my Soul sisters, Anne, emailed me from Copenhagen that she was in meditation that morning and I appeared to her, I was a bit surprised. I guess I'm still a bit shocked when people tell me that they feel my presence when I'm not actually there. Anyway, the message that came with her awareness of me was that I needed to come to see her this summer.

At first, I thought that she just missed me and wanted to get together, and my concrete mind kicked in with questions: *Could I afford it? Did I really want to go to Europe again, at my age? What about jet lag?* I felt a bit resistant. *I'm so comfortable here, with my life right now, why make another big plan?* The whole litany of ego concerns presented themselves, but I promised her I would sit with it in meditation myself and see if I felt the "nudge" of my Soul.

So, that very morning I was in meditation and I posed the question. *Give me a sign if this is something my Soul has planned for my next step.* I didn't understand that a simple visit to a friend could have Soul purpose, but I was willing to ask. What came was unexpected. I felt a surge of energy in my body. I sat up straight, spine erect, filled with what I can only describe as a downpouring of will energy. After sitting with that for a few minutes and just breathing it into my body I felt myself relax into a more expansive state. Then, surprisingly, I began to write, in my head, a description of a talk I could give at an upcoming conference. The whole paragraph played itself out in my mind. I know, when that happens, to write it all down immediately so it won't be forgotten.

What is surprising about this is that I had only given slight consideration to even going to this conference, let alone presenting a talk. I had given talks before at this conference, so it had crossed my mind, but I somehow felt lethargic about it and not too interested in creating it. Then suddenly the energy was there to offer it.

In a manner uncharacteristic of me, I immediately wrote the organizer and submitted my proposal. Amazingly, she wrote back within the hour and accepted it. Wow, that was stunning.

Now this energy was still running through me and I started thinking about Copenhagen. All of a sudden it felt completely doable and I even came up with the idea that I could do a book signing there to a group my friend belongs to and then it would be tax deductible.

I wrote her and made that proposal. Now I was on a roll and my mind went to the fact that if I went to Copenhagen I would most likely stopover in the UK.

A friend in Canada had told me that any time I wanted to go to England she could probably arrange a book signing there. So, I emailed her, and she got right back. She would see what she could put together.

Another friend emailed me then, totally out of the blue, about doing a presentation at a retreat center on Orcas Island. By now I was pretty much blown away, but I decided to try to confirm or reject the message I was getting by checking my horoscope.

Why was I not surprised when I saw that this year was all about expanding my career, getting out into the world more. Basically putting myself out there, being adventurous and not getting stuck in a rut, breaking things up a bit?

Pluto crossing my Ascendant had always brought up fear and trepidation in me, and this was happening right now. But as I researched it a bit more, I discovered that this transit isn't just about death (Pluto is the Lord of Death), but it is also about fusion, synthesis and integration. It is about claiming new levels of power, self-expression and autonomy. This felt much more like what was happening.

My feelings of strength and confidence and power were coming into an embodied state within me. Also, I read this interesting description of Pluto transits: "Truth above kindness. Resolution over comfort."

Good reminders for those of us who are always so determined to be kind and so attached to the comfort of the way things are.

Then I remembered that there was also an eclipse last month, in February.

This first eclipse in February sets your career ablaze. It is encouraging you to make the most creative strides forward that you can. This flare can help you garner the attention that you need so make sure that you start the year off with a firm dedication to what you most want to see flourish here.

So, what started as an innocent invitation soon morphed into this message from the universe about what I am to do next. One would think I would be used to the magic of the way things work in my life, but somehow it always sort of stuns me. I do believe that this particular set of messages came about mainly because I had earlier opened myself up to a greater sense of my own power and strength. I'm sure my resistance would have been much stronger had I not felt that strength pouring into me.

I aspire to trust more deeply in my own strength and not be surprised by the magic that appears in my life.

I aspire to think big and not be held back by my self-perceived limitations.

I aspire to live my life with ease.

Live today as your Soul dictates and the future will round out itself in fruitful service.

—Alice Bailey, *Discipleship in the New Age, Vol I*

June 2016
Warrior, Warrior, Wherefore Art Thou, Warrior?

I had been feeling so strong and confident after my download of "warrior" energy a few months ago. I had no fear or trepidation about my upcoming presentation at the conference in Arizona until just a few weeks before I was actually going to present.

Suddenly anxiety and fear were once again present. I know that if I can get a handle on the anxiety of presenting, I reach a place of true excitement, but at this moment there was only apprehension. *Where was that warrior energy?* Search as I might it did not seem available.

The Universe doesn't usually give me direct, explicit injunctions. They are usually much subtler. So here are the ways the Universe responded to my question of, *What happened to the warrior energy. Where did it go?*

One bright day, on my walk through the woods, I was listening to a podcast by someone I had never heard of, but the title of the podcast had the word "warrior" in it and since I was searching, I decided to tune in.

This person defined a warrior as "someone who is willing to engage in the world." That was a new definition for me and I could relate to it.

I know myself to be someone who is "willing" to engage, even if I'm afraid, uncertain, and nervous. In fact, one of my *mantrams* has been, "My job is to just show up," with whatever I feel I'm being guided to do. I then try to let go of however things turn out, knowing that I am working in cooperation with Spirit and it is a partnership. It's not just my show.

So, I knew this, but I had never associated it with being a warrior. I could really breathe into that.

The next piece of clarity came from an email I received from the person coordinating all the talks that the presenters were giving. She said at the end of her email, "And never forget that as you get up to make your presentation you each have an angel standing beside you." Whoa, I could really breathe into that.

I am a part of two different groups that I consider my "spiritual family." In both these groups we ask for the kind of support we need from each other during the month we are not together. We make a commitment to hold those requests in our hearts as we meditate each day. So, I made my request for an easing of my anxiety. Each day when I meditated I not only held those friends in my heart I made a conscious decision to spend a few minutes opening my heart to receive their blessings.

One member, who is a Reiki Master, said she would send me a shot of Reiki at the exact moment of my presentation.

Just tuning into these energies each day began to seriously diminish my anxiety and I began to feel a bit of the warrior creeping back into my consciousness.

The next piece of understanding came while watching an ice skating competition on TV. It was an amazing display of beauty and motion and connection. It was really perfection in every movement. I remember saying to myself, *Look, you don't have to do three triple salchows, you just have to give a speech. Get a grip.*

Then I was sitting with a client who was concerned because he didn't feel a strong connection each time he meditated, and he feared he was somehow losing it. I responded, "Just because you don't feel it doesn't mean you've lost it." (Note to self.)

Now that the presentation is over, I feel again, the confidence that always comes when I step out of my comfort zone. I actually have a quote somewhere, by someone, that says, "Life begins at the end of your comfort zone."

Keep dedicating your energy to what serves your work and in turn helps you to serve those that need your work the most.

—Chani Nicholas

November 2017
Did Curiosity Kill the Cat? I Don't Think So

Remember the old saying, "Curiosity killed the cat, but satisfaction brought him back"? I've been reviewing lately my relationship to curiosity. Not the type of invasive curiosity that drove my mom to steam open all my letters from my boyfriends and then glue them back to make it look like she hadn't done it. And not the type that says, "I just can't stand not knowing." I'm also not talking about the type of curiosity that some people have where they ask the questions that are really none of their business, just because they want the thrill of knowing or being able to pass the information along.

The type of curiosity I'm talking about has to do with changing my own perspective on things. Here's two examples from my own life that I've experienced in the last month.

As some of you may recall from a previous blog, I got an email from a friend in Copenhagen, early this year, saying she had connected with me in her meditation and felt that it was important that I come to visit. I was aware of a lot of resistance, *I'm almost seventy-six, do I really want to do any more international travel?* But I promised her I would take the question into my own meditation. When I did, I was suddenly infused with an energy that felt warrior-like, strong, and invincible. There was no hesitation, of course I could do this. What's the big deal? So, based on nothing more than that, I made my plans.

As it turned out the plans evolved into me promising to give three presentations at the local Theosophical Society. As the day of departure drew closer, I became aware of my own internal anxiety voice, *What if I can't sleep? How will I give a presentation if I'm sleep deprived? What about jet lag? What if it's too much for my friend to put me up for 10 days? Will I drive her crazy?*

When I recognized this old habitual internal negative loop, I paused to consider, *How would my perceptions about this trip change if I just became curious?* What if I said to myself, *I'm curious about how this is going to turn out. How will it all unfold? I wonder how the plane ride will be. It will be interesting to see if I make all my connections.* Immediately I began to feel excitement instead of anxiety.

I realize this is not rocket science. Many spiritual, psychological, and philosophical traditions espouse this form of inquiry as a way to work with emotional states, as in, "Hmmmm, I am afraid. Okay, I'll just notice my fear, allow it to be there, hold it in compassion and gently be curious about it, exploring it with tenderness." This takes us out of the total identification with the feeling and lets us get to know our fear, so we can recognize it more quickly when it reappears. I've known this approach for a while, but just this month I've actually put it into practice.

What happened? Well amazingly everything went so smoothly I was pretty blown away by it all. My friend and I were like two peas in a pod, compatible in so many ways and we thoroughly enjoyed each day together. The talks were very well received. I slept fairly well with little jet lag. I'm not saying that this all occurred because of my attitude, but everything became much more enjoyable, manageable and smooth, because I wasn't anxious or projecting my fears into everything.

The second incident occurred when I attended a Tom Kenyon workshop a day after returning from Copenhagen. Tom is a world-renowned sound healer and I have attended many of his workshops in the past, but this day I was a bit jet lagged, so half way into the first day I became agitated.

We had done some clearing work so I'm sure that played a part in it, but my mind went to, *Is he ever going to stop talking and just get on with it? Maybe this was a mistake. I probably shouldn't have tried to squeeze this in so close to returning from my trip.* You get the picture. The old negative loop again. I really did want to participate, and I wanted to be open and receptive to whatever needed to happen, so I didn't want this negativity to override my intention.

Then I remembered curiosity. What if I just came into the next day with a curious mind, instead of a negative mind set? *I wonder what this day will bring? How will it unfold?* I didn't have any more agitation, and the second day proved to be a powerful experience.

He talked about the heart being as light as a feather instead of heavy and burdened. I could relate to that because when I am worried or anxious, I can feel anything but light.

I wondered how I could help my heart become lighter. One thing that came to me was to begin my day with curiosity. Sometimes in the morning before I get up I run through my "to do" list in my head. Not exactly a light-hearted way to begin my day. But what if I made a habit of beginning my day with the curiosity question? *I wonder what today will bring? How will it unfold?* I can feel the visceral reaction in my body when I do this. There is a fluttering in my heart, an excitement, an anticipation that does make my heart feel lighter.

I'm going with that.

PS: The more I practice using this, the more it comes into my mind throughout the day. So, I have begun asking that question for every little thing. *I wonder how my walk will be today? I'm curious about my meditation this morning. How will it unfold? What will the trip to the store be like?* Somehow this practice energizes me, and I walk around with more of a feeling of excitement and anticipation.

At this age, of almost seventy-six, anything that enlivens me and lightens my heart is well worth the effort.

In a *Peanuts* cartoon I have on my refrigerator, Snoopy says to Charlie Brown, "What if today we were just grateful for everything?"

I'd like to add, *"What if today we were just **curious** about everything?"*

CHAPTER 10
BOUNDARIES AND CODEPENDENCE

There's so much I could say about boundaries and codependence. These are issues I've struggled with my entire life, starting with my Christian upbringing which stressed always doing for others. I even carried a card in my wallet till I was in my twenties that said, "God first, others second, I'm third."

Many years as a married woman trying to deal with an alcoholic husband fine-tuned my enabling, codependent behavior.

Later, as I began my own healing journey, I realized the ramifications of a Cancer moon, a recipe for codependence. You've heard me mention this often in these entries.

You've also heard me talk about the Seven Rays Conference that I attend each year. I hypothesize that I have what is called a Second Ray Soul. This ray is called the Ray of Love and Wisdom. A beautiful energy, if the love part doesn't leak out into codependence.

Then there's the Enneagram, which is another system that tries to categorize personality types. In this system I am a Two, which is the caretaker.

So, there are many elements in my make up that lend themselves to this issue of boundaries and co-dependence.

You can check the Appendix if you want to know more about these systems.

In case you are not familiar with the qualities of a codependent let me share with you some of the notes I have taken, over the years, on this subject.

From the book, *Whatever Arises, Love That*, by Matt Kahn (mattkahn. org):

Co-dependent empath is someone who has to make sure everyone is feeling ok in order to relax, (it's) when the quality of your experience is dependent upon the actions or behaviors of others.

Some other qualities of a codependent:

Becoming overly involved in people's lives and getting our validation from their need for us.

Feeling compelled to help someone solve their problems by offering unasked for advice or trying to fix their feelings.

Anticipating another's needs before they even ask for help.

Making an underlying assumption that they can't take care of themselves, so you must jump in.

Not expressing what your needs are in any given situation.

I can relate strongly to all these tendencies and am still working on a healthier way to be in the world.

February 2014
Taking People at Their Word

Lately I've noticed another one of those wonderful patterns that sits in my endless reservoir of habitual thinking. And it sits there quite comfortably, thank you very much, until my awareness kicks in. If I'm lucky it kicks in before it has to hit me over the head.

Pondering on an interaction I had a few weeks ago, what I noticed that I offered to help someone, not really wanting to, just sort of to be polite. I didn't really expect them to take me up on it. I expected them to defer, as I usually do, and say, "Oh, thanks, but I've got it." Instead she said, "Great, here's what you can do." OMG, she took me at my word. It wasn't a tsunami of insight, I just noticed it.

Later, another conversation. My daughter was asking a friend of mine for a favor. My friend said, "sure." My daughter says to me, "Do you think she's just being polite? Maybe she feels obligated." I heard myself say to her, *Well maybe you can just take her at her word.*

It got me thinking of all the times I have wasted energy trying to figure out if people really meant what they said. It hasn't been easy for me to ask for help in my life, but this awareness has provoked me into thinking in a new way. What if I did just take people at their word? PERIOD, end of story.

I began to experiment. At my recent book signing several people came up and asked me if they could help me set up. I said yes without a second thought.

At a weekend seminar at my home a few weeks ago, I asked a friend to take charge of the coffee. Not a big deal, but I didn't worry about imposing. I just assumed, "He's an adult. He can say no." What a revelation. If I have a need, I can ask, and just assume people will tell me the truth, and if they don't, it's not my job to figure out why or agonize over whether they really meant it. I'll just take them at their word. I'll just *assume* they have the ability to say no.

I also want to be more mindful of when I *offer* to help. I am a Type Two, on the Enneagram, so I'm almost out of my seat before anyone asks for anything. Now I am learning to pause and ask myself, *Is this offer coming from a conscious choice to help or am I just falling into the old habitual reaction?*

Here's what I have figured out about myself. Usually when I *deflect* an offer of help it's because I *assume* the person is offering out of obligation or to be polite. (It is not hard to see where my daughter came up with her questions.)

Another reason I deflect is because I want to feel competent. *I can do this by myself.* The need to prove this to people and myself has lessened with age and the reality is that it really is harder for me to do some things alone.

Sometimes I refuse offers of help because I have a genuine desire to make things easier for others, like when my children come over for dinner and I take charge of everything. I know how busy they are, how stressed, trying to manage kids, careers, relationships, so in an effort to give them just a few hours of not having to do anything, I offer to do it all. But lately I've been clearer about asking them to take charge when I don't feel like it.

Probably the biggest lesson in all of this is for me is something I've been working on for a long time, asking for what I need without trying to decide ahead of time whether or not I'm imposing on anyone. Let the adult in them tell me it's too much or it's inconvenient or they just don't feel like it.

How much easier, clearer, and more direct is that?

August 2014
When Understanding is Not Enough

I think we can all agree that understanding one another is a good thing. Walking in someone else's shoes, giving them the benefit of the doubt, etc. etc. etc. I have a strong empathy gene, so it comes fairly easily for me to see and feel where someone else is coming from. That has mostly served me well in my life and in my profession as a therapist. But I realized some time ago that I spent many years in my marriage "understanding" instead of speaking up, standing my ground, and stating my needs and expectations about how I wanted to be treated.

So recently when I was disappointed in a friend's behavior, it sparked a memory of this awareness. She had agreed to call at a certain time on a certain day. I was looking forward to hearing from her and catching up, but the day came and there was no call. It wasn't like I was sitting around just waiting for the phone to ring, but I noticed I was disappointed.

I realize in the scheme of things this is not a huge deal, and this is how I often talk myself out of saying what I feel. I "understand." I minimize my feelings. I mean, truly, it's just a phone call, right? So, I debated in my mind how I wanted to handle it. Most of me just wanted to ignore it and pretend it wasn't a big deal. I can easily understand how someone can forget a phone call. See, I'm doing it again, even in this blog!! Yikes! And it truly *wasn't* a big deal, but there is a principle here that I discovered anew in my morning shower. Someone once told me, "People treat you the way you train them to treat you." I think there is a lot of truth in that. So, I asked myself, *How do I want to be treated as a friend?* I realized that I appreciate and respect someone who honors their commitments, even the small ones, like a phone call.

So, I understood, *and* I spoke up, because I want to be treated with consideration and thoughtfulness in my friendships. And guess what, she actually thanked me for letting her know how I felt and agreed that that's one of the components of a good friendship, sharing the easy stuff and the hard stuff.

It's one of the many lessons I'm learning these days. It has to do with the courage to be vulnerable. To share even when you think you might be judged for being a wimp or, heaven forbid, *too **sensitive***, and believe me I've been exposed to that a lot.

These are small little awarenesses, for sure, but I believe that every little shift in our consciousness adds up to a stronger, clearer expression of our authentic self.

So, let's hear it for understanding *and* courage, *and* directness, *and* honesty, *and* vulnerability.

August 2014
Every Day, in Every Way, I Just Keep Learning

In my last entry, I wrote of how we train people to treat us in certain ways and if we want to be treated differently, we must speak up and let our feelings and needs be known. Since that opportunity keeps presenting itself to me, I have decided to write another blog about a different situation with the same undercurrents.

I have a friend of several years whom I have a great deal of respect for and admire in many ways. The last year or so I have felt her criticism of me on several occasions.

At least I have interpreted some of our interactions as her being critical of me. I acknowledge that I am extremely sensitive to criticism, having lived so much of my life with that energy. Also, I have that Cancer moon that just adds to the mix of sensitivity in general. So, I'm pretty certain that my friend would not categorize her comments to me as criticism, but nevertheless I felt the hurt in my body and it didn't go away.

My pattern in these situations is to process it all inwardly. I'm very courageous about examining my part in any uncomfortable situation. What I'm not so brave about is actually talking about my feelings with the other person. I tell myself, *Well, good, I've figured that out. I will be more aware in the future, of that tendency.*

But I noticed this time that I was closing down a part of my heart toward my friend. When that happens, I create some distance and withdraw a bit.

A few days ago, we were together and within the course of a few hours there were three incidents of that same type of comment. I didn't respond to any of them and then noticed that I couldn't wait to get away from the discomfort of that situation. The uneasiness did not go away.

I value my inner process and what I learn from it, so I sat with my feelings and asked for some illumination. I got clearly that it was my personality (ego) that was hurt. I got clearly that I wanted to not take it personally. I remembered that my friend is kind hearted, generous, understanding and would not do anything intentionally to hurt me. Usually this is where I stop but remembering the pattern I have of understanding and keeping quiet, I began to feel like I wanted to handle this in a different way.

I have also been asking in my meditation time to be shown whatever is in me that needs transformation, so I sort of took this on as a cosmic mission...

even though it felt scary.

I called my friend and asked if we could get together, that I had some things I needed to say. We met for coffee and before I could say anything she apologized. She went on to completely take ownership for her comments that day and as we discussed an earlier incident we discovered that we had both completely misinterpreted the others' words and intentions. I thought she said one thing, so I responded, but in reality she had meant a totally different thing and took my comment as a dismissal and then reacted in anger.

We talked about our "edges." Where we are struggling in our personalities. I related my sensitivity to criticism and she told of her desire to channel her big energy in a healthier way.

Later I realized how refreshing it was to have a conversation with someone who could listen without becoming defensive, who could take ownership for their part of the incident, and who kept her heart open to me during the entire process.

These are the qualities I want in a friend. I'm sure this is not the experience I would have with everyone, but didn't I start this post by saying how much respect and admiration I have for this person? Well, that's why.

It also inspired me to risk being authentic and vulnerable more often, but I want to be discerning in this. I believe we need to choose carefully the people we decide to open ourselves to. Not everyone deserves our trust and if we don't have a lot invested in the relationship it might be time to just dismiss the whole thing and move on.

Unconditional love, conditional access.
—Author Unknown

May 2015
Taking My Stand, For Others

I am involved with a small group of friends that I've known most of my adult life. We don't see each other on a regular basis, but at least a few times a year two or three of us make the effort to get together to catch up on our lives. Jill and Sam are a part of this small group (obviously not their real names, and not a couple).

The last few years when we have gotten together, I've noticed that Jill seems to be carrying a lot of animosity, verging on hatred, toward Sam.

Right off, let me say that I deeply love Sam, and I do care about Jill, but not with the same depth.

It would be easier to bear if Jill were to keep her feelings to herself, but often she disparages, demeans, and questions Sam's integrity and character to his face, and in front of the rest of us. And in the few times when I am alone with Jill, she invariably steers the conversation toward her anger and frustration with Sam.

The therapist in me recognizes that Jill's emotional reactions to Sam go much deeper than any conflict she may have had with him. I know for a fact that there has never been any harm done to Jill that would account for her hostility. This is a projection of mammoth proportions. So, I understand it has very little to do with Sam, per se.

The Buddhist in me believes that for someone to have this depth of anger must mean there is a commensurate amount of inner suffering going on. So, there is reason for much compassion and I can usually get to that place within myself. I can ache for Jill's suffering. Who hasn't suffered and felt that kind of deep pain? Empathy is present in me most of the time.

But the question remains, is that enough? *Do I take a stand? Is that what is required of me? How do I be in integrity with what this destructive energy brings up in me?*

I recognize that I often avoid conflict. I literally hate the messiness. So, in the past I have tried to neutralize Jill's feelings by explaining Sam to her, or by changing the subject, in an attempt to diffuse the situation and to ease my own discomfort. But lately that doesn't feel like enough.

I am reminded of a story attributed to Maya Angelou, and I will paraphrase. The story goes that she had invited many people to her home to some kind of a party. During the course of the evening she overhears someone make a disparaging comment of some kind, cruel and judgmental, as I recall. She states very strongly, and without hesitation, "These kinds of comments are not allowed in this house." And if I am remembering it correctly, she asks him to leave. This struck me so powerfully because I remember asking myself if I would have the courage to do something like that. But it did inspire me to not let those kinds of negative comments linger without a response. Yet here I was vacillating in this situation. What to do?

Well, this is a friendship and even though it is longstanding I do have the option of bowing out of it altogether. Because of this animosity and negativity, I have chosen to limit my exposure to Jill but that leaves me feeling a bit like a wimp, taking the easy way out.

In a past blog, ("When Understanding is Not Enough") I talked about how I need to stand up for speaking my truth when my needs are not being met or when I am being treated badly. In this case it feels like I also need to stand up and speak my truth when someone else is being mistreated.

So, I have begun having imaginary conversations with Jill in order to prepare myself for the next time this happens in my presence. At first these conversations in my head were quite lengthy with a lot of explaining and trying to be nice, my old pattern of dealing with conflict. Then I realized I just needed to state directly and clearly the essence of what I wanted to convey, and it went something like this:

"Jill, could I tell you something? Often when we are together and almost always when Sam is present, you say very hurtful things to him or about him. I want you to know how deeply those words hurt me and so I am asking you not to share your feelings toward Sam with me. And if I am in your presence when you attack him, I will stand up and ask you to STOP!" (This is not unlike what we have been teaching my three-year-old granddaughter to say when she is in the presence of a bully. Oh well, it's only taken me seventy-plus years to get this.)

So here I am "taking the high road" in this situation. I will come from a place of compassion and an open and understanding heart, and still say what needs to be said to stop this form of violence.

Get ready, Jill, here I come.

True compassion comes from standing for and with others and acting on behalf of others. Knowing that to serve others, serves us all.

—Charter for Compassion, contact@charterforcompassion.org

April 2017
Breathing In

I've been thinking a lot this month about my friends and family members who have strong water signs in their chart: sun, moon or rising sign in Cancer, Scorpio or Pisces. I'm included in this list being a Scorpio sun with a Cancer moon.

These are the signs with deep sensitivity to the outer world. Pisces can easily lose their energy to anyone in pain. Cancer gives it away to anyone in need of nurturing or mothering. We water signs meet the world first through our feelings. We are sensitive, empathic, compassionate people. So, this world is not always easy for us to deal with, especially this particular world, in this particular time.

With the sun in Pisces this last month and with several planets aspecting it, we have been hit doubly hard with that sensitivity. It came as no surprise then, really, when I once again found myself in the pool at the gym with my water aerobics class.

Now, this is a new gym, a new pool, and a new class since my insurance company dropped my other membership. So, I knew no one. But still that same old judgmental mind kicked in when two people were laughing hysterically and talking loudly the entire class. Some of you might remember this scene from a previous entry entitled, "Lessons From the Gym." I thought I had conquered that particular lesson, but here I was in a new place with the same old reaction.

I recognized my sensitivity to noise, to distractions and I knew I wanted to have a different reaction. I tried Pema's *mantram*, "Just like me," trying to remember there were times when I was insensitive. It didn't work. I was still rather pissed off.

Then I sort of saw how my energy had dispersed outward, as water signs are prone to do. We lose it easily. I took a really deep breath and visualized myself breathing my energy back into myself. I asked myself, silently, of course, *What would happen if I just paid attention to my own energy, if I just focused on how my body feels in this water, if I just breathed myself back into myself?*

Amazingly, I lost almost all of my sensitivity to the outside environment. I just fully inhabited my own body. I know this isn't rocket science, but the shift was pretty dramatic. The noise in the room noticeably diminished, at least to my ears.

So, I am pondering this month the challenge it is for us sensitive types to stand in our own being. How do we create a boundary between the outside environment and ourselves without shutting down? Shutting down is easy for most of us, but do we really want to go around clenched in and constricted, keeping out the good stuff as well as the disturbing?

For me, when I breathed my energy back into my body, I felt strong and grounded. I acknowledged, *This is me.* I was still aware of the energy in the room, but it didn't draw me out of myself.

Discernment is difficult. What is mine and what isn't? It's one of the important practices for water signs. Where does my energy go when I'm triggered? Can I hold onto it? Being such strong compassionate types, we can sometimes just let everyone in and then wonder where our energy went.

I remember a story that one of my favorite writers, Daniele LaPorte, relayed. She was talking to her teenage son who had just suffered his first heartbreak. She said to him, "Always keep a gate on your heart. Then you stand there and decide who enters and who doesn't." I thought that was a great story because again, discernment includes knowing when someone else's energy will not support our wellbeing. The Buddha is reported to have said to someone, "Never throw anyone out of your heart." Sylvia Boorstein, a Buddhist teacher added, "You may have to throw them out of your house, but never out of your heart."

Some people deserve to come in, some come in and then need to leave, and for some we need to lock that gate as tightly as we can, but with a loving heart.

Just for fun:

There are over 7 trillion nerves in the human body. Some people are capable of getting on every damn one of them.

—Anonymous

July 2017
Ouch (x3)

Again!!! I did it again. Not intentionally, not with forethought and certainly not to upset, but I gave someone I care about an unasked-for suggestion. He was sharing a feeling with me and I just slipped into the old pattern of trying to make it better.

We have talked a lot about this issue and how it affects our relationship, but sometimes those old patterns just creep in and I find myself in deep water again. *Just listen*, I tell myself later. *That's all; just listen, listen, listen.* I keep forgetting to bite my tongue.

The "suggestion" I gave was only a sentence, but his response was immediate and angry, "I'M HANDLING THIS!!!!" Ouch, I could feel the hurt in my heart and I don't even remember the rest of our conversation. I just wanted to get off the phone.

I have a habit of handling hurt feelings by "understanding." I've written about this in the past and it's still easy for me to slip into. After hanging up I had a conversation in my head. *I know he cares about me. He wouldn't intentionally hurt my feelings. He's not himself these days because of the pressures of his own life. I should be a bigger person and just forgive him.* Then I noticed that I didn't want to talk to him again. I wanted to distance myself, shut down.

If this was just an acquaintance and this reactiveness was a pattern, I would probably just decide it was not the kind of relationship I wanted to invest in, but I want this person in my life. Still, I held onto my hurt.

Then two things happened. First, I read a post on Facebook that quoted a person named Sophia Nelson. It said, in part, "Be a woman another person can trust. Have the courage to tell another directly when he/she has offended, hurt or disappointed you." Wow, that hit home. The reminder that trust depends on total honesty, even when it's hard and I am afraid.

And this also harkens back to my age-old issue of valuing my own needs and speaking up when they are not being met, even if I have judged my needs as being too petty, or unimportant, or, heaven forbid, I'm just being too sensitive.

I've written so much about this issue in the past that I'm really getting sick of it, but it keeps coming up for me so when that happens, I seem to need to write about it.

The second thing that happened was that I was sitting in meditation the next day, totally into it and miles away from any feelings of hurt, when the pain from that conversation hit me with a force I couldn't ignore. It ruined the rest of my meditation, but I got the message. This was something I needed to attend to.

I sat for a while thinking of how I wanted to speak my truth and what came up was this imaginary phone conversation. *Have you got a few minutes? I need to share something with you that is really hard for me to do. Yesterday during our phone conversation, I crossed the line and gave you a suggestion that you hadn't asked for. Your response was really harsh, and it hurt my feelings. I know you would not intentionally hurt me, but I'd like to ask you if you could try to be a bit gentler with me when I forget to honor the boundaries we have created? I also want you to know that my first response to being hurt was to shut down and distance myself from you, but I realized that I care too much about our relationship to do that. I hope you can see that this is my attempt to create a deeper level of intimacy with you. I don't want anything to be in the way of our closeness.*

It took me a few more days to actually screw up the courage to call and say what I needed to say, but I felt so relieved when it was over. He was gracious and admitted his part and thanked me for my honesty. I was grateful to be received in that way.

I think the larger picture here is that it's not so much about this particular conversation or me getting my feelings hurt as much as it is about me developing the muscle that makes it easier for me to be vulnerable and admit when I'm hurt.

My warrior self needs to stand up for what is true if she is to fully embody her power, and since I have been searching to reconnect with that strength and confidence, I am grateful for another opportunity to practice.

Warrior am I and from the battle I emerge, triumphant.
—Scorpio *mantram*

A week later, another difficult situation with another dear friend. My feelings of disappointment and hurt required a few days of inner processing before I could say what needed to be said. But I did it.

A few days later: WTF??? Three times in one month?

Another opportunity to speak up about my feelings, with another friend. Feeling hurt, not heard, and not acknowledged. Equally as hard, but after a night of tossing and turning I spoke my truth again and felt my vulnerability, but also my strength and authenticity.

Then as I was preparing my article on the new moon in Cancer for the Soul Bridging website, (www.soulbridging.com) I realized that many of the aspects of this new moon have to do with our wounds, (hurts from the past) and communicating our feelings. So, I guess I'm feeling the impact of those energies as well. Besides which, the full moon is hitting my Cancer moon at the exact same degree and "digging up the dirt" and Pluto is sitting right next to my moon. Whew!

And is it just a co-inky-dink that I came across this quote, from Matt Kahn (at mattkahn.org), at the same time?

One of the most commonly overlooked spiritual practices is daring to be completely honest with everyone you encounter. Some may say others cannot handle their honesty, but true honesty is not a strategy or a weapon of any kind. It is the willingness to be open and absolutely transparent in sharing how any moment feels in your heart. It has nothing to do with confrontation, accusation, or any form of blame. True honesty is the willingness to stand completely exposed, allowing the world to do what it may, and say what it will, only so you may know who you are – beyond all ideas.

I also began to wonder if there wasn't a deeper message here. Three times in one month just seemed too coincidental. Then I came upon the answer while reading a book by Ram Dass, called *Polishing the Mirror*. His words popped right out of the page and into my heart. I knew this was the core of what I was struggling with. "Just allowing your humanity and that of others **to be as it is**, is the beginning of compassion." I needed to feel compassion for the sensitive, easily triggered, Cancer moon that I am, but I also needed to feel love and acceptance for the other person's personality expressions.

I have pondered a lot about the line between fully accepting someone, as they are, and still asking for my needs to be met. In this sentence, from Ram Dass' book, something got clarified for me. I need to express my needs. I need to be vulnerable, honest and authentic, but I have to accept people where they are and not hold onto the hurt. I have to keep my heart open even when I feel like distancing and shutting down. They are expressing their humanity just as I am expressing mine, nothing more.

CHAPTER 11
INJURY

February 2015 was the mother of all "perfect storms". The main thing that happened, was a major fall. I was babysitting my three-year-old grandson. We were getting ready to go outside and take a walk. I put my walking shoes on and tried to step over the baby gate which I had done many times, but usually without shoes. The toe of my shoe caught on the top of the gate and I fell flat - splat - no time to cushion the fall, on the right shoulder, fracturing it in two places.

Thank God/dess my daughter happened to still be in the house. Usually she took off as soon as I got there. My cell phone had fallen along with me and had landed way across the room. I don't know what I would have done had she not been home. I couldn't get up.

My grandson witnessed it all and stood stock still, in shock, as I fell. I yelled for my daughter and she came, gave me two ibuprofen and called 911. Luckily no surgery was required, but I was in a sling for six weeks and then many months of physical therapy. It took me a little over a year to feel really back to normal. Don't forget this was a seventy-three-year-old body.

The entries that follow are my musings about that challenging February and what I learned about myself in the recovery process.

January 2015
Mindful Attention

I've been working on my mind for a long time, trying to force it into submission, railroad it into cooperation. During meditation I have learned to quiet the "monkey mind" somewhat, to turn down the volume on the chatter and that has helped, but recently I've been reading again about the power of the mind to dictate our emotional state and I decided I wanted to become more aware of that connection.

What were some underlying mental patterns that had me in an unconscious loop and how did they impact the way that I felt? I made a one-day commitment to be especially mindful of my thoughts.

Driving to an appointment that day I tuned in. What I heard was, *I'm tired. I wish I could just go home and take some time for myself.* I did a reality check. *Had I really not had any time to myself for a while?* No, last week was pretty clear, lots of time. So, the thought was not relevant to the reality of that moment. It was just an old belief that I never have enough solitary time, that I never have enough energy, that I just want to be home reading, like all the time.

So, I decided to choose a different story. I said to myself, *Wow, this is a chance for me to get out of the house. I need some balance in my life between solitude and being out in the world and this appointment has all of the ingredients to uplift and energize me.* (Which was all very true, by the way.)

Then I immediately noticed, because I was determined to pay attention, that my body responded with more energy, a feeling of lightness and anticipation, rather than subdued dread. *What will this experience be like? Let's just go and see.* I was pretty amazed at how quickly everything turned around, and I went on to have an energetic, fun filled, afternoon. Who knew?

That night as I was getting ready for bed, the old anxiety began to creep in. Since going off my hormones several years ago and still dealing with recurring hot flashes, my sleep has not been very restorative, lots of tossing and turning. Sometimes I have to get up and read for a few hours because I can't settle down and get back to sleep. This pattern has created a thought loop that kicks in almost every night. *I wonder if I will get a good night's sleep tonight? I'm afraid I won't be able to sleep through the night and then I won't have much energy tomorrow and then my mind will be fuzzy... and then... and then...* All of this, of course, plays out in my body, tense, constricted, anxious. Who could sleep well with all that going on?

Before bed that night I gave myself different information. I said, *I know I will sleep well tonight. I will rest calmly, I will ease back into sleep if I wake up, I will wake up tomorrow refreshed with plenty of energy to do all I need to do.*

I remember waking up slightly two times during the night and repeating those words each time. My body relaxed, smoothed out. It never got triggered into anxiety. This was very unusual.

The next day I felt great, not just because I'd had a good night's sleep, but also because of the excitement of knowing how I could use this new awareness to improve my life.

Certainly, this is not a new concept, watching, monitoring and reprogramming the mind. It is the famous maxim of the "positive thinking" movement. It's the foundation for the Science of Mind philosophy. It's Cognitive Therapy. However, I had never really noticed the connection between what I thought and how it affected my energy.

For many years I have been frustrated with my energy levels, never being able to count on a sustained high degree of exertion, motivation, and impetus. Only now am I beginning to realize how my thinking has affected my energy.

None of this negates truly paying attention to how we are feeling and honoring that. This is about noticing repetitive thinking patterns that consistently depress our energetic system.

How do we want to feel?

Can we influence this by choosing a different perspective, by reframing a situation?

And is that negative loop really true for us in this moment or is it just an old habitual thought?

The concept is really pretty simple, I believe. With mindfulness I can choose the thoughts that make me feel the way I want to feel.

I want to feel liberated, free, and authentic so my choice is to continue this practice of paying compassionate attention to the thoughts that play across my consciousness. I want to be present to my true self, in the moment, and experience the joy in that.

How about you?

The moment you change your perception. Is the moment you re-write the chemistry in your body.
—Dr. Bruce Lipton

Addendum: The next month (February 2015) turned out to be my "Pity Pot" month so this reminder helped me deal with the opportunities that were presented to me that month. I had to practice a lot!!

March 2015
The Pity Pot

Okay, my friends, I'm going to just lay it all out there and call this what it is. It's a dump blog, an unload blog, a "just get it all off my chest" blog.

There will be no pithy words of wisdom, no spiritual "ahas", no funny t-shirt sayings, no poetry. In a word, or maybe several, "I've had it with the month of February." Okay, I know, Mercury retrograde can be challenging, but OMG it was off the charts this month… sudden death overtime. Here it is in a "not so small nutshell," and in chronological order. Remember, I'm just dumping here, no need to get all hot and bothered just hang in there and listen, if you want.

I guess I really need to start in January, so I can't blame it all on Mercury. My one totally relaxing vacation of the year with my sis and her hubby to Palm Springs and I came down with the mother of all colds the day we arrived!!!! So, okay, my mind reframing was pretty okay with that, "If I'm going to be sick I might as well be in the sun." Then when my brother-in-law, caught it, in spite of all my attempts to wipe doorknobs and sneeze into my elbow, I felt really guilty. His bug immediately turned into the mother of all ear infections, and he was due for surgery on his nose right after we got back. Yikes, more guilt.

I finally recovered from the cold and then walking to my son's house to babysit one night, in the dark, I missed the bulge in the sidewalk and took a complete header onto the cement. Sat outside for several minutes to wipe up the blood so I wouldn't completely freak out my three-year-old granddaughter. As it was, she was busy worrying about me all evening.

I woke up the next day with the right side of my face the color of an eggplant. Okay, I didn't break any bones, my newly mindful mind tells me.

Then in rapid succession my refrigerator dies, my phone dies, and the On Demand feature of my TV goes out. Now we're definitely talking Mercury retrograde.

I make it through the loss of the Seahawks at the Super Bowl (boo hoo). My bruise is almost gone, the cold is finally over, and one evening I take three bites of a "little bit too long in the new fridge" turkey meatloaf. That night I'm up for almost nine hours straight with diarrhea and vomiting. You know the scene, sitting on the pot with a bowl in your arms. At one point, I'm totally out of it and wanting to die and the glass bowl filled with vomit slips out of my hand into the toilet, breaks into a thousand pieces and I just start to cry.

This is probably wayyyyyy too much information, but it speaks to the mood.

The next three days I'm living on Saltines, Gatorade, and Campbell's Chicken Noodle soup.

I make it to the weekend workshop on the Enneagram, still not eating, so pretty weak.

Saturday afternoon of the workshop I get a phone call from my friend who lives in my downstairs apartment telling me there is water gushing out of her ceiling into the hall, the bedroom and the storage room. Long story short, a pipe burst in my bathroom upstairs, covered the floor and the hardwood floor in the hallway and made its way downstairs before anyone caught it. I was still in a semi-food-poisoning-fog so handling all the details was a major challenge.

Two days more days go by filled with a million phone calls and service people in and out of the house, but I think I'm finally on top of it when I get another call.

Swear to God/dess this is the truth. An apartment house that I own with another couple has a burst pipe in one of the units and water is gushing all over the kitchen. The manager can't find the source and by the time the water detectors get there (didn't even know there was such an outfit) the room is flooded; the cabinets and floors are all damaged and it looks like we will have to gut the whole kitchen. The poor tenant has to move out.

Now my home has seven dehumidifiers blasting hot air 24/7, upstairs and downstairs, to dry out the moisture from the floors and the walls. The noise is deafening so I can only sit in the closed off family room or my bedroom, if I put in ear plugs. That level of noise is extremely disconcerting.

The first night the humidifies are in my hallway I go out in the dark, forgetting they are there and take another header as I trip over one and go down. The next day I am bruised and sore and I have a monster sore throat, probably from the dryness of the air with all the machines on. Besides which it is eighty degrees in my house from the heat.

Today I'm walking down the stairs to the basement apartment to make yet another scheduling arrangement and I trip AGAIN!!!!, falling down the last four steps with my bad knee buckled underneath me. YIKES!! So, I ask you, just WTF is going on? One thing I know I need to do is to get outside and put my feet on the earth again. Haven't done that for a week or so, so I'm sure I'm not very grounded right now.

Several years ago, I was having lunch with my friend, Marie. I had had a breast cancer scare and was waiting for the results of a biopsy. I was on the pity pot then also and started bemoaning my fate. "I just want to get on with my life," I wailed. She looked me right in the eye with so much love and tenderness and said, gently, "Honey, this is life." So, I get that I'm just having a sh*tty month and that this is no life-and-death matter. I need to accept that this is just life, messy, frustrating, and unpredictable.

My tolerance for being on the pity pot has gotten less and less over the years mainly because it's so uncomfortable. My body really doesn't like the drama and the negativity. So, I'm fairly certain I will be sick of this "poor me, ain't it awful" attitude very soon, but in the meantime, I'm feeling a bit like swearing, a bit pissy, a bit edgy, a bit discouraged. I'm not immersed in it, but it's there.

When I have a moment of calmness some clarity sneaks in and I can see and be grateful that:

I'm alive.

I didn't break any bones or my hip.

I didn't have a concussion.

My whole house didn't flood.

The whole apartment didn't flood.

I actually like Gatorade and saltines.

But then the moment fades away and I'm back to just wanting to swear. The FGO (F*cking Growth Opportunity) mindset has yet to set in completely.

Done ranting.

Thanks for listening.

Addendum #1

Just when you think the worst is over your shoe catches on the top of the baby's gate as you are trying to step over it and down you go, fracturing your right humeral bone in two places, and doncha know, it's my right shoulder, and I am immobilized in a shoulder sling for six weeks. Prayers and good healing thoughts greatly appreciated.

Addendum #2

And the beat goes on. Yesterday my hair blower blew up and the freezer somehow got unplugged... everything has to be thrown out.

Lordy, lordy will the fun never end?

My *mantram*? It's only food and no one has died. Sometimes you have to look really hard to see things in a different light.

April 2015
We All Need Somebody to Lean On

Insights at the edge, or, what I have learned from being incapacitated for six-plus weeks:

It's almost impossible to wash under your left armpit when your right arm is in a sling.

It takes about thirteen-and-a-half days to get nauseated just thinking about another game of spider solitaire or scrabble, especially one handed.

The Dog Whisperer is actually fairly entertaining at 3:30 in the morning.

I never fully appreciated the beauty and ease of typing with two hands.

It's humbling to have to ring a bell to summon someone to help you out of a chair or bed at 2:00am in the morning, even if that someone loves you a lot.

I'm really pretty okay with not having any obligations or commitments even though my inner critic has had a field day trying to tell me I should feel guilty for being so unproductive. And my spiritual inner critic says I should still be serving others in some way in spite of physical limitations. Or at the very least spend all this extra time reading all my spiritual books and meditating more. (None of which I have been able to do, by the way.)

Some deeper learnings:

Since my divorce back in 1996 I have prided myself on my independence, my ability to be self-sufficient, my, "I can do it myself attitude." Well, when you can't even get out of a chair without help, that little piece of pride has to give way to a humbler reality. I needed help.

I am blessed to have so many people in my life willing to help. The stumbling block was entirely mine. The truth? I absolutely hated asking.

A session of EFT (Emotional Freedom Technique) with the wonderful, Karin Granstrom, cleared that pretty quickly (karingranstrom.com).

Still it was sobering to realize that this is probably how we all will end up, incapacitated in some way and dependent on others for our care. So, I began to look at it as good practice, a graceful, grateful dependency. This song helped.

Lean on me, when you're not strong, and I'll be your friend, I'll help you carry on

—song by Bill Withers

You can catch it on YouTube.

My wonderful acupuncturist, Dr. David Martin, who often acts as therapist and a medical resource, suggested perhaps, just perhaps, since I have spent many years in co-dependent relationships and also as a Type Two in the Enneagram (we live to serve), perhaps the universe was telling me that for once I really needed to just focus on taking care of myself... Ya think?

I've never been one to be overly concerned with my appearance but when you are reduced to only having three tops you can get into, and one pair of sweats (with an elastic waistband), and you can finally shower and wash your hair by yourself, but no way can you hold the hair blower and *fix* your hair. Well, you just have to let it all go.

My biggest challenge has been the nighttime. Under the best of circumstances, I am not great at getting a good night's sleep. We're talking major tossing and turning. So, when I'm forced to lie on my back, unable to change positions, I get frustrated and my body gets restless. It really wants to move. Maximum time in one spot: about one and a half hours, assuming I can even get to sleep.

So, each night I beat a well-worn path down the hall from my bed to the recliner to try a new position. Then an hour or so later, back to the bed, interrupted by time on the computer (Remember spider solitaire and scrabble?) the TV (Remember *The Dog Whisperer?*) and any good mystery novel I am currently reading. Those are my nights.

Well, after a few weeks of this I'm pretty sleep deprived and that is when my gremlin mind kicks in. It has a very loud voice, "THIS SUCKS. YOU'RE NEVER GOING TO GET A GOOD NIGHTS SLEEP. DO SOMETHING!!!"

I do try relaxation CDs, meditating, saying *mantrams*, a few sleep aids that only end up making me feel hyper. Nothing seems to work.

Finally, my daughter says, "Maybe you can just go into the frustration, just be with it."

That seems to resonate so I begin remembering what I had forgotten.

Byron Katie: "Why argue with reality?"

Sylvia Boorstein:

Can you meet each moment just as it is? Can you meet it as a friend?" That really stuck. How can I become friendly with the night, with all of my frustrations and anger?

Well I have to say that those words alone didn't magically cure all my sleep problems, but I was able to come to a place of more acceptance, this is just what is, in this moment. Can I just be with it? When I can the nights become softer, gentler. And my inner gremlin sort of nods off. At least one of us gets some rest.

So, that is what I know so far. I'm sure as this whole episode unfolds more will be revealed.

> Slow down you move too fast. You gotta make the moment last.
> —Paul Simon

Resting In Each Step

Have patience. Slow down.
Because the gap between
'Where I am'
and
'Where I want to be'
is full of possibility.
So don't rush through it.
Take time.
Find the dignity in slowness.

Learn to love the gap.
Grace it with your presence.
It is bursting with life, and creativity,
and it holds unexpected treasures.

Have patience. Slow down.
Life is only Now.
Find rest in every step.

In presence, there is no gap.
— Jeff Foster

May 2015
A Note I Sent Out to All My Friends and Family

So, my friends, here is my list of PTVEs: Post Traumatic Virgin Experiences (named by my sis, Joybelle).

For the first time in 8 weeks I ...

– drove my car
– fed myself with my right hand
– blew my hair dry
– pulled up my pants with both hands (What a relief!)
– picked up my purse and took it with me (Way too heavy to do that again for a while!)
– unscrewed the lid on my Kombucha drink by myself
– slept an entire night in my bed, as opposed to my "man chair" as my daughter calls my recliner
– walked my old route through Woodway (about two-plus miles)
– put my socks on using both hands (So much easier.)
– tied my shoe laces (It's the little things, don't cha know?)

So, thank you for all your healing thoughts and prayers and the generous offerings of food.

I have decided that everyone over the age of seventy should have a meal train service. It's really the best invention since sliced cheese.

I am so well taken care of and so grateful for all of you. Only ten more weeks (of physical therapy) to go!!!

June 2015
Change Me Prayers

Last week I was feeling a bit impatient, restless, a tad pissy. I just wanted to be done with the recovery period of my injured shoulder. It had been over three months and I wanted to be back to normal full time, not just a day or two per week.

I know I'm in another "in between time." I've been here before. Right after finishing my book I took a deep breath and said, okay, that's done, now what? Then there was this period of several months where it seemed like nothing was happening. I hadn't really thought beyond the finishing of the book.

I'm not one to make a five- or ten-year plan and then create another one just to keep working toward my goals. I'm more of a let it happen, watch it unfold, wait for the energy to be there, type of person. But last week I was not living much in that frame of mind. I was struggling to remember that I *can* trust the unfolding.

My creative juices seemed not too juicy and I was feeling a bit barren, no internal stirring of excitement. Okay, I will take exception to Thursdays, when my kids bring the grandkids out to play with me. I get excited about that. But I was hungry for a nudge from my Soul about my next step.

I liken this particular "in between time" to the times when my kids were little, and they were sick. The first few days they're feeling so bad they just sort of lie around in a stupor. That's was me the first six weeks after my accident. Then comes the time when they are feeling well enough to be up and around, but they are bored and restless because there isn't the energy to do what they want to do.

That was me this last month. Feeling better, wanting more, but not much energy and certainly not feeling back to normal. I was mostly feeling kind of irritated.

I know that I preach about accepting what is, and I love the quote by Jeff Foster about falling in love with the present moment and that helps when I can really feel into it. But I couldn't really get there until I picked up a book called, *Change Me Prayers, the Hidden Power of Spiritual Surrender*. The author, Tosha Silver, relates little vignettes of people she has known or worked with over the years, and then talks about their dilemmas. At the end of each short chapter she creates a little prayer that speaks to what they are struggling with. Several of these prayers touched a chord with me and my state of mind last week.

I translate "Divine Beloved" into "my Soul."

Change me Divine Beloved *(my Soul)* into one who trusts Your timing in every way. Let me accept stretches of quiet and rest, knowing they recharge me for future action. May I trust that change always comes at the perfect time.

Change me Divine Beloved into one who can offer all decisions to You, *(my Soul)* breathing and flowing with the unknown. May I trust during times of transition that the perfect actions will be shown. Grant me patience to allow events to line up as they need.

Amen, I say, and again Amen.

PS I guess some of those creative juices are flowing. I got up out of bed inspired to write this blog at 2:30 in the morning. Maybe those prayers are already changing something.

A week later:

I'm here to tell you that there is magic in these prayers. I swear I said them only once before bedtime the night I wrote the blog and the next morning I woke up with a different person. I got dressed, did my five-mile walk (which I haven't been able to do since the accident), sat down at the computer, and did some writing. I actually was busy all day and my mind was still alert and functioning into the evening, a rare occurrence. It's been several days now and I'm still feeling remarkably normal, back to myself.

Amen, I say, and again Amen.

Then just yesterday, this poem. Co-inky-dink??? I think not.

The Rhythm

In any creative feat
(by which I mean your work, your art, your life)
there will be downtimes.
Or so it seems.

Just as the earth is busy before the harvest
and a baby grows before its birth,
there is no silence in you.
There is no time of nothingness.

What if,
during the quiet times, when the idea flow is hushed and hard to find
you trusted (and yes, I mean trusted)
that the well was filling, the waters moving?

What if you trusted
that for the rest of eternity,
without prodding, without self-discipline,
without getting over being yourself,
you would be gifted every ounce of productivity you need?
What would leave you? What would open?
And what if during the quiet times you ate great meals
and leaned back to smile at the stars,
and saw them there, as they always are,
nourishing you?
There are seasons and harvest is only a fraction of one of them.
We forget this.
There is the rhythm that made everything.
The next time you stand in the kitchen, leaning,
the next time a moment of silence catches you there,
hear it, that rhythm, and let it place a stone in your spine.
Let it bring you some place beautiful.
—Tara Mohr

June 2015
Listening to My Body

I think for most of my life I have undervalued my own worth.

Certainly, being raised to be a good little "Christian girl" did nothing to validate my own intrinsic goodness. Indeed, I believed I was in "need of salvation" because I was born in sin. Where is there room in that scenario for a trust in oneself? If I couple that with a long-term marriage in which I very rarely felt "seen" for who I really was, then you have the backdrop for an adult struggling to feel her own self-worth.

Going to graduate school at the age of forty-five to get my degree in Psychology began my conscious journey of self-discovery and healing. I worked very hard to face my shadow and to "improve myself" and I know that is valuable work, but it's only been in the last ten years or so that I've come to realize that it's also important to acknowledge my own intrinsic goodness. That has been a much more difficult pill to swallow, but I have been opening more and more to that understanding.

Still, when I had my disastrous month of accidents, malfunctions, and illness I realized there was some deep level learning that was wanting to emerge. What was this all about?

The first realization came when I became aware of how hard it was for me to ask for help. Why was that so? Well, there was pride involved in telling myself I could do everything myself, but clearly that proved to be inaccurate. Then when there was such an overwhelming response from friends and family to help out I was rather stunned. The deeper level truth began to seep in. I was valued. I think if I had made no progress in valuing myself this wouldn't have struck me so deeply. But I absorbed it on what felt like a cellular level. My outer experience validated what I was beginning to accept about myself.

Withdrawing from all outer activity gave me time to focus more deeply on caring for myself and what I needed in any given moment. I began again to feel the "rightness" of following my own inner voice. I came to realize that I needed to cut back on my commitments. I enjoyed the solitude, the quiet, the slower pace. It felt like I was tapping into my own natural rhythm and I could feel how nourishing that was.

Then I decided to visit an old friend from graduate school who is a therapist and gives intuitive readings. I was curious to ask her if there were other learnings that I needed to be aware of through these months of recovery. Her insights were so helpful because they clarified my situation from a perspective I hadn't really considered.

She said, this was very much a time of a "knitting together" (interesting terminology since that's exactly what my broken bones have been doing), a knitting together of my life experiences that I might walk with greater confidence and trust upon my Path. I am experiencing a greater sense of wholeness within myself and I have a sense of peace about that.

She mentioned that I have to acknowledge that I have a mortal body that is in transition. My body has its own pacing, its own wisdom, its own timing and I need to honor that. My ego wants to believe I am indestructible and can carry on as if I were still twenty-five. So, this is a wakeup call that the ego needs to work in harmony with my body. The body has primacy. Can I surrender to the needs of my body? Can I take the wisdom of the body seriously, not just as a temporary measure but as a way of life? My life will be smoother, and more satisfying if I can do that. When I try to push through and ignore the fatigue in the body my body feels it as a punishment.

She mentioned how stunned I was by my accident and that on some level I felt I had made a mistake. Did I really think I had the capacity to *not* make mistakes? It would be helpful to assume an attitude of humility here and accept the fact that I don't have the power to navigate perfectly all the time.

The bottom line for me is the commitment to surrender to the wisdom and needs of my body. I want to make it a habit to check in first with what my body wants/needs and act from there, and to trust fully in the intelligence and wisdom of the body. What better way to value myself?

When people talk about their lives, often they describe a life characterized by qualities previously valued only in industrial contexts: speed, efficiency, productivity, and multiple moving parts. People are busy, and while they might complain about it, they also can't imagine life otherwise.

The idea of margins, of generous space for engaging life, seems to have vanished from our vision, and instead we nurse a bitter cup of guilt and anxiety when we aren't "making a difference.

—*Slow Living: Choosing an Unhurried Life,*

What do religious and spiritual traditions have to say about this? How can we make room within ourselves for peace, for slow and careful appreciation of life? How do our traditions help us attune ourselves within to slowness? What internal practices and foci help us slow down?"

October 2015
And My Life is Really Very Blessed

A few weeks ago, my daughter asked to borrow a book of mine, *Awakening Joy*. This book was written out of a class that has been offered online for a few years now. The authors, James Baraz and Shoshana Alexander, began teaching these classes in Berkeley, California many years ago and then decided they would teach it online as well.

I took the eight-month class and was so inspired that I began teaching the class myself, here in Seattle, to groups of mostly women. It's a wonderfully uplifting book with so many helpful ideas and practices, based mainly on Buddhist teachings, but the principles are very universal.

While my daughter was busy gathering her things to leave, I began to leaf through the book and came upon a story that James tells about his eighty-nine-year-old mother. I sincerely believe these serendipitous occurrences in our lives always hold meaning for us if we are paying attention, so I was curious to re-read this inspiring story and discover the truth it held for me at this moment in my life.

He tells the story of a visit to his elderly mom. He happened to have with him a magazine that had an article on the benefits of a gratitude practice. Over dinner he began to tell his mom about the article. She thought it was a good practice but didn't believe she could do it because she always saw what was wrong, not what was right.

She admitted she had a lot to be grateful for, but she didn't see herself adopting this practice. James asked her if she was willing to make it into a game and she said okay. So, for the next few days every time she complained about something (and she did that a lot) he would stop her and say, "And?" She had agreed to complete the sentence with, "My life is really very blessed."

What started out as a game became a part of their time together and as the week went on, they both noticed a shift toward more positive feelings and a sense of lightness about their time together. It began to have a real impact.

James continued to practice with his mom every day for a while after he left and sometime later, he got a call from his sister who was back in town after being gone for a while. She said, "What did you do to Mom?" She had noticed a dramatic shift.

So, James suggests beginning this practice, realizing that at first it might sound false. Every time you find yourself worrying or complaining, just say to yourself, "And my life is really very blessed."

He goes on to say,

Remember you're in a learning process and be patient with yourself. Every time you succeed in shifting your outlook to a more relaxed sense of gratitude, tune in to how good you feel, and pause to anchor that in your body and mind.

You can catch James' mother describe how her son "ruined her life", on a YouTube video where she is speaking to his "Awakening Joy" class. It's hilarious.

October 2015
Sugar, and Caffeine and Popcorn, Oh My!!

I know that I'm in a Category I, first class, funk when "Joy to the World," (of the Jerimiah-was-a-bullfrog, variety) doesn't snap me out of it. It doesn't happen often, that I get in these funks, but one has been going on for about ten days now I'm start getting really tired of it.

It began with an acute attack of BPV, Benign Positional Vertigo. I woke up one morning and the room was swirling so fast I could hardly get out of bed. I did all the right things, called the Ear, Nose, and Throat doc, went in, had him do the Epley maneuver. It's a maneuver that readjusts the neck. I had it once before several years ago and that took care of it, so I was optimistic. But when it hadn't gone away completely in two or three days I began to slump. At least I could get out of bed, but I felt wobbly, disoriented, not able to think clearly. That is still going on and I'm getting impatient and frustrated.

Now, here's what I believe, in my head. Funks come and go, like the tides. This too shall pass (my mom's favorite coping skill). Don't add to the suffering by telling yourself a story about how you feel. I believe this, on the level of my rational mind, but my rational mind is on vacation and I can't seem to find her.

So here is my reality. I crave sugar. I was doing so well. I went on a three-week anti-inflammation diet to help my shoulder heal, but basically, I couldn't eat anything good. No sugar, no dairy, no wheat, etc. etc. etc. I made it the three weeks and then the vertigo hit me.

When I'm not feeling well, physically, what my emotional body craves is comfort food. There is still a part of my brain that believes that these foods will make me feel better. So, I go to the store and pick up a twelve pack of Magnum double chocolate, caramel ice cream bars and start having one or two - okay sometimes three - a day. Then because I can't think, I escape by watching movies, but of course I can't watch movies without a big bowl of popcorn. Forget the olive oil. Pure butter for me, with lots of salt.

On the way home from an acupuncture appointment, my car, without any urging from me, turns into Dunkin Donuts and I come away with three cream filled yummies and they are gone by the time I get home.

By now my body is beginning to rebel and I am more tired and cranky and feel hungover, so of course I must have some coffee to get me going in the morning.

This is the cycle of my funks. Try as I might I can't access my will. I think it's gone on vacation with my rational mind. I don't want to go to the gym. I don't want to take my walks. I really don't feel like doing much of anything.

I think the most toxic part of my funks, besides the food thing, is what I do to myself internally. I start doubting myself, I begin to question my decisions, I try to figure everything out, and I lose touch with my belief in the flow of life, with the natural cycles, the in breath and the out breath. I feel like I'll always lack energy, focus, and motivation.

Now I know that the two are related, that what I do to my body greatly impacts my state of mind, so I'm reaching for that ounce of determination to end this cycle.

I found part of it just a few days ago so I'm pretty sure I'm on the upswing. I remembered, *really* remembered, that my funk was partly due to what I was putting in my body (duh), so I determined to switch it up. Cut out the sugar, cold turkey. Same with the caffeine, and went back to the gym. Made another appointment with the doc. Still not feeling a hundred percent, but at least I'm not adding to the discomfort with the toxic foods.

Sometimes when I'm feeling crappy like this, I remember what I have told countless clients of mine. "If you could imagine that this little part of yourself was your child, what would you say to her?"

I think the conversation would go something like this, *Sweet little one, it's no wonder you are feeling blue. You've been "recovering" for the last 8 months, since you fractured your arm. Of course, you're tired of it, how human is that? I think it's perfectly okay for you to pig out on sugar and caffeine. I know there will come a time when you have had enough, and you will get back to your old healthy routine. See if you can just be with the frustration, just lean into it, sit with it, just as it is. Everyone has felt this way at one time or another so maybe just fully accepting where you are right now will bring you some peace.*

I will have this little talk with inner child, rest and breathe and love myself without condition until this cycle passes. And cut out the toxic self-talk.

Okay, now I'm feeling better and there is the beginning of optimism and hope. I'm starting to believe that this will eventually run its course, or just disappear. But in the meantime I'll do what I can to be gentle with myself and try to focus on accepting, with grace, what is, not what I wish it could be. I think I need to re-read my last blog on how blessed I am.

PS The day after I wrote this blog I was sitting outside, bare feet on the earth, and I began to *feel* how solid my connection was to Mother Earth, how she supported me and held me. Then I began to notice I <u>was</u> grateful, for the smell of the salt air, the chirping of the birds as they fed at my feeder, for the silence and the stillness. I think my mental funk has been liberated. Now my body just has to catch up.

PPS A few days after I wrote the above, I went to the doc, again, and tested positive for a UTI. What the heck is going on? Okay. Not trying to figure it out, just resting in what is and being grateful for the discovery of antibiotics.

October 2015
Over the Funk, Part II

Today, Wednesday, sitting again outside, feet on the earth, I feel the warmth of the sun, and a familiar sensation of calm and ease and gratitude creep into my body (definitely over the funk).

Okay, it's true, I'm three days on antibiotics and had an acupuncture appt yesterday so that all helps immensely. Then this thought began wiggling its way into my brain, *What if I could give myself permission, even when feeling healthy, to put my body's needs first? Why not be okay with the snail's pace? Why not fill the day with ease and grace instead of activity?* Today I didn't even look at the time until it was 12:30pm and I felt so free, to not be a slave to the clock, or appointments or agendas.

I've always lived with the mindset that you get your work done, get your obligations out of the way, take care of the "to do" list, then you can relax. Well, I want to reverse that and there's nothing in my life preventing that from happening.

I'm single, retired, and my kids are on their own. I'm free in every way except by how my mental perceptions limit me, and of course, I'm learning about my physical limitations as well. That's reality, but my mental perceptions I have some control over.

It's sort of the same feeling I have when returning from a restful vacation. I always think to myself, *I'm going to try to take some of this ease, this peace, back with me into my daily life.*

So now I'm going to try to take this pace, this mindfulness, this attention to the body that this year has required of me and bring it back into my normal daily life, assuming my life ever becomes normal.

That means that I must weigh more carefully where I put my energy. Not just because I want more ease in my life, but also because my body is demanding it.

Yesterday I looked at the pile of laundry that had accumulated since my vertigo attack two weeks ago. (I couldn't bear the thought of bending over). Anyway, I just said no, I can't do that right now. Today I looked at it and it was no big deal, but then I walked down the hall to the grandkids room where there were blocks, trucks, books, blankets all over the place and I just closed the door and said, "Maybe later." I mean this is not rocket science. I get that, but it is the kind of discernment I want to carry with me.

Learning to give myself permission to honor my own needs has been a life long journey. It's always been especially difficult when meeting my needs has meant that I disappointed someone I cared about. But this isn't about that. I'm not letting anyone down by not cleaning the grandkids room. No one is disappointed in me if I don't look at the time until its afternoon. So, I have no excuse to keep giving this voice a microphone and letting it decide if I can relax or not.

This is about giving myself, just myself, permission in every moment to live from the inside out, connected *to* and in tune *with* my heart and my body,

I know I'm repeating themes here, but themes keep repeating themselves into my life and I want to remember these moments of subtle clarity, these moments when truth breaks through in a deeper way and I am embodied more fully with their wisdom.

My friend, Heidi Robbins, wrote this beautiful poem that describes our periods of pause and renewal. She graciously allowed me to reprint it here.

The In Between

Extremes have always been comforting to me for their clarity and stark contrast. The all or nothing approach has made sense and doesn't leave time to ask questions. The caffeinated, driven, scramble up the mountain-side way of life has been my way.

Funny then that I now find myself in a world of soft edges and blurry next steps-- a world of increasing stillness and humbling uncertainty. I am living in the in-between, the middle, the soft center. I am firmly lodged in the realm of the unknown.

At first as this blur begins, I think I'm just terribly depressed. I'm uncomfortable with the pace of my life, the lethargy and lack of direction. In moments, it feels terrifying. I lay in bed at night and think 'Will I always feel this way? Am I just getting old? When will I know what's next?"

Though I have been uncertain in my life before, I have never been here.

But I write to you now because I begin to sense a glimmer in the darkness. In the last few days, I sense a new and tender trust with this unknown territory. In moments, I feel spacious. I can only do what I can do and I can't do a lot right now. Shall we call it surrender?

To-do lists aren't making sense. The day begins to unfold in a more organic way. I find myself sitting at the kitchen table and loving my little blonde boy's vivacity and just wanting to steep in it. I look at my daughter and drink in her laughter. There is time for this. Imagine that.

I could never imagine that. There is TIME for a life to unfold in an organic way. There is no rush. This is the realm of quality, the realm of the soul. Quantity cries out at every turn. We do not always have to answer. We do not always have to answer.

I am deepening. I am like a field, now fallow, but being nourished and prepared for a new planting. It takes time. My fallow field must sit in the sun for days. It must soak up nutrients for weeks. It must be whole unto itself no matter its state of fecundity. It must realize its beauty even in its emptiness.

This is the necessary in-between, the quivering at a threshold, the vast quiet without apparent end. This is a time of true perspective. This is living into what matters, what is material, what has substance.

The space in between matters. The space in between you and me, the gaze that we exchange, the words that reach out and touch us or pierce us or soften us. The search matters-- the search for meaning, for unraveling the mystery, for the heart of things. What is felt matters -- and it's okay to feel it all, allowing it to move through, allowing it to change us. The unknown matters. It is not yet defined. There is magic in that. Anything can emerge.

It comes down to this. I'm discovering that this in between place allows me to be more deeply with myself and *with you*. It allows me to feel you. Before I can move into my next work, I want and need to feel you -- *to feel us*-- to feel our heartache and our yearning to live more fully expressed.

Close your eyes and meet me here. It's time out of time. You can arrive in a single breath. There is nowhere to be but here, with one another, in the thick of the in- between-- in wonder, in awe.

—Heidi Robbins

November 2015
Honoring the Pause

This week (November 17 – 22), I am supposed to be on Whidbey Island at a retreat house, called Earth Sanctuary, which is connected to the Sakya monastery in Seattle. I had looked forward to this solitary time for several weeks and had planned carefully so I wouldn't have to go into town for anything other than emergencies.

Bags were packed, groceries bought and stored, books and writing implements included. My intention was to spend some uninterrupted time writing, catching up on some reading, and meditating. I was to check in on Tuesday, November 17th at 2:00pm.

I woke up that morning with the beginnings of a nasty cold, but I determined to carry on. *Might as well recover there as here,* I reasoned. Then the news of the storm hit. Then my tenant downstairs informed me that the Mukilteo ferry was really being affected by the winds. I paused, settled down, and listened. *I think I'll go tomorrow and see if I can extend my stay by one day.* I called the caretaker and that was fine. So, I settled in, here.

Then at 3:30, another message, from the retreat center, "The power is out, there are fallen trees everywhere, I'll call you when we get power back" Another pause, sinking into my body. *I don't really want to go at all now, to not feel good, to maybe be with no heat or electricity, to not be able to cozy up, and pamper myself. No, definitely don't want to go.*

I called and canceled, was reassured of a refund and then another moment of stillness and the thought emerged, *What if I just stayed here, at home, and made this my retreat? Everyone already thinks I'm gone which takes care of obligations, phone calls, and details. I can do everything here that I had planned to do on retreat and will not allow myself to be sidetracked by cleaning up or noticing everything that I could be doing around the house."*

So, I gave myself a beautiful five days and everything within me deepened and solidified into an incredible stillness. Honoring the pause is pretty synonymous with tuning into the body, for me. This whole year of being forced to slow down has been so rich with rewards and a new pattern has developed, at least most of the time. When I am moving slowly through the world, I *remember* to pause, to go within, to ask, and to listen deeply and then my body leads the way.

Pushing through, soldiering on, being fearful of letting someone down, and making my choices based on those out dated mind sets, just doesn't work for me anymore. I much prefer this feeling of alignment and connection and walking through my days with ease and a deep sense of peace, even in the midst of all the terror and violence going on in the world.

I can access those feelings when I am quiet and slow. Rushing around, not taking time, I can easily get caught in fear and negativity.

So, this day, I choose peace.

I choose compassion.

I choose ease.

And my body is very grateful.

December 2015
Lessons From The Hermit

A few months ago, at the Fall Equinox ceremony, I mentioned how being in sync with nature has become such a big driving force in me. I've mentioned before how it started many years ago when I was introduced to the books by Machaelle Wright (perelandra-ltd.com), and the idea of co-creating with the Nature Intelligences.

The kingdom of nature holds all the information about life in this physical reality so doesn't it make sense that we should join with those forces to help create a better world? "Nature is powerful beyond belief and humans are powerful beyond belief. But when nature and humans act together that combined power is intensified a hundred-fold." (*Perelandra Garden Workbook*, Machaelle Wright)

So, at the ceremony this year I remembered what Machaelle said, "At the fall equinox the focus is on nature's infusion of the life vitality that initiates and triggers the new year's cycle." As part of our ceremony each person went into the silence and asked to be shown, through the drawing of a Tarot Card, what this next cycle might hold for them. We asked to be open to receive the information that the card might hold for us. I was not surprised when I drew the Hermit. Here's the explanation, taken from *The Mythic Tarot*, by Juliet Sharman-Burke, and Liz Greene:

The lesson of the Hermit is one which cannot be learned through struggle and conquest, for struggle will not stop time. Only acceptance of time yields the rewards. Through enforced limitation and through circumstances which onlytime, not battle, can release, the Fool develops the reflective, introverted, solitary stance of the Hermit. The Hermit teaches us how to endure and wait in silence. On a divinatory level the card of the Hermit augurs a time of aloneness or withdrawal from the extraverted activities of life, so that the wisdom of patience maybe acquired. There is an opportunity to build solid foundations if one is willing to wait. The mature Fool has developed a mind and a heart, a firm sense of identity and finally a deep respect for his own limitations in the great passage of the round of time.

I think I have already begun this cycle as my learning continues around the theme of accepting limitations, especially those of my body. Fracturing my arm early in the year certainly taught me humility and patience as I struggled with the feelings of helplessness and my issues around being "productive."

I guess the lessons will continue for this next year. My body certainly feels the truth of the need for more quiet time to reflect and a general acceptance of slowing down to accommodate the needs of my body.

Just like the song by Simon and Garfunkle, "Slow down you move too fast... you got to make the moment last."

May 2016
Claiming My Space

A few months ago, in preparation for the full moon in the sign of Pisces I was reading up on all of the energies that would be descending as well as the symbology of this last sign of the zodiacal year. I learned that as the last sign for this astrological year, we were ending a yearly cycle.

We started in Aries, the first sign of the zodiac and now twelve months later we contemplate what we have learned and what needs to end for this new beginning to be birthed. Not unlike our New Year's Eve where we ponder the past in anticipation of the future, I started asking myself some questions.

What was I leaving behind?

What was I letting go of?

What needed to be cleansed, cleaned out in order to move into the next new cycle?

These questions were reinforced as I held my full moon ceremony and asked those present to ponder on what this ending meant to them.

At this ceremony we also acknowledged the lunar eclipse. What was the meaning of those energies? Significantly, the eclipse was also asking us to identify and be willing to let go of any long-standing patterns that we felt might inhibit the birth of the new cycle.

Holding all these thoughts in my consciousness I went to bed the night of the full moon and had a profound dream. In it I am on a bus with Joe Biden. (I know, cheesy right?) Anyway, he is a man that I admire so I felt drawn to him. We sat and talked for what seemed like hours and there was such a good feeling between us. I felt seen and heard and listened to and felt deeply connected to his presence.

Then later in the dream we are sitting in a restaurant and he says to me, "I so enjoyed our conversation, but I don't feel like you really shared anything of yourself." I was stunned and was sure I hadn't heard him correctly, so I asked the woman who was with us to explain to me what she had heard. She confirmed exactly what he had said. Well, I'm still in the dream and I decide to try to analyze what this may mean. (Forever the therapist. Even in my dreams.)

I am surprised when the meaning comes through so clearly. I get the message that deep, deep down I haven't believed that people really want to know me. It's not that I don't share, it's that I don't *feel* like people are really interested. I often hold back. This awareness was so strong that it woke me up and I immediately wrote it down. I've been sitting with it for a few weeks now and the deeper understandings continue to be revealed.

First of all, I realized that even though I am not acting out this particular pattern most of the time, it is still there, and it definitely wants to be released.

Another awareness came when I related this pattern to my Type Two in the Enneagram. Twos have a need to have other people think well of them so they can become more attentive to others in an attempt to manage other people's perceptions of them. That may partially explain why I don't feel people are interested in me. Not everyone I meet is a Two and so intensely focused on others as I am. With all this attention on the other I'm not present to what people may be sending *me*.

All these revelations brought me to a moment in which I stated my willingness to be done with this pattern and I rededicated my energies to my right to *claim my space*. My *right to be here and to be heard*. I even wrote it in big bold letters in my journal. I have to say it has made a remarkable, if subtle, difference in the way I feel. It's hard to put into words but there is a new confidence, a new self-assuredness that is informing the way I walk through my day.

I am ready to birth this new beginning with a little less baggage holding me back. I read a sentence somewhere, during this time, that perfectly described how this shift feels. It feels like, "Personal confidence and the ability to operate from a new level of personal mastery."

Once I opened up the space within me to more deeply believe people were interested in me, I began getting all kinds of affirmations to that effect. I'm here at a conference in Arizona with many from the worldwide esoteric community attending. I missed last year and so I haven't seen these people for two years, yet every single person I saw greeted me like an old friend. I'm sure that has happened before but this year I took it in as confirmation that I was seen and heard and welcomed by others.

There are also some interesting correlations with the astrology of my chart that may be connected to "claiming my space."

I do love it when I notice the many threads that weave themselves together to create a new awareness. Dreams, synchronicities, astrology, the Enneagram, quotes from a book, etc. all leading to a deeper understanding.

Anyway, in my natal chart I have the planet Saturn sitting exactly opposite my sun. The sun is where we shine, where we embrace all that we are and unabashedly shine it forth, without reservation, full of confidence about who we are. Then Saturn comes along and says, "Wait a minute, not so fast. You have limitations you know, responsibilities, duties to perform." So, this has been my lifelong challenge. Go for it? Or, wait a minute, you must do all the hard work first then someday you will be ready.

Often in my meditations when I ponder what my service would look like without the obstacles of my personality it always comes down to greater self-confidence. I see myself, teaching, writing, presenting in front of groups, without anxiety or hesitation. It would feel spacious and free… liberating.

I feel like I'm *being* that now, since the shift of "claiming my space." It's hard to describe the shift in words. I just feel different, more empowered, less fearful, more of the feeling that I have a "right" to take up space. And if I don't take up space it's because I choose not to. So, it's a choice instead of a misguided belief that people aren't interested.

Everyone who has looked at my chart here has commented on how this is going to be a pivotal year for me. A dramatic shift in some way and I can't help but think it has to do with finally releasing this deep underlying belief of unworthiness, I guess I could call it.

This whole year, since my accident last February, has been about purification, cleansing, releasing, accepting limitations, and coming to peace with that.

I made peace with my Cancer moon because of that accident, learning to set my boundaries. I refocused on living my life. I had a deeper experience of detachment. So, there's no way this is not all connected. Getting a handle on Saturn, resolving Cancer, a rededication to my Soul's work, all with confidence.

The other astrological aspect is Pluto is crossing my Ascendant, as we speak. Whatever is frozen in form, Pluto dredges up. This belief of unworthiness was definitely frozen. Pluto digs it up, so I can see what needs to die, to be reborn. For me this means I need to die to my lack of confidence, to not enough. I need to untangle my preoccupations and focus on shining my light into the world.

What am I putting to death in my life, so I can live more fully? My old pattern of less-than, of, no one is interested.

The next step is "yes" to wherever I'm led.

CHAPTER 12
ALL ABOUT SCORPIO

Scorpio, we're told, is the sign of tests, trials, and triumph. It's a sign of death and rebirth and transformation. One of the symbols of this energy is that of the Phoenix who arises out of the ashes to become the eagle. The eagle flies above the clamor of the world, triumphant in his wholeness and filled with the wisdom he has gained from being in the fire.

This theme of death and rebirth and transformation has certainly been true in my life. Three major examples come to mind.

In my twenties, after leaving home, I began the dismantling of the dogma of religion in which I was raised. It was the death of a belief system that I had entered into fully, with my whole being. It was a slow process of testing out each belief on its own and seeing if it was truly mine. It would have to make sense with what fit for me.

It started small. Did I really want/need to go to church every Sunday? I tried it out to see if I would feel guilty, if I would miss it, if I was drawn to it? The answer that came, surprised me. No. None of the above. What took its place was a delicious feeling of using that time for what did feed me, what felt nourishing. That turned out to be peacefully sleeping in and upon waking, enjoying a cup of coffee as I read the Sunday paper. What a joy!

This was the beginning.

The second death occurred in the late sixties when I was 27. My then husband and I had just purchased our first home in San Jose, California. We took great joy in furnishing it and making it our own. Then one fateful Sunday afternoon we were watching the movie *Zorba the Greek* on television. Totally inspired by Zorba's zest for life and his inner joy we both looked at each other and said, "We're not done traveling."

Both of us were teaching school and had taken every opportunity to travel when we had time off. Thinking we were done for the time being we purchased the house. But after Zorba, we quickly began to plan for a year-long trip around the world.

We would go where we were led. No definite plans, no reservations anywhere. We would stay as long as we wanted in any one place and move on when we felt like it.

Six months into our journey we had traveled through all of Mexico, Central and South America. We were on an immigrant ship for thirty-seven days that took us from Rio de Janeiro, up the east coast of Africa to England then back down to Cape Town, South Africa.

Making our way through Africa and up to Kenya, we flew over to Bombay, India. A few days after we arrived we received several telegrams from our families saying our house had burned to the ground and arson was suspected so we needed to come home right away. We had lost everything. Something was definitely dying.

The last example was the death of my marriage. This was probably the most gut wrenching. After thirty-three years, how did I let go of a fantasy dream that everything would somehow work out? I was forced to face my fears of being on my own while my children were not yet launched. I was just out of graduate school and beginning my private practice as a therapist. I certainly was not financially self-sufficient yet. My old life was dying and even though I initiated the divorce I was terrified.

I share these three examples because the dying part was not the end of the story. With each of these deaths a greater sense of freedom was born.

Leaving the church and my old belief system allowed me the freedom to find my own way, to forge my own path. Dying to the habitual patterns of being a good Christian were rather superficial deaths. The more significant shifts came from relinquishing the idea that there was one way to God, and our church had the way. Everyone else was doomed. I also let go of a belief in heaven and hell as an actual place. I do believe in the higher spiritual realms, but I believe that hell is the belief that we are somehow separate from our Divine nature and heaven may be that dimension that we are lifted into when we die. But I don't believe it's all gold lined streets and being in a constant state of bliss. I believe it's a pit stop on our evolutionary journey. We go there for a time to review our past life, to weave together the lessons learned and to see what karma is left to resolve and we continue to serve according to the capacities we have developed. When it is time, we re-enter to take another step on our journey, hopefully wiser and more aware.

The interesting part about losing the house and everything we owned was that coincidently just a few weeks before we got that fateful telegram we had been talking about how we still didn't feel finished with traveling. We said, "Let's not stop until we've seen everything that we're dying to see." If we would feel tremendously disappointed by not going to Thailand, for example, then Thailand would be on our list and we wouldn't stop till we had seen it. Mentally, the decision was made that when we got home we would sell the house, save up more money and take off again. So weirdly enough, we didn't mourn the loss of the house, we only mourned that fact that we had to go home and cut our trip short.

As it turned out, we went home, sent the arsonist to San Quentin, rebuilt and sold the house at a profit, saved up for a year while renting a beautiful cottage at the beach, and then took off for another thirteen months of traveling the rest of the world.

This death gave us the freedom to do what we most desired and the clarity about what our priorities were at that time.

The death of my marriage has led me to a place in my life I could never have imagined. Released from the effort and energy that I was putting into trying to hold the dysfunctional family system together I was now freed up to create the life that was truly mine.

These are dramatic examples of how the Scorpio energy has impacted my life. And of course, it's not all about astrology. There is karma, life purpose, and other forces at work as well. In each of these cases, however, the test was presented, the death occurred, and I believe that the courage of the Scorpion helped me go within and face the death. Once I could see clearly, I gained the perspective I needed to allow the freedom and transformation to occur.

The examples you will read about in this chapter are not nearly as dramatic. I think as I've gotten older and have paid closer attention the tests have become subtler. They seem to center more around transforming my inner life. What is blocking a fuller expression of my essence? So, the nudges come, and I pause and take a look at what is going on and because I'm committed to my own spiritual and psychological development, I will work on transforming whatever is brought to my attention.

November 2013
Scorpio and the Hydra

This is my birthday month and as the Scorpion, I know that part of my job is to go into all those secret, dark places of myself and unearth all that is hiding there. It's a courageous and heroic act, this digging deep and uncovering, being *willing* to see, acknowledge, and bring to light all the unfinished parts of myself. And *how* to transform, once the light has revealed? For surely, this is also my task, not just to *see*, but to *redeem*.

In the ancient legend of Hercules, the Great Presiding One gives Hercules twelve tasks that are symbolic of the challenges we face in each astrological sign. The task in Scorpio is for Hercules to go into the deep, swampy land (the unconscious) where the Hydra sleeps and slay him. He is given only three instructions on how to do this:

We rise by kneeling,

We conquer by surrendering,

We gain by giving up.

Hercules is a warrior and believes totally in his own strength and ability to subdue this monster. He finds the Hydra and notices that he has nine heads (each head symbolic of the personality tendencies that must be redeemed). He attacks with ferocity and manages to sever many of the heads, but to his surprise each time one head is cut off, two more appear in its place (when we try to repress or kill off those unwanted parts of ourselves, they come back stronger and more powerful).

Finally, desperate and exhausted by his own efforts, he remembers the words given to him before his journey began. He kneels in humility, he surrenders his own agenda for how to subdue the Hydra, he gives up his own will in service to the Greater Will. He lifts the Hydra up to the Light, and the Hydra is redeemed, transformed.

I take this legend into myself and realize that all of my "heads" need to be lifted up into the light of the Soul, that only the pure unfettered Love of the Soul will redeem the dark places within myself.

On the day of the November full moon, I was sitting in meditation and pondering this journey of Hercules and what meaning it might have for me. This is the poem that emerged:

Make of my heart, a resting place,

Where all can come to be blessed,
To be cleansed,
To be immersed in a cauldron of Love.
'Enter, …fear,
Welcome,… anxiety
Come in, …confusion and uncertainty.'
Come and rest,
Lay your bodies down.
Be cradled in the waters of Love.

November 2014
Scorpionic Revelations

Those of you who have followed my blog for a while know that my birthday month is November and that every year part of my spiritual practice is to be particularly mindful of what aspect of my shadow will be brought to my consciousness.

As a matter of fact, I consciously *ask* to be shown and then proclaim, somewhat hesitantly, my *willingness* to see.

Sometimes when the cycle is over, I say to myself, *I actually asked for this? What was I thinking?* But most often I am grateful for the lessons learned and the new awareness's that I have been shown.

In some regards this newest cycle began in the spring of this year when I signed up for the Tom Kenyon workshop on "the shadow." The workshop was to be held in October and I thought it the perfect time to visit the underground of my psyche, one month before my birthday.

I really had no idea what would emerge as there were no outer experiences to clue me into what was coming, until a few weeks before the workshop when we were asked to keep a dream journal. I filled ten pages in the next several days. It was so startling clear that it was almost embarrassing. Okay, it was really embarrassing.

Up came all my insecurities, my lack of self-acceptance, jealousy, my "where do I belong" stuff, boundaries, my need for validation, my fear of losing myself... On and on and on.

So, my assumption, going into the workshop, was that I would explore these issues in greater depth. Instead, some miraculous healing took place.

The first day of the workshop we focused mainly on White Tara, the goddess of compassion and mercy. Tom took us into a deep and profound experience of her presence. I took in so much love that I felt like I couldn't contain any more. I was bursting.

That night I had this dream:

I'm having a party and many of my extended family are present, mostly those who have already passed over. It was as if a brilliant spotlight was shone on each family member, and they seemed to light up with love. When it came to one member with whom I have had a lifelong conflict, I saw his entire family and I could feel the suffering and dissension within that group. When the light shone upon them there was only understanding and harmony.

It felt lovely and warm.

I woke up not feeling all that different, but within a few days I realized something had shifted. Even with all the healing work I have done around this situation, whenever my thought would turn to this individual I would have a visceral reaction of repulsion. Since that dream, I have felt only compassion and understanding when he comes into my awareness. I am able to send him healing light when I do my morning meditation and prayer, and it feels absolutely authentic. I think that is a miracle.

The second healing took place a few weeks after the workshop, but I am certain it was connected to the intention we held during the weekend to clear away and transform whatever was in need of healing.

I was sitting in a circle with friends and we were celebrating the "Day of the Dead" (Halloween). We invoked our ancestors and asked for them to communicate with us if they had something to say. I may lose some of you here, but that's okay. My mom and dad, both deceased, came to me. They looked right at me and said, "We see you."

It was as if I knew they had this expanded vision and they could let go of their fundamentalism and accept me for who I really was, because they could *see* who I really was. I felt their support, their admiration, and respect. They also asked my forgiveness for the way in which they tried to "tamp down" my energy. I understood how my energy was so foreign to them that it made them afraid.

Whether this really happened or it was just an imaginary conversation isn't important to me. What is important is that I *know* some layer of my woundedness was transformed.

These thoughts are not necessarily new to me, but the embodiment of the energy was what was transformative. *Something* shifted deep inside and not just mentally.

How do these two situations relate to my dreams of insecurity? I believe that these are a few of the deepest roots of my unconscious habits. Bringing them into the light of my awareness and holding them with love and compassion freed up something in me. There is a spaciousness that was not there before.

Blessed be to Scorpio and all that she brings.

December 2016
The Aftermath

The day of my seventy-fifth birthday, November 9, 2016, we had elected a new president. To be honest, I must say this was the most depressing birthday of my life. I stayed up late on election night until there could be no doubt. There would be no last-minute comeback, no saving grace.

The next few nights I was unable to sleep, bathed in fear, as all the "worst-case scenarios" played their way out in my mind. We know what those scenarios are, no need to go into frightening detail.

Most of my birthday was spent in a feeling of disbelief and shock. The intense grief would come later. I tried to practice what I preach, *just be with it, it is what it is, don't argue with reality.* I tried to be the witness. *Fear is present, but I am more than my fear.* I really tried to hold all of my despair and fear and sadness in the cauldron of my loving heart, but on this birthday day, it was way too soon. I just needed to feel everything. Just that, nothing more.

After a few weeks, after much meditating and supportive conversations with my tribe I was able to see more clearly. The emotional impact leveled out. I had let my feelings have their way with me. I had tried to honor them as best I could.

I knew then that I was at a moment of conscious choice. Did I want to be seduced back into the dark swamp of emotional turmoil or did I want to choose peace? Not passivity, but active peace? I chose peace.

Something had been awakened in me, some strong sense of standing up, standing firm, speaking my truth, and embodying my truth. I made the choice to **be** strength, to **be** power, to **be** truth, in my own life and then I put on my safety pin and headed out to Greenlake to stand in peaceful unity with 3,000+ of my fellow humans who were demonstrating for equality.

I made some conscious decisions:

I would not follow all the news.

I would not get entangled in Facebook posts.

I would not read anything that might shake loose my fragile equilibrium. Part of me did want to stick my head in the sand and pretend that nothing would change, or that even if it did it wouldn't impact me, but reality was hard to avoid so that really wasn't a choice.

What could I focus on that would be balanced, reasonable, and helpful?

I decided to deepen my meditation practice to include a powerful prayer for the Soul of our country. For a recording and a written copy that I made of this meditation follow this link: soulbridging.com/3560.

I made a commitment to myself to be as proactive as I could about political issues. I'm not an activist, by nature, so this was a stretch for me, but I found ways that I could contribute that didn't include knocking on doors or proselytizing.

I decided to:

Read only that which,

listen to only that which,

be with only that which:

Uplifted, encouraged, inspired, and held me in loving support and understanding.

I made a habit of reminding myself, daily, sometimes hourly, of the fact that most of humanity longs for peace, for justice, for harmony. This helped keep me in a state of hope and optimism, rather than dejection and despair.

I reminded myself of what I believe is true:

We are at the end of an age, astrologically and rayologically. Any time new energy comes in and meets old energy there will be disruption.

The old, entrenched mind sets are never going to give way without a struggle, but evolution always moves forward so I'm trusting in that. We may be in a dip that feels like regression but from the largest perspective we continue to evolve and expand.

To heal anything, it must be brought to the light of day. We are seeing the manifestation of the shadow of our collective psyche. Now that it is seen, there can be no denying that this darkness resides in each one of us and we are being shown where our own healing needs to take place. Hasn't this example of blatant sexism, racism, and misogyny forced you to examine your own attitudes or deeply hidden tendencies?

There is a new age coming and it will embody all the qualities of cooperation, collaboration, equality, and a right distribution of resources. The timing of this age of Aquarius depends on the choices we make, as a species. So, part of my "political activism" includes a commitment to embody these qualities in my everyday life. Every step we take individually has an impact. I deepen my faith that I can make a difference in my own small way.

I rest on the fact that I know I am not alone in this endeavor. There are unseen helpers that are always available to help me stay strong, to impress upon me what right action needs to be taken next, and to uplift and raise me up when I am discouraged and doubtful. I know these same Beings of Light are doing what they can to assist us in transforming our planet to its rightful destiny as a beacon of Light in the Cosmos. They hear our appeals and they respond, pouring more light into our sacred earth.

May we all be blessed with strength, courage and clarity as we face these uncertain times. May we strengthen our alignment, hold fast to our balance and remain calm and centered in the midst of the storm.

January 2018
Acceptance, Loving Attention, and Clarity

I've written before about my Scorpio nature, digging deep, courageously seeking, questioning endlessly. As my birthday month approaches, I am almost always hit with a powerful emotional experience. I've come to look upon these moments as indicators that something within me needs further examination. More digging, more questioning, more seeking.

One year, several people close to me died very suddenly and unexpectedly. I was rather swept away by the emotions that arose within me. Then I realized my birthday was coming up, and I remembered the pattern that I had identified earlier of being confronted with some form of unfinished business around the month of November. So, I mused, *Guess I have some work to do around how I handle grief and the fear that arises when I face my own mortality.*

This past year, I was sort of waiting for what would emerge, but it occurred in such an odd way that it still took me by surprise.

I was sitting at my computer reading an article from *The New York Times* about the likelihood of a major earthquake hitting the West Coast. I had heard of this before, of course, but for some reason I was compelled to read the entire article, very carefully. I finished in a terrifying state of panic. This was not some "fake news" report. This was authored by an expert in seismology. When he stated that everything west of I-5 (our major freeway), would be toast I nearly lost it. I live west of I-5 and so do both of my children and grandchildren. Yikes!! I went to bed and dreamt of earthquakes.

I awoke in the same state of fear. It literally took over my mind for the entire day. The worst-case scenarios playing themselves out in my imagination in vivid detail. *Would I be swept out to sea in a giant tsunami? Would the houses behind me come sliding down the hill and demolish my home? Should I move to the east side of I-5? But then, I reasoned, my children and grandchildren would be gone and why would I want to be around then?* On and on it went. My body was now in a state of painful constriction.

Finally, I paused. I noticed. I stopped and sat. I breathed deeply and became quiet. I acknowledged the fear, opened my heart to it, tried to welcome it, tried to remember that fear is a human emotion and I was not alone in it. My heart went out to all beings living in a state of fear. I sat for several minutes just allowing whatever was there to be there. Slowly the intensity lessened and finally dissipated.

Here's what emerged for me, after I reached this place of acceptance and calm: **clarity**. I realized that I have no control over whether an earthquake hits my home, so fretting and stewing about it was pointless and now that the feeling of fear was minimized I could really accept what I couldn't control. I also noticed that it wasn't dying that scared me, it was how I would die that made me fearful. Knowing that I will probably not have any control over that either, made it easier to let go.

So, what could I control? I asked myself. Well, I could finally make the decision to have my home retrofitted, which would minimize the damage of any normal earthquake. If the big one really did hit, and the epicenter was right where my house sits, well, then I am toast, but I can't control where it hits or the magnitude, so just get on with it.

I discussed with my tenant downstairs the possibility of taking an emergency preparation class together, so we would both know what to do. We talked about creating two emergency boxes of supplies, one downstairs and one in the garage. It felt good to take some action that would prepare me as much as possible.

Even though I have no control over how I might die I have had the conversations with my children about my wishes. I've even created, at my daughter's suggestion, a "death file", which I continually make additions to as I think of other ideas about how I hope the end of my life will unfold. I've written my obituary, created my own memorial service, picked out the music, and poetry that I love.

Now, I let all the rest go.

November 2018
What If Today We Were Grateful for Everything?

I've been thinking a lot about that famous Snoopy/Charlie Brown quote because for a while now I haven't been able to push that particular "on button" in myself. It's mostly due to a reoccurrence of the old insomnia issue. The frustration and anxiety have been particularly intense. This intensity may be due to the fact that we are entering my birth month, November. Traditionally this has meant that some emotional issue usually arises for me to look at. Scorpio is the sign of the underworld of our psyches, so part of me is not surprised.

After a week or so of this continual mind-f*cking, I finally realized what I was doing. I watched myself be in a perpetual bad mood, feeling a bit depressed and catastrophizing the worst-case scenario. I would never, ever again have a good night's sleep. You've heard me bemoan this before so I won't belabor it but what was different this time was that I realized what my thoughts were doing to my body and my mental health.

Then a couple of things happened that helped shift things for me. I was reading a blog by David Spangler in which is tells the story of his very first car. He loved that car and every time he drove it, he felt such love and gratitude that it was his. And the car never broke down. It drove like a charm for him. His father, who gave him the car, really didn't like it, but bought it because it was a good deal. Well, every time his father happened to drive the car something went wrong. David's sixteen-year-old mind concurred that the car must respond to whatever energy was directed toward it.

This wasn't a new thought for me, but it got me to thinking about it in connection to my insomnia. How must my bed feel when every night I come to lie down with a sense of dread or anxiety? Would things be different if I slipped under my covers each night grateful that I had a bed and that it held me so comfortably? Could I give thanks to whatever subtle energies inhabited that bed? For me it seemed more than just a gratitude practice it made me more aware of my connection to the subtle realms. There really is an energetic connection between my bed and me, my computer and me, my chair and me, and when I express my gratitude to my bed, or my computer, or my chair, I begin to feel that connection as an energy flow between us. This is not rocket science. David has been preaching this for years through his books and talks on subtle activism, but suddenly it hit me in a real way.

The second thing that happened was an email from Tom Kenyon, the sound healer. He posted an article and a meditation from a group he calls the Trillium. He suggests in this article that they are beyond our dimension but are willing to help us during these chaotic times with whatever we need to stay centered and grounded. He suggests we listen to the five-minute sound meditation while holding in our intention in our awareness. The effects, he says, will be more powerful if we can do this while in a state of deep gratitude or appreciation.

So, here's how these two events changed things for me. I began listening to the CD while doing my gentle stretching right before bedtime. My intention was simple, deep sleep. I pictured myself lying peacefully in my bed, totally at rest with no agitation or mental anxiety. After those five minutes I made my way to my bedroom and crawled into bed. Lying there I took a few minutes and felt my gratitude for my bed, sending it my good feelings and feeling the comfort of its energy holding me. Then I gave thanks to my pillow, my comforter, the wind gently blowing in through my window. I thanked the nature spirits that help keep the plants in my bedroom healthy. I invoked the spirit of my bedroom and asked her to work with me to create a space that would feel like a peaceful sanctuary. I was deep in gratitude and felt the blessing of connection.

It's only been a few days, so I can't claim that this will last forever, but I've had great sleep for two nights now. And this feeling/awareness has spread into almost every area of my daily life. It's like walking into the world with new eyes. Everything is alive. Everything has consciousness and the more I acknowledge that and radiate my gratitude out to meet it, the more blessed I feel.

Sending my gratitude now to my computer, for taking this all down and not crashing on me.

Update:
A few weeks later I am still not sleeping as peacefully as I'd like, but it seems like what was really important about this experience was the expanding of my awareness around my living environment. I walk around my house now with an increased desire to transmit the gratitude that I feel to those unseen beings that share my space. In return, I feel the connection we are making with each other and I am grateful for the feeling of support that gives me. I feel held and uplifted. It's an energy exchange that benefits us all and I am beyond grateful... regardless of how I sleep.

CHAPTER 13
HOLY DAYS

The section below was previously published by the Lorian Association, the organization affiliated with David Spangler and his work, and originally appeared on their website, lorian.org.

I am reprinting it here as a way of introducing this chapter on Holy Days, because it explains how I came to honor the significance of nature's cycles and began to see these important events as sacred and holy: Christmas, Easter, Summer and Winter Solstice, full moons. They all took on a deeper meaning when I viewed them from the lens of the unseen worlds.

Some of the information in this article will be repetitive, but it will give you an overview of what led me to this larger perspective.

In the mid-eighties I think the universe must have conspired to catapult me into a whole new level of consciousness. Several life-altering circumstances converged to expand my concept of the world. The first thing that happened was I came across the material put out by Machalle Wright and her research center in Virginia, called Perelandra. I began using her flower essences and reading about the deva kingdom. She introduced me to the concept of co-creating with nature, that nature is a living intelligence and that we are hardwired to work in cooperation with these living beings. They hold the blueprint for our evolution, and they desire to work with us to assist us in our own processes of expansion. This was a completely new idea to me. At first, I have to admit, I resisted it because I suddenly felt overwhelmed that I now had to consider nature in making decisions… about my garden, about how I treated the earth, about my life. It seemed like just too much to take in.

About the same time, I came across the Findhorn experiment and started reading Dorothy Maclean and David Spangler's work. It reinforced this idea that the subtle worlds were real and accessible. My resistance vanished, and I realized that I carried a deep longing to be more in sync with nature and her cycles.

It was then that I decided to go to graduate school to get my master's in transpersonal psychology. I wasn't at all clear about what I would do with an M.A., but I felt compelled to begin this study. With young children at home I studied part-time and it took me five years to complete my work. During that time there was another huge expansion of consciousness for me as I began processing and looking clearly at my own life. I emerged committed to begin a practice as a psychotherapist. But as I unraveled some of my own issues, I began to see the dysfunction in my own life and my marriage.

Three years after graduating, in 1990, I ended my thirty-three-year marriage. Terrified and uncertain, I began to use some of the tools elucidated in the Perelandra work. I connected with a MAP team, beings in the subtle realms, who worked specifically with me and whatever issues were coming up for me. I would enter these sessions full of fear, doubt and uncertainty and would emerge forty minutes later in a complete state of calm. Nothing external had changed. Internally my whole perspective was transformed. With the understanding that I had learned from David's work and the Perelandra material, I was even more convinced of this field of subtle energy. And connecting with these special beings several times a week strengthened my belief and washed away any lingering resistance.

During this transitional time another practice I incorporated into my life was connecting to trees. I had always loved walking in the woods, and now that I understood the true nature of that world I began walking in a different state of consciousness. I began really noticing the trees, asking to be connected to them, asking to be blessed by them. I decided to pick a tree that was along my walking route and just sit with my back against its trunk. Every day I would go there in so much anguish and fear and would feel the energy of the tree filling me with strength and solidity. I would visualize the roots of the tree supporting and grounding me. That earth energy was palpable and healing and sustained me through this life transition I was experiencing.

Each of these practices helped me to deepen my faith in this unseen world. I began to long to be in sync with nature, to somehow honor and participate in her changing seasons. I began a practice of going out each morning to sit with my bare feet on the earth, giving thanks and sending gratitude to the over-lighting deva of the land and blessing the angel of my hearth, feeling my connection to the subtle worlds deepen. I could then begin my day from a place of peace and alignment.

My longing also led me to begin holding full moon meditations in my home as I was drawn to a practice that would align me more deeply with all of nature's cycles. I have been holding these ceremonies now since 2002.

It is through these monthly gatherings and the practices inspired by my work with the subtle realms that I am strengthened and empowered. Each month I feel the qualities of the astrological signs pouring into me. Consciously receiving them, I strive to express them from my highest nature.

Before every full moon gathering, I invoke the four directions, the astrological energies, my MAP team, the deva of the land and the angel of my hearth and other beings of light I work with, giving thanks for their participation. I ask that they bless each person who enters my home, that they may feel welcome and safe and receive whatever they might need. I have heard from so many people that entering my home feels like being in a sanctuary. One day my daughter came to visit, and I was not home. She sat in my meditation chair and as she meditated this is what came to her.

"May all who enter this house feel truly welcome, just as they are.

"May all who enter this house dwell in ease of body and mind.

"May all who enter this house feel the comfort of belonging to family.

"May all who enter this house receive that which truly nourishes.

"May all who enter this house be inspired to communicate that which is honest and true.

"May all who enter this house know that in this place they may rest, free of judgment, scorn or expectation.

"May all who enter this house feel the trees, the sky, the light and the birds surrounding and supporting them.

"May we all take the strength and goodness we receive here and

"Share it with the world."

This is my prayer to those unseen beings every month when we meet, and I am forever grateful for their presence in my life and in my home.

December 2013
Pwetty Wites

It all started when I began reading David Spangler's new book called *Starheart* (lorian Press LLC, Holland, MI. 2013). It's five short tales all about magic, mystery, and the unseen worlds. It's wonderful.

I hadn't planned on decorating this year. My adult children and grandchildren and I planned to do something nontraditional this holiday season and go away for three days to celebrate in another city, not too far away since the little ones still don't travel long distances in a car very well. So why bother? I thought.

Well David woke me up. In one of the stories he talks about how angels are attracted to beautiful lights. That was all I needed to hear. Out came the tangled, some missing, some not working, sets of lights stored in the basement. Who doesn't want the angels visiting their house, especially at Christmas? So, my bedroom, the living room, the deck, and the front yard were all decked out, and I began waiting for the angels.

It just so happened that this last week my son's house was getting painted on the inside. "Mom, could we come and stay with you for a week while the painters are here?" The "we" includes his beautiful wife and my precious almost 2-year-old granddaughter. So how could I refuse? I began imagining how I would wait until dark then take her to every room that I had decorated. The lights would be off, and I would say, "Wait now, just look." We would hold our breaths; the plug would go in and we would clap our hands in excitement. So that's what we did. It was magical. Every morning after that she would wake up, come in to meet me in my bedroom and she would begin the day with, "Grammy, turn on the pwetty wites. More pwetty wites, Grammy," until every room was lit up. Then with looks of wonder and awe she would just sit and look.

So, I began also to look through her eyes. What a joy to re-experience Christmas from the heart of a child.

I think my angel came this year dressed as a little girl with magic in her almost two-year-old body.

I am blessed.

April 2014
Preparing for Wesak, An Invitation

Dear fellow students of the Ancient Wisdom teachings, and anyone else who may be interested.

In just a few weeks we will be celebrating the Wesak full moon, said to be the most powerful full moon of the entire year. This full moon always occurs during the Taurus month of April.

I am writing to invite you to begin your preparations now, as the sun enters Taurus. Taurus is said to be the sign of the Buddha and this festival honors that great Lord as well as the Christ. They come together on this auspicious night to blend their energies and to bestow a wonderful blessing upon humanity.

During our celebration I will take you on a guided journey to the Wesak Valley where this healing ceremony takes place. We will partake of the water that has been blessed so that we may use it for the healing of the planet and for our own bodies.

I wish to emphasize the importance of gathering together in groups to meditate at this time, if possible. It is said that the strength and intensity of our invocation during these three Spring Festivals (Aries, Taurus, Gemini) impacts the spiritual energies that are available to us for the entire year. When we invoke, pray, and ask for love, light, and power to descend on earth, we are heard. And we evoke a response. The power of these prayers is magnified when a few or more are gathered together and hold the same intention. Our world desperately needs these spiritual energies right now.

For those of you who wish to participate, either in our ceremony or with your own group, or even on your own, I'd like to offer a few suggestions that might be helpful as a preparation.

Keep the upcoming festival in your awareness throughout the days leading up to the time of the full moon, holding the intention to be open and receptive.

Consistently maintain your spiritual practices, or even increase them, in an effort to raise your consciousness to as high a level as possible.

Watch your diet and health. This preparatory time is a time of purification so be aware of any toxins you might take into your body, i.e. caffeine, alcohol, etc.

State your intention inwardly to be a vessel for service. How can you use these energies for the upliftment of humanity?

If possible, make the few days before the festival ones of quiet, inner repose. Not that you must be in silence but holding an inner calm as you go through your day will help keep the energies intact within you.

Hold in your awareness that this is a time when a great expansion of consciousness is possible for us, individually as well as collectively. New spiritual awareness's can be accessed, and the inner realms are very close.

Here are some additional suggestions, given to us from the Tibetan Master, Djwhal Khul:

…I would suggest the following. Refuse to allow yourselves to be swept by any fear psychosis or to be stampeded into any attitude through which the anxiety and unrest and distress in the world can overwhelm you. Strive to stand in spiritual being. Each morning, in your meditation, seek to take that attitude with a new and fresh definiteness and to hold it during the hours of service which lie ahead each day. Between now and Wesak, let each of you gain that control of speech which has often been your goal but seldom your achievement, and remember that the most powerful factor in the control of speech is a loving heart. Wild and fearful talk, hateful gossip, cruel innuendo, suspicion, the ascribing of wrong and wicked motives to persons and peoples brought the world to its present distressing situation. Guard yourselves strenuously against this.

It will be good also to cultivate the joy that brings strength. This is not the time for gloom, despair or depression.

Will you, therefore, carry with you the following ideas?

First that the Hierarchy of spiritual Forces stands in spiritual Being.

Second, that we too can stand steady in spiritual Being.

Third, that the silence of a loving heart should be our keynote.

Fourth, that strength to stand is the result of a joyous attitude and a true orientation to the soul. (Alice Bailey, *The Externalisation of the Hierarchy*, pp.81-83)

So, my friends, let us stand in our own true spiritual natures these next few weeks. Let us remember the joy and beauty of that nature and may we purify our thoughts, words, and deeds that we may be harmless in all we do.

December 2014
Illuminating Hope

On this Solstice day I am thinking of the light of the Sun filling my heart and illuminating all my hopes and wishes, for myself and my world. Here are a few of the hopes I can feel are alive in me.

I hope that my adult children continue to welcome me with love and warmth into their lives.

I hope that my beautiful grandchildren continue to feel safe and nurtured in my arms.

I hope that my heart continues to open, expand, spill out all the love that is in me.

I hope that the leaders of the world can open to the light that is within them and act from that place.

I hope that everyone who is hungry is fed, that everyone who looks for shelter, finds it, that everyone in grief and sadness is lifted up.

As I sat today in meditation at the moment of the Solstice, connected subjectively to my larger group, I wanted to feel my deepest intention and affirm it as mine. And true to form, my mother showed up, from the "other side," in the form of an old hymn. She often visits me this way, knowing how I loved those old hymns. I'm convinced that this is the way she passes on her wisdom to me.

It may not be on the mountain height, or over the stormy sea,
It may not be at the battle's front; My Lord will have need of me;
But if, by a still, small voice He calls, to paths that I do not know,
I'll answer, dear Lord, with my hand in Thine,
I'll go where you want me to go.

I'll go where you want me to go, dear Lord,
Over mountain, or plain or sea;
I'll say what you want me to say, dear Lord,
I'll be what you want me to be.
—Mary Brown and Carrie Rounsefell

So, in my own words, I do affirm that I am willing to follow the voice of my Soul, no matter where it takes me. And when it invites me to step out of my comfort zone, which it invariably does, I humbly ask for courage.

Thanks, Mom.

December 2015
Stepping into Stillness

As the busyness of the Christmas season begins, I would like to declare publicly that this year I am determined to walk through these days differently.

My intention is to attune myself to nature and this cycle of darkness. Autumn has passed, and the vibrancy and light of the sun is not as available to me right now. So, what does nature have to teach me about this cycle? I think She's *inviting* me to do as she does, to hibernate, go into the cave, listen to my body. She reminds me that this is a time to sink in, to pause, to listen, to ease up and let the darkness hold me. I see myself cozy in front of the fire with a cup of hot chocolate in my hand, and yes, lots of marshmallows on top.

When I pause and take this in, I realize that in this state of receptivity to the darkness I can actually kindle more strongly the light that is within. And I think that is the deeper meaning of this season. I am invited to bring more light into my *inner* being and let that be the focus of my days, not whether I can find just the right present for Aunt Milly.

When I don't resist the darkness, there is a space created that allows me to notice what gifts it brings me. (I did say lots of marshmallows, right?)

Are you aware of any gifts that the darkness brings to you?

As the Christian world celebrates the birth of Jesus, I like to hold these questions in my mind.

What is wanting to be born in me?

What am I birthing this season?

I'm pretty sure my answer this year would be freedom and a releasing of past conditioning. My time in the Scorpionic underworld has revealed this to me.

As I release more and more layers of my conditioning, I am freer to be a more authentic person, expressing from a deeper level of knowing and understanding. Cords have been loosened, ties broken, and a new freedom is now celebrated.

I want to expand on this feeling of freedom and commit to slowing down, settling in, and being more mindful of my connection to the light that is within me. I want to connect to the meaning that Christmas has for me.

In my belief system this has to do with the light of the Christ, which is unconditional love, taking up residence in my heart. More and more Love equals more and more Light. Then, as I walk though my days, I can consciously radiate that Light to everyone in my life. What greater way is there to honor this holiday season?

May the light of the Christ shine within your heart this Christmas season and all through the year.

When winter comes to a woman's soul, she withdraws into her inner self, her deepest spaces. She refuses all connection, refutes all arguments that she should engage in the world. She may say she is resting, but she is more than resting: She is creating new universes within herself, examining and breaking old patterns, destroying what should not be revived, feeding in secret what needs to thrive.

Winter women are those who bring into the next cycle what should be saved. They are the deep conservators of knowledge and power. Not for nothing did ancient peoples honor the grandmother. In her calm deliberateness, she winters over our truth, she freezes out false-heartedness."

Look into her eyes, this winter woman. In their gray spaciousness you can see the future. Look out of your own winter eyes. You too can see the future.

—Patricia Monaghan, www.patricia-monaghan.com

In December, let's be extra mindful of this truth: Each time we say YES to something, we are saying NO to something else. Yes, to that party can mean no to snuggle time on the couch. Yes, to that favor for a coworker can mean no to an extra favor for your spouse. Yes, to one more PTA duty can mean no to self-care. Instead of allowing a smiley YES! SURE! OF COURSE! to be our knee jerk reaction- let's make a conscious effort to take a holy pause and ask ourselves: If I say yes to this, what am I saying no to? To give myself time to consider this I usually say: 'That's such a nice offer! Let me get back to you about that! This December let's make sure that it's either an "OH, HECK YES!" or a "No, Thank You." December is a really, really good time to hoard your yeses for yourself and your peace and your people. The world will keep spinning.

—Cindy Ratzlaff and Kathy Kinney, www.queenofyourownlife.com

While active in the world, at no time are we to lose sight of our inner orientation and recollection. All the time we are outwardly busy, we simultaneously are occupied with a constant realization of a retreat inward, a heightening of our vibration and a raising of our consciousness.

—Tibetan Master DK

December 2015
Welcoming Winter Solstice

Today, the longest night of the year brings us the hope of the light returning. The Winter Solstice always falls on the day the sun enters the sign of Capricorn. It also falls in the middle of the holiday season.

What if we looked at the holidays as "holy days," where we celebrate and honor the light that is within us? The energy of the sun is not very available to us right now, so it is up to us to nurture, strengthen, and protect our inner light.

What is that light within? It is the light of the Soul, the light of the Christ that burns within all of us. That Christ consciousness that is present in every human being.

We are invited, at this season, to cultivate that Christ light. It is especially important in these chaotic times that we be a beacon of light in a dark world. One way we can nurture this light within is through stillness. It is difficult in this busy time of year, but don't you feel your body longing to settle in to be nurtured, and received with love? When we are in sync with nature we can learn from her. She is resting now. Can we slow down, ease up, sink into winter and honor this opportunity to rest, to become still?

Through stillness we can tap into that light of the Christ more fully. We can expand our capacity to hold and radiate more light. Then we can walk into the darkness of the world and be a healing force for goodness.

Blessing in the Chaos

To all that is chaotic
in you,
let there come silence.

Let there be
a calming
of the clamoring,
a stilling
of the voices that
have laid their claim
on you,
that have made their

home in you,

that go with you
even to the
holy places
but will not
let you rest,
will not let you
hear your life
with wholeness
or feel the grace
that fashioned you.

Let what distracts you
cease.
Let what divides you
cease.
Let there come an end
to what diminishes
and demeans,
and let depart
all that keeps you
in its cage.

Let there be
an opening
into the quiet
that lies beneath
the chaos,
where you find
the peace
you did not think
possible
and see what shimmers
within the storm.

From the book, *Book of Sorrow. A Book of Blessings for Times of*

Grief, by Jan Richardson, Wanton Gospeller Press, Orlando, Florida, 2016
Used by permission, www.janrichardson.com

December 2015
Entering 2016, Gently and Lovingly

This time, between Christmas and the beginning of a new year, is like a sacred pause. The hustle and bustle of Christmas is over, and we have these few remaining days, between years, where we can choose to become quiet, to be still and review, look back, and contemplate what the past year has taught us.

What are the themes that wove in and out of our everyday lives and what were the learnings that emerged out of those themes?

One year I opened my home for an afternoon and invited friends to come and sit in the silence, asking them to bring their journals, writing implements, pictures, etc. I put out art supplies, tea, soft music, and created sacred spots in every room where people could sit and just be with their musings.

I went through my year of journals and noticed the themes that ran through my year. It was an interesting experience to see how the threads wove themselves into a tapestry that was much clearer to me having spent that time with my words.

I think it was that year that I discovered Danielle LaPorte. Many of you may already be familiar with her, either through my frequent posts of her writings or your own connections.

Her voice called to me that year to abolish New Year's Resolutions. *What a concept.* Her radical idea was that instead of trying to set goals, or trying to accomplish, or trying to "do better" maybe we could just notice what it is we really desire to *feel* in our life and then do whatever it takes to feel that way as often as we could. She called these our "core desired feelings."

Here are some of the feelings she listed:

Seen
Light hearted
Bliss
Aligned
Joyful
Harmony
Powerful
Inspired
Clarity
Delight

Flow
Sensuous
Bold

Her idea was then to choose three feelings that jumped out at you. (Of course, this is just a partial list and you can make up your own.) Then list as many things as you can think of that will help you feel the way you want to feel.

As I recall my three most desired feelings were aligned, delight, and clarity. For me to feel aligned I must be disciplined about my spiritual practices, meditation, reading, and staying connected to my spiritual community.

If I am in a state of alignment everything about my life seems to flow easier. (I think flow was my fourth choice.)   I am more able to take right action, I am more mindful of being harmless, my thoughts seem to vibrate at a higher octave and I have more control over my emotions.

I chose delight because I was rather tired of responsible, heavy duty Saturn running my life. Feeling burdened by responsibilities, putting my nose to the grindstone, pushing, pushing, pushing. A little more spontaneous fun was definitely in the picture, so I signed up for dance classes because dancing is the quickest way for me to get a joy fix, aside from my grandkids. I even asked my son to make a CD of all the tunes I most like to move my body to so that when I am home, I can pump it up and really get into it. (Let's hear it for "Old Time Rock and Roll".)

My third most desired feeling was clarity because it gave me a feeling of ease. When I am clear, I don't fret and fuss and worry. I know what is what, and I rest in that. What brings me the most clarity, besides meditation? Being out in nature. So, I joined a meetup group of people who go on hikes once a month. Needless to say, I've had to take a vacation from all these wonderful adventures while I've been in recovery this past year from my broken shoulder, but even though I was immobilized and slowing *way* down, there were many moments of clarity.

Once I got past the worst of the injury, there was more time to devote to my spiritual practices thus a deeper alignment took place. There were many moments of delight, like just sitting and watching the birds come to my feeders. And surprisingly, a new desired feeling emerged for me. *Peace with what is.*

So, my friends, I invite you to a new way to begin this year. Take some moments to pause and contemplate how you really want to feel in 2016 and then do whatever it takes for you to feel that way, at least some of the time. That's what I'll be doing the next few days. If you really want to get into this, look into Danielle's book, *The Desire Map*. It's a helpful resource (daniellelaporte.com/thedesiremap).

The following prayer, that I will paraphrase, is from another one of my guru goddesses, Tama Kieves (tamakieves.com):

I bless the life I have lived this past year. It offered me a lot and I am grateful for all I received. I am grateful for everything that I tried this year, even if it did not work. I thank myself for the many times I believed in myself, even if I couldn't hold onto that feeling for as long as I would have liked. I am grateful for all the times I got things right and for all the times I stepped out of my comfort zone to try something new. I thank myself for all the times I stood tall, in my own power, and spoke my truth. And for all the times I searched for my truth. Now, I ask for blessing as I begin this new year. May I enter it with love and appreciation and may this new beginning bless myself and all those that I touch.

And so, it is.

June 2016
The Great Root on Which We Live:
Honoring the Summer Solstice

Today I was thinking about the upcoming Solstice, when the energy of the sun is available to us for so many hours. I start to ponder what this means.

What does it mean to be the recipient of so much solar energy? How can we let that light ignite the spark that is within each of us? Can we use it to expand our consciousness, to radiate more fully the love that is our essence?

Surely it is a day to honor the Mother, Gaia, our precious earth. We give thanks for her abundance, for her beauty. Perhaps we can use this day to connect more deeply with Her essence. We do have a co-creative relationship with the earth. We can learn to tune in and connect to her wisdom and guidance. It is a partnership. I think this involves sitting in silence, asking to see what our part is and then doing it. From there we practice letting go. We release our idea of how things should turn out. We surrender our time line for when things should manifest, and we trust in the "deep root on which we live."

This, from Anne Hillman, author of *Awakening the Energies of Love, and The Dancing Animal Woman* (annhillman.net):

I tend to think that new life emerges from seeds and forget a far more ancient truth. Today, I find myself celebrating the way it can also arise from the very old----like tiny seedlings sprouted from the living root of a giant redwood tree. This new life *simply claims the giant's root as its own,* surrenders to its impetus, and grows towards the light.

How do we cooperate with life's gradual shaping of the human mind---its painstaking work of drawing us toward the light of greater awareness?

As I see it, the action required is to trust the great root on which we stand---and learn to surrender. Some see surrender as defeat, a capitulation to an outer force, but it is really an inner relaxation---into the root. What does the use of the word 'root' mean to you? *That matters.* For when you know what you rest on and can relax into it, your heart opens to life's secret---its creative impetus conveyed beneath thought: a feeling, an intuition, an image, or a confirming synchronicity. Subtle clues like these remind us that there is infinitely more to life—a reality we barely notice but that the body knows intimately---a wisdom *built into* the great root on which we live.

When we remain exquisitely attuned to life's presence in this way, it will often surprise us: nudge us to be more authentic, to improvise, to move in a new direction. Its whispered hints may feel absurd, even impossible. But if you dare to follow them, you will be adding more light to life's deep need for it at this time.

July 2016
I Build a Lighted House and Therein Dwell

This is the *mantram* for the sign of Cancer. On this day of the full moon, sitting in meditation these thoughts come to me.

How big is my lighted house?

Can it house the whole world?

Can I invite all of humanity into my "house", into my heart to be fed and nurtured and loved?

How do I do bring more light into my house? Do I invoke? How do I open? Am I willing to receive?

Sacred light can dissolve the obstacles, transmute the hindrances, dispel the illusions.

I welcome this light into my life, into my "home."

How much light can I tolerate?

How do I expand my capacity to hold more?

Through purification, aspiration, dedication, and steadfastness.

Usually the light does not come as a blinding flash. It creeps in slowly, one ray at a time until the body becomes a radiant expression of love.

My prayer becomes, "Pour down upon me the love, the light of the Christ."

This is my dwelling place, within this love.

I reach into the light,
And bring it down to meet the need.
I reach into the Silent place
And bring from thence
The gift of understanding.
Thus, with the light I work
And turn the darkness into day.
—Alice Bailey, *A World Problem*)

January 2017
The Prayer Tree

In a big cardboard box in my bedroom closet there are twelve files, one file for each astrological month. Inside these files are my notes from the research I do each month for my full moon ceremonies and the articles I write for soulbridging.com. Since I have been doing ceremonies since 2004 you can imagine how big the files have become. Nevertheless, each month I retrieve my notes from the past year and review them to see if I want to include any of the information for the upcoming full moon.

Last month when I was planning the full moon/solstice ceremony I came across some notes I had written many years ago and had completely forgotten. Unfortunately, I did not note the source, but I was so taken with the ritual that I incorporated it into the ceremony and repeated it again at my family's Christmas Eve gathering. Here is a synopsis of the notes I took for the Sagittarius full moon.

In Siberia, trees are seen as sacred because they are believed to be the bridge between heaven and earth. So, each year at this time there is a gathering where people from the community come together to create a prayer tree. Offerings of food and drink are left under the tree and the shaman of the community chants and gives thanks to the helping spirits for carrying the prayers of the people up to the universe so that their dreams manifest back on earth. People tie ribbons on branches symbolizing their prayers for individuals, families, and their community.

I thought this was a perfect ritual for the Sagittarius energy since it is a sign of vision and big dreams. Doesn't our world need that right now? So, I asked people this question: *What is your vision, your prayer for the people in your life, for your community, for our planet?*

Since I believe that writing things down makes them more powerful, we then wrote our words on colorful pieces of paper that had ribbons attached. Each person then brought their prayers and put them on a branch of the small tree I had purchased. When everyone had participated, we closed with this prayer.

We offer our prayer of gratitude and love to this tree for the energy it brings into this house, for the light it brings us at this Christmas/Solstice time. We ask now that this living being work in partnership with us and the angels and we send forth these prayers on the wings of the angels, that all who receive them may be blessed, may be protected, may be healed and may be at peace. And so it is.

I don't usually buy Christmas trees, but when I read these notes I felt impelled to buy a small little one, so I might have a place to welcome all these prayers and so that my home would be filled with the dreams and hopes of everyone who gathered together.

Blessed be.

April 2017
A Sweet Easter Blessing

On the day before Easter I was preparing to take a nice long walk. I must admit I'm a "fair weather" walker. The weather must be reasonable, the temperature pleasant, and I must be really motivated to make the trek up my long steep driveway and then three intimidating hills before I get to an even stretch. But on this day the sun was shining (a rare occurrence this winter) and I was determined to get outside.

Most days, when I take this walk, I plug in my phone and listen to podcasts, so I can be distracted from the discomfort of those four hills, but on this day, I remembered something I had read recently in the book *Aging As A Spiritual Practice*, by Lewis Richmond. The suggestion was that when you begin any walk you take the first fifteen minutes and just focus on gratitude, a "gratitude walk" the author called it. I liked that idea so decided to try it out, bringing the phone along, just in case.

I was ambling along, slowly, because of all the gratitude I was feeling, the smell of the spring flowers in bloom, the warmth of the sun on my face, the beauty of the trees, when I noticed a bench. I had passed this bench a million times on my walks but this time I paused to take a good look. I think because I was in such a state of grace I really saw it. To my surprise, and delight, tucked away in the corner was a painted rock, with hearts that surrounded the head of an eagle, and the message, "You are loved." Wow, I was blown away. I know that I am loved, by my family and my close friends, but I don't always remember that there is a bigger love. This felt like the universe was wrapping its arms around me and whispering, "You are loved". It felt transcendent.

Well, I tell you, that love carried me through the rest of my three-mile walk without even a thought of turning on the podcasts.

And by the way, a big dose of gratitude to whomever took the time to perform that sweet act of kindness.

Blessed is the season which engages the whole world in a conspiracy of love.
—Hamilton W. Mabie

December 2017
Signs and Synchronicities

On Saturday, December 2nd, at the Sagittarius full moon ceremony I was talking about how in ancient times in the old mystery schools, Sagittarius was called the "sign of silence." This was because they recognized that with the fire of Sagittarius meeting the mental agility of Gemini (its opposite sign), the potential for destruction was great. Their discipline became silence, and their keynote, harmlessness. After talking about this for a bit at the ceremony, we took a few moments to go within and contemplate these questions.

How would this season be different for you if your keynote was silence and harmlessness?

What energy do you want to bring to this season? (Frustrated, harried, burdened? Or open heartedness, inner peace and ease?)

We then talked about how we do have choice here. We don't need to go blindly into the holidays doing what we've always done. Perhaps we've always gone into the this season slightly frantic and feeling rushed. Maybe we are dreading time with the family or trying to get just the perfect gift for everyone. We can set our intention to daily hold that inner silence, that quiet repose, that *knowing* that everything will get done in its perfect timing. We can choose this. We can commit to this. Sagittarius is, after all, a lot about commitment and dedication.

The influence of Neptune is powerful at this full moon and I spoke of how Neptune speaks to us through dreams, symbols, and images. It is the planet of imagination and the invisible realms. So, paying attention to the way Neptune is talking to us is important. The messages from Neptune won't likely come through our logical left brain. We need to open our minds to the higher levels of insight and look for synchronicities and signs that come to us through the subtle realms.

The feeling of expansive energy from the ceremony was palpable, as it almost always is and on Sunday, I spent a quiet day of just basking in the glow that seemed to fill my house. This is my secret motive for holding full moon ceremonies. I get the benefit of the wonderful, sacred energies filling my home.

But Monday was a different story. I awoke with a scratchy throat, stuffy head, and feeling like I was coming down with something. I immediately began worrying, as I am wont to do. I had committed to taking dinner and caring for a friend recovering from surgery for several hours on Tuesday and I was concerned I wouldn't be able to do that if I was sick. My mind kicked in and I began stewing and fretting, such helpful feelings for warding off a bug, right?

I began to think I should go to the store, that day, while I was pretty okay. I should begin the cooking so it's all ready for tomorrow in case I can go to help my friend. I should really make those muffins my grandson loves so I can have them all ready on Wednesday when I go to babysit. You know how it goes.

Then I opened my computer to these lovely words by my astrologer friend, Heidi Robbins: "The moon enters the sign of Cancer today. Use Cancer for its feeling sensitivity. Stay open to what feels nourishing. Make choices that care for the quieter parts of you. Be tender with yourself and others. Allow tender." I began to take that in.

When I went to sit for meditation, I noticed a book that was sitting on my altar, *Outrageous Openness*, by Tosha Silver. Keeping Neptune in mind and wondering if I could get a message this way, I randomly opened the book to the chapter called (Are you ready?) "The Ease of Flow."

In it she recalls a friend who emailed her about a shift that had occurred to her around how she goes through the holidays. I noticed that I had previously underlined this passage twice!! "Somehow a change has occurred this holiday season. I'm moving from a place of ease and effortlessness, allowing things to happen as they wish to happen." Tosha goes on to say that even if our logical, critical mind can't take this in that our receptive, intuitive mind will absorb it. Then she states, "This idea harmonizes so well with Divine Order. If you align in any moment with the flow of life as it presents itself, all will unfold in the right way at the right time with a certain spontaneity and ease."

I was a bit taken aback at the synchronistic way in which both of these messages spoke of the same truth. Ease, flow, tenderness, surrendering to Divine Order.

These are the intentions I wish to carry with me this season.

As Abraham says (via channel Esther Hicks), "Worrying is using your imagination to create something you don't want."

I don't want to use my imagination in that way.

So, I'm going to go take a hot bath, grab some turkey soup from the freezer, put on my jammies, and settle down for a long winter's nap.

I choose to let go of my worried mind and my to-do list for today. Thank you, Neptune.

All will be well.

August 2018
Lughna... What?

I have to admit I'd never heard of the Celtic Festival called Lughnasadh until a few days ago, although I was familiar with the English name given it, Lammas. Still I was intrigued and looked it up.

Wikipedia describes it as:

...a Gaelic festival marking the beginning of the harvest season. Historically, it was widely observed throughout Ireland, Scotland and the Isle of Man. Traditionally it is held on 1 August, or about halfway between the summer solstice and autumn equinox. However, in recent centuries some of the celebrations shifted to the Sundays nearest this date. Lughnasadh is one of the four Gaelic seasonal festivals, along with Samhain, Imbolc and Beltane. It corresponds to other European harvest festivals such as the Welsh *Gŵyl Awst* and the English Lammas.

But first the backstory.

In trying to finish up this book, I had to research a lot of the poets and writers that I had quoted. Copyright issues come into play when you are selling something that contains other people's words. One of the people I googled was Miriam Dyak who is the author of "Spring Cleaning", one of the first poems quoted in my book. Much to my surprise I found she lived right here in Seattle, my home town. I called her, and we had a lovely conversation. I realized we had much in common as she is only a few years younger than I and she is also a therapist. I asked for her permission to include her poem and she graciously gave it to me with no strings attached, except that she be acknowledged. Then she told me that she had written poems for each of the Celtic holy days and she would love to send them to me.

On the day they arrived in my email box I was having a mini crisis around the book. Doubting myself, wondering if I would ever finish it, if anyone would be interested in publishing it, if it was really something people could be helped by.

That was my mindset, having a "doubting Thomas" moment. Then I read her first poem dedicated to the festival of Lughnasadh.

Care Of The Growing Crop

Since corn needs all the light it can get
you will want to avoid planting other tall plants nearby
you are growing yourself remember
you deserve your day in the sun
you deserve your own ripeness
and you will want to make sure each plant
has every opportunity to make good use of the rich soil you have
        provided
so that at last these dreams you've been holding will fill out
in precious clusters of milky pearls and silky yellow moons
Sweet corn is at its sweet juicy tender best for only a few days
and you have labored a whole season for this perfection

Trouble shooting
we hope none of the following problems will be yours
Insect infestations like a swarm of worries
take measures in your own soul before there is a full-scale invasion
The corn earworm lays about 1,000 eggs in her twelve days of life
We know how these hatch into hesitation, fear, doubt, self-deprecation,
        inertia how they eat tunnels into the mind
Cut them out and give them back to the earth for compost
You have grown too far to give up now

Diseases
wilt and smut and blight out there in the world
Don't let these attack your own small patch
Develop a resistant strain
go against the grain of expectations
be an original a treasure
Give yourself a new name:
Golden woman
Moon Maiden
She Who Stands Tall And Proud

Thieves

raccoons, woodchucks and deer are probably the worst four-footed sweet corn thieves

they are the distractions that come just when you're getting somewhere

when you almost have success in the pot

and steal you away from your own life

They have an uncanny way of knowing just when the ears

have reached their prime

They are other people's needs you always put before your own

They are love affairs that want you to be somebody you aren't

They are larger bigger better purposes/harvests than yours

You can try to spook them with rock music

You can plant pumpkins in their path

You can even cover your ears with paper bags...

But I am here to tell you

this night on the festival of Lughnasadh the time of ensuring the harvest

your personal harvest the village harvest

and the safety of the good we are all growing in the world

I am here to tell you what the ancients know

that if you give up your crop along the way out of carelessness or
   nobility

it doesn't matter

your spirit will be a hollow husk and no one not you not others

will be fed

But if you tend your own patch to completion

(no matter how insignificant it seems)

if you let yourself swell with joy with the rich nourishing milk of
   fulfillment

you will have raised a miracle

Your small garden of life, of art, of love, of work, of mothering and
   building and

being a wise woman

whatever you have planted and tended and grown

will feed yourself your village

there will be corn for feasting, for flour, for popping over winter fires

and enough to plant next year

There will be seeds that open spontaneously in the hearts of other women

and wild possibilities will appear in dreams on the other side of the world."

—Miriam Dyak, www.voicedialogueworld.com/en/miriam-dyak

WOWSA!!! I am inspired, and I will continue.

I am She who stands Tall and Proud.

CHAPTER 14
SHIT HAPPENS

Every now and then no matter how lofty our intentions, or how carefully we have planned, the Universe steps in and says, "Really? You thought you were in control of this? Ha! Think again."

This particular event seemed auspicious mostly because everything I had planned fell to pieces. Not just one thing, but everything.

Seriously though, when that happens there's nothing left to do, but laugh and say to the Universe, "Ha, you thought you could trip me up but look, I even made the most of this shitty week."

August 2017
A Five-Day Personal Retreat? Hmmmmm, Not So Much

Every year I try to get away alone to a beautiful place and give myself some time to be away from all distractions. Even though I live in a lovely home, I'm always looking around and seeing what needs to be done and getting interrupted by phone calls, and my own addictions (mystery novels, magnum bars, and spider solitaire just to name a few).

In the past, I've walked into Earth Sanctuary, on Whidbey Island and just sunk into the stillness that pervades this Buddhist retreat house. Arriving there on a Tuesday afternoon, I couldn't catch that quiet vibe. I was restless, edgy, and not able to settle. I know this is common on retreats, so I thought that by the next day I would be fine. But my insomnia kicked in that night and I was tossing and agitated all night. The next day I woke with a foggy mind and sluggish energy.

Nevertheless, I tried to persevere. My intention had been strong. This will be a spiritual retreat, meaning only spiritual reading, some writing for a possible new book, or articles for the full moon and new moon, perhaps a blog, and lots of time to meditate and walk in the woods.

So, despite my tiredness I managed to go through all three of the spiritual books I had along and got some writing done, but the restlessness continued. Even a long walk in the woods was interrupted by all the mosquitoes that I had promised not to kill. By that evening I was feeling a bit desperate. What now, I thought? I've got three more days and I'm so not into this.

Unable to reach a place of peace or tranquility, at 8:00pm of the second night, I gave it up, got in my car and drove the few miles into the small town of Freeland. I paid for my package of Magnum bars and my two mystery novels and headed out to my car. Turned the key into the ignition and, nothing. The car was dead. Only then did I realize I'd left my phone at the retreat house.

Luckily, I've been practicing asking for what I need so when a young man came out of the store, I didn't hesitate to ask him for a jump. I was pretty sure it wasn't the battery since I had just put a new one in, but it was the only thing I could think of. Well, that was a bust. Now I began to feel sort of stuck and a little sheepish, but I asked him if I could borrow his phone to call my insurance tow service. He was very gracious. The insurance person had no idea where Freeland, Washington was (he was in Tennessee), but finally found it on Google and then tried to find a local tow truck and auto repair. It took forever, and I was constantly checking in with nice young man to see if he's still okay not going home and putting his groceries away. He assured me was fine, waiting.

Well the local tow truck guy had already gone home, but the insurance guy gave him my sob story and he agreed to pick me up in forty-five minutes. So, eating my humble pie I asked the nice young man if he would be willing to drive me the mile and a half back to the house to pick up my phone, so he wouldn't have to wait for the tow guy? He agreed with no hesitation.

On the way back, I was gushing my appreciation when he made an amazing comment. "I knew there was someone at the store who needed my help tonight, that's why I went." I was astounded and of course tried to pry more information out of him, but he was reticent to share any more.

Getting back to the store, I was sitting in my car, waiting for the tow truck guy, and here's what happened. At least ten people (I counted), came by and asked if I needed help, could they give me a jump, did I need a ride somewhere? When I expressed my amazement to one person, he said, "That's island life." Wow, how great is that?

Eventually the tow truck guy came by and I decided to try one more time to start the car and, it started right up. After talking it over with the guy I decided to go ahead and drive it to the repair shop, which was now closed, and have them look at it the next day. Tow truck guy took me in his truck to the shop and drove me back to the house. I felt so grateful and blessed and also a bit stressed out, so no writing or meditating now. I went straight for the Magnum bars and my mystery novels.

The next day I was on the phone every few hours to check on my car which they couldn't get to till late afternoon so that made it hard to concentrate, but I did get some writing done. My mind began to go to "worst-case scenario" however and I began to worry that I wouldn't be able to get home on Saturday, in time for the full moon ceremony, Sunday. *What if they couldn't fix it in time, what if I was stuck here? How would I get home?* Finally, I heard from them and they told me it would be fixed by Friday afternoon and they would come pick me up. So, I was relieved and again, grateful.

Friday morning, I was taking my chair out to do my usual morning routine, which is to sit on a chair outside, with my bare feet on the earth. The chair was cumbersome, and I was having a hard time getting it through the door but finally it was through. But on its way, it snagged something on the door and the door slammed shut. I reached to open it and realized it was locked. The moment of total panic hit. I was there with no shoes, so I couldn't walk anywhere. My phone was again, inside on the table so I no chance to call anyone.

I vaguely remembered reading the instructions on the day I checked in that there was a lock box somewhere with a code to get a spare key and that I should write the code down and put it under the mat, but of course I didn't do any of that, so I didn't remember where the lock box was, or what the code was. But, I did have a chair and I remembered that I opened my bedroom window a bit the night before because it was hot. So, I hauled the chair around to the side of the house and looked at the window. It was rather high up and there was a huge bush right in front of it.

Okay, I can do this. I swung that chair up with all my energy, tried to stabilize it as best I could, then tried to haul myself up to the wobbly chair and pull myself up to the window and into the house, all the while thinking my kids would kill me if I injured myself trying to do something so foolish. I finally managed to get in but that pretty well shot Friday's energy. It was back to the Magnum bars and the mystery novels.

Seriously, I couldn't believe all this was happening. I began to wonder, facetiously, if the Universe was sending me a message that it's not wise to be so easily distracted from your intentions.

The other disturbing part of my visit this time was that I did have to agree not to kill any bugs and there were three lovely spiders in the bathroom that were in corners where I couldn't easily get them out, so I just left them. Well spiders and I don't have a friendly history, but I did promise, so each time I walked into the bathroom, especially at night, I was on edge just hoping they hadn't moved.

I started thinking about going home Friday night instead of Saturday morning, but I didn't feel like cleaning up and packing so I stayed until my check out time on Saturday.

After cleaning up, doing laundry, remaking the bed, and packing up all my stuff I was ready to go. The last item on the checkout list was to leave the key in an envelope under the back-door mat. I lifted up the mat and guess what was there?

THE CODE TO THE KEY BOX, that someone else had written out and left. And I finally really looked at the house and saw exactly where the key box was.

REALLY? The code was there all the time, with access to an extra key?

By this time all I could do was laugh. It's was all just too funny.

I was so happy to get home.

Lessons learned:

The key is always there to open the metaphoric door if one is willing to look carefully.

When I am stuck, whether metaphorically or literally, there is always help available.

The most important thing is really holding the strong focus for how I want to use my time... and if I do that, I can retreat anywhere, including my own home.

There is no spiritual law that says you will incur bad karma from eating Magnum Bars and reading mystery novels.

CHAPTER 15
SURRENDER

What does the word "surrender" conjure up in your mind? Giving up? Passivity? Loss of control?

I'd like to redefine it from a Spiritual perspective. One of the foundations of spiritual surrender, I believe, is faith, or trust in something greater than yourself. Without that, it probably does feel like giving up or being passive and losing control.

It's not important how you define "something greater than yourself," you just have to believe that it has a power. The power to take your burden, your worry, your anxiety from you and give you some peace.

Of course, we have to be *willing* to let go and that, I think is the difficult part. It feels scary to admit we have no control of some things. We like to believe we are powerful and can adjust life to our liking, but of course this is not true. We are powerful, for sure, but life doesn't hang around waiting to please us, or give us our version of happy and serene.

It helps, I think, if we believe there is a plan and a purpose to our lives. It's easier to surrender when we know it is for a greater good, even if that greater good is just living our life with more ease.

What is true for me is that I have to get pretty sick and tired of the energy it takes to worry constantly, to be in a perpetual state of anxiety, before I can surrender. It's exhausting to try to control people and things just so I can pretend I'm safe or so everything turns out the way I want it to.

Part of the truth, as I see it, is that the only thing we truly have control over is how we react to what life brings us. We can't control outcome. We can't always control timing. We certainly can't control or change how other people live their lives.

What are our choices here? The author Hugh Prather, in his book *The Little Book of Letting Go*, says it pretty succinctly:

Some things are simple and here's one of them. You can either relax and let go of your life, in which case you will know peace. Or you can try to control your life, in which case you will know war.

The examples in this chapter reveal some of my little acts of surrender. Certainly not life changing in and of themselves, but I believe every time we become more aware and are willing to look at what we're being shown we participate in our own healing process. Practicing those little acts of surrender might strengthen the muscle that we will need when we have to tackle the really big surrenders in our lives.

September 2015
A Little Act of Surrender

Yesterday I did something unheard of for me, I stopped asking questions.

I woke up feeling off, misaligned, out of sorts. I wanted to stay in bed and just doze all day, but my mind told me that was impossible. Think of all the things on my "to do" list. They *must* get done and they *must* get done today.

Then, remembering the learning for me of the last several months since my accident, I tuned into my body. I felt the fatigue, the soreness in my back, the queasy stomach. If I had stayed with that, I probably would have been fine, but I reverted to my questioning mode. *What could this be? What's wrong with me? Is it the New Moon and the solar eclipse, is it the flu, is it, is it, is it????*

Then I just stopped with the questions. In that moment I surrendered to what was. My body was asking for attention. *Could I just give it what it wanted without all the mental dialogue?* Yes, I could.

I curled up in my "man chair", got my favorite blanket, snuggled in, read a few lines in a book and promptly feel asleep. It was only 11:30am. I didn't wake for two hours. This may not sound like rocket science to anyone else but to me it was a *moment,* and I believe these small moments eventually add up to a shift in consciousness.

So, this moment was all about just listening without questioning. Just following without explaining anything to myself. Just surrendering to the moment, as it was, *without argument or questions.*

There is a power in the act of surrendering. When I stop all the mind chatter, it makes everything easier. No endless back and forth, trying to figure it all out, trying to decide something. Energy is released to tune more fully into my deep Self and just listen. Imagine how much simpler life would be if we just gave that busy mind a rest. If we just let it curl up in the man chair, snuggle in and be still.

In surrender we give back to God our demand to understand the big picture of why things happen the way they do. We give back our insistence that life behave a certain way in order for us to feel good and the mistaken belief that well-being depends on outside circumstances rather than our inner connection with the Source of all life and love. We release the desperate scrabbling at control. We unfetter our lives, and the life of the world around us, into Mystery, that wisdom which is beyond our capacity to understand.

Surrender opens us up to trusting the wisdom of uncertainty, the ability to be flexible and open-hearted no matter what comes down the pike. In surrendering we find a deeper seat of power and wisdom from which to act in our life according to our own true values and visions. Surrender frees us to act from our deepest core in the present moment, without losing precious energy fixating on a specific outcome.

With surrender we tap into something much greater than our own personal energy. We have moved into the force field of God/Goddess, the "electromagnetic field of love." Far more love and intelligence is available within this field than we can ever find within just ourselves. By letting go of resistance to what is, right now, we surrender to the present moment, the holy field of love and power. The present moment is our opening to God/Goddess.

—Melissa Gayle West, *Silver Linings*, www.melissagaylewest.com

June 2016
An "Aha" Moment in the Dentist's Chair

There is no one I know who thinks that going to the dentist is fun. Necessary, but certainly not how you would really like to be spending your afternoon.

Sometimes it is difficult for me to not be in fear of it since I experienced a childhood trauma sitting in that chair. I don't remember how old I was when I first had a dentist appointment, but my sense is that I was pretty young. I already had a fear of needles so when I saw the needle coming my way to give me Novocain, I pretty much freaked out. I refused to let him put that in my mouth. So, for the next several minutes I sat in pain, my hands clenched to the sides of the chair while he drilled away. Now, I wonder why anyone would agree to treat a child who refused anesthesia?

Nevertheless, when my current dentist told me I needed to have a fifty-year-old filling replaced in preparation for a crown (there were also a few minor fractures in that tooth), I was not a happy camper. An hour and a half in the chair, yikes!!!

Before we started, she asked if I would like to have gas (nitrous oxide). Wow, really? I'd never had that before, so my immediate response was, you bet!

While breathing in the wonderful gas she gave me the dreaded Novocain, absolutely pain free. Okay, so now I'm sitting there with a wedge in my mouth to hold my mouth open, plus that rubbery thing they fasten in your mouth and the drilling going on and on and do I care? The answer to that would be NO. I'm pretty much in la-la land. So, I'm floating along when all of a sudden, a clear, distinct thought comes into my mind, *This is what it feels like to not worry.* Whoa, really? Freeze this moment, I want to say. I really want to remember this feeling, because it's fairly new to me. It reminds me of the first time I got a massage. I distinctly remember getting off the table and being startled by the revelation that this is what it felt like to be totally relaxed in my body. Evidently a rare occurrence as well.

I know, as I'm sure most people do, that worry does no good, but that hasn't stopped me. I'm sure it's all tied up with what I have thought made me a good person, a good mother, a good friend. What kind of a mother would I be if I didn't worry? Isn't that part of the job description? My children are so grateful I passed along this gene to them. Not! Aren't we supposed to worry about our friends? Well, I believe it's all a matter of degree. To what degree do we let worry block our joy? Our faith? Our ease?

One day when I was stressing over an upcoming surgery, not life threatening, the worry gene had taken over. My sister gave me a refrigerator magnet. It said, *"Good morning, this is God. Today I'll be handling all your problems and I won't need your help, so relax and leave everything to me."* I think this a great antidote to the anxiety producing worry gene. Even if you don't believe in God, or a Higher Power, or a universal intelligence, you might as well hand it all over to something.

It's really an act of surrender since we really have no control over what might happen to our loved ones or our friends.

The other antidote I've found helpful is prayer. It's a way of handing it over, but also it does send out an energy of healing and protection to the person and to the field, and I happen to believe that it works. It is a law that energy follows thought. At the very least it can lessen my anxiety, since when I'm sending love and healing, I'm not embroiled in worry. And this is a Gemini month and Gemini is all about transmitting and distributing.

This month I wish to transmit my faith that everything is as it should be, and all is working out according to a larger purpose and plan.

When I can rest in that, I am back in the dentist chair, floating along in la-la land without a care in the world.

March 2017
At War with Nighttime

It is 3:45am on a Sunday morning as I sit writing this, one of those periodic nights of insomnia. The sheets on the bed lie rumpled and torn up, a warzone.

The battle is between my mental body (which loves nothing better than to wake up, energized and ready to fight, the minute my head hits the pillow) and my physical body's need for deep rest.

It wasn't always like this. I can remember a time, not so long ago, when my bed was a cradle of welcome. Inviting me into her warmth with a loving embrace, I would drift sweetly into dreamland.

Now it has sometimes become a thing to be dreaded. Before crawling in, the mind is already convinced it will win this war. The body, fearful, curls up in constriction. What to do? Dialogue only seems to activate the monkey mind. *Mantrams*, meditation, deep breathing work for a few minutes and then succumb to the anxiety that this will never end. Worst-case scenarios take over. *I will forever be tired, I will never sleep through the night, my mind will slowly lose its edge (if it ever had one) from sleep deprivation, I can't possibly babysit, teach, hold my full moon meditations, write what I want to write because I won't have the energy, or the clarity that I need, etc. etc. etc.* The anxiety increases, so more tossing and turning. Stillness eludes, relaxation becomes impossible. When I do feel myself drifting off it only takes one moment of that insidious fear to bring my body to attention.

I have yet to find a solution to this dilemma that doesn't include narcotics with their nasty hangovers. So, I offer no words of wisdom here, no platitudes. I'm still seeking resolution.

I would like to be able to say to myself, just this moment, this is just a moment in time. Can I be with it fully, not resisting what is? But obviously there is much resistance. I have spent lots of time theorizing about the underlying cause of this situation. Is it rooted in a fear of letting go? A deeply buried unwillingness to welcome the darkness?

The truth is I just don't know and honestly, I'm sick of thinking about it. Sometimes it helps to just get up and read my mystery novels for a few hours, but then it feels like giving in to the restlessness. I've tried to eliminate the most obvious causes, no caffeine, no TV or computer after 9:00pm, stretching before bedtime to relax my body, getting my exercise in, watching my diet. I have acupuncture treatments once a month and regularly get body work. So, I'm at a loss. Sometimes I blame it on aging, or on solar flares, or whatever astrological configuration is happening, or the full moon, or hormones, but it doesn't always add up. And like I said, I'm totally sick of trying to figure it all out. So, for now it will just remain a mystery, like the stack of "whodunits" lying by my bedside.

I welcome your comments but please, no suggestions, or fixes, trust me, I really have tried almost everything, and at this particular moment I just needed to get it all off my chest. Maybe now sleep will come.

Many months later:

I've been reading a book called *The Surrender Experiment* by Michael Singer. After several profound spiritual awakenings Michael decides to experiment with just surrendering everything to the Divine, every decision, every situation, every moment, really. His book is a chronicle of his life experiences as he takes on this new perspective.

It was a totally inspiring read and it made me want to experiment with it in my own small way. I had several nights of restless sleep again, and I was fuming and struggling with the whys and wherefores. And then I decided that this was the perfect place to start. Why not turn my nights over to the Divine? (You can use whatever language works for you. Just "turning it over", works, or "let go and let God.") It's certainly not a new concept. But I began repeating the *mantram* every time I thought about my insomnia, especially right before going to bed. *I'm just leaving this with you. You can have this night. Use it in whatever way you want. It's yours to do with as you wish.* I think the following statement was probably the most important: *However this night plays out, I will be okay.*

Well, I'd like to report that I went on to have a perfectly deep and uninterrupted sleep, but there was some tossing and turning. The difference was that when I became the least bit restless, I repeated the phrase, *I surrender this night to you. Whatever happens I will be okay.* Amazingly the anxiety went away. Now it's only been a few weeks that I have been doing this but so far, the anxiety has not returned.

I will probably never sleep like my sis (dead to the world the minute her head hits the pillow and stays almost in the same position all night). Some things are just not fair, so I still toss and turn but I am sleeping and I'm not getting up to read or play spider solitaire for a few hours every night.

I'm encouraged by the power of this practice and have begun using it in more and more areas of my life.

I'm going to a party where I know only a few people.

I surrender this party to You. Let happen whatever needs to happen. I will be okay.

I have a presentation I need to make.

I surrender this presentation to the Divine, trusting that my words will reach those who need to hear them. Either way, I will be okay.

I surrender my morning to the Divine, trusting whatever needs to unfold will do so, without my pushing or effort or trying to make something happen.

I surrender this blog to the Divine. May it reach those who need to hear these words, and may it go forth as a blessing to all who read it.

Insomnia Blessing

For you awake
In sorrow.
For you awake
In pain.
For you awake
In illness.
For you awake
In grief.

For you awake
In worry.
For you awake
In fear.
For you awake
In loneliness.
For you awake
In rage.

May peace
Lay itself
Beside you.

May rest
Enfold you with
Its grace.
May solace
Breathe into
Your being.
May sleep
Come and call
Your name.

That you will
Close your eyes
In comfort.
That you will
Spend this night
In peace.
That you will
Give yourself
To dreaming
That you will
Waken into joy.

From the book, *Book of Sorrow. A Book of Blessings for Times of Grief*, by Jan Richardson, Wanton Gospeller Press, Orlando, Florida, 2016 Used by permission. janrichardson.com

CHAPTER 16
OPENING THE HEART TO GREATER LOVE

In the following entries I share my process of attempting to open my heart to a greater love. In other words, taking love out of the personal and elevating it to the level of the Soul. Seeing another as a Soul, not just an ego. Inviting humanity into my heart, not just my personal friends and family.

Acknowledging that we are all Souls, living in a human body, allows me to see how we are all connected. We are a family. Perhaps with this perspective I can look pass your foibles, your idiosyncrasies, the things my personality doesn't like about you and see your essence, your true Self.

It's a practice that will take a few lifetimes, I'm sure, but I'm trying to act "as if" it was an active principle within me now.

June 2018
Can I Love More?

We're in a Gemini month right now and I've been pondering what this might mean for me. Gemini is the sign that transmits the energy of unconditional love and wisdom. It is the love that translates into a desire for right human relationships, for a resolution to whatever separative tendencies we may hold.

Here's how it played out for me. I got an email from a person that I used to be fairly close to, but partly because of the way I was treated in that relationship, the friendship sort of died. We didn't see one another anymore.

Then I got this email from him asking if I'd like to get together for coffee and "catch up." My first impulse was, "NO," but I didn't know how to gracefully decline. I sat with it for a few days and then decided to accept, although I felt half-hearted about it. I recognized that I didn't have good feelings toward him. Maybe I still held onto the hurt, but I had confronted him about it and he had taken responsibility. I made the decision at that time that I didn't trust him as a friend and sort of closed off my heart to him.

Then the universe began working on me. First it was a chapter in the book my women's group is reading called *Awakening Joy*. I read the wrong chapter, which I took as sort of a sign. Instead of reading the chapter on Self Love I read the chapter on Loving Others. In this chapter the authors, James Baraz and Shoshana Alexander, talk about how when we focus on the negative feelings we have about someone, we may be closed down to all the good things that person might have displayed. We forget.

So, I started thinking about all the good times this friend and I had shared and how, at one time, I had respected and admired him because of all the positive qualities I saw in him. That shifted things a bit, but not altogether.

Later in the chapter I read about the lovingkindness practice where you wish someone well.

May you be at peace.

May you be free of suffering.

May you remember the beauty of your own true nature.

May you live your life with ease.

The suggestion is that you start wishing yourself well and then after a time extend the blessing to those you may have difficulties with.

I began doing that with this person.

I tell you, it's hard to hold onto many bad feelings when you are wishing someone well, every day.

The discomfort eased some as my heart began to crack open a bit more.

The final piece for me was realizing that at this full moon we are being graced with a downpouring of love and wisdom. We are being asked to love more.

How do I want to use this energy? Gemini is all about establishing right human relationships, with myself, with others, with my environment. *How can I bring that energy into my relationship with this person? How can I shine the light of Love into our connection?*

Here's what I finally came to.

This person has been somewhat abusive to me in the past, so I won't give him complete access to my heart. I still choose not to be in a close relationship with him. That feels like a healthy boundary to me. But I will meet him for coffee with my wishes for his well-being foremost in my energy field. I will hold him in my heart with compassion and understanding, remembering all the good qualities that he embodies. And if the issue of our friendship comes up I will bravely share with him my struggle with this. That feels like an important way for me to stay in integrity with him.

Somewhere, during this time another note from the universe appeared that helped me a lot. It was an old quote that I happened to remember, and it fit this situation perfectly.

"Unconditional love, conditional access."

May the blessings of this full moon pour down upon you and may you find the love that helps resolve the relationships in your life that are troubling and difficult.

PS It's been proven to me over and over again in my life that once I'm aware of an issue in need of resolution, if I give it mindful attention the Universe will invariably provide me with the information I need to heal it. The above stories are perfect examples, and so is the story below.

After I wrote this entry I went for a walk. Listening to a podcast on "Healing the Judgmental Mind" I heard the presenter give her formula. One step really struck me. She said, see the situation as if for the first time. The Buddhists call this beginner's mind. Each time you sit on the cushion for meditation you do so for the first time. Just be open to whatever appears to you that day.

I wondered how I could apply this to my situation. *What if I came to the coffee date open to just seeing who showed up? As if I was meeting him for the first time? Seeing him as he was that day, leaving all the stories behind?*

I'm willing to try that.

January 2016
I Want to Know What Love Is

This story started way back in November, 2015. Two friends of mine who happen to be spiritual teachers and have a retreat center in Finland began a worldwide livestream meditation. Twice a day, Tuija Robbins and her husband, Michael, brought people together to focus on a country that was at high risk for terrorism. We would spend the first fifteen to twenty minutes learning about the country then Tuija would lead us in a meditation.

We aligned, we invoked, we demanded, we blessed each country. We asked that the Forces of Restoration and Light descend on that country. We visualized the Christ standing in the center of the country, radiating light and magnetizing the good. We invoked a defending, protective, unifying wall around the country to draw in the light and repeal all negative and evil actions. Then in the evening we did it all again with another country.

It is powerful work and I have begun to look forward to the 9:00am, 9:00pm schedule partly because it coincided with my morning meditation time and my evening preparing for bed time, but more than that, after several weeks I began to notice that my awareness was expanding. I felt more connected to the world. My heart began to expand as well, becoming more inclusive and open.

For so long I have been focused on my own path, my own evolution, my own growth. It occurred to me that it might be time to open my heart to the world.

Then a few weeks ago after babysitting my grandson, my son-in-law gave me a CD he had made for me. It was Krishna Das' *Sri Argala Strotram*.

Toward the end of the CD he chants in English, "I want to know what love is, want you to show me. I want to feel what love is, I know you can show me." Well, these words hit me like a ton of bricks and I couldn't stop playing it. Those words went right to my heart.

Do I really know what love is, and can I really contain a larger love, the love of humanity that those meditations were stimulating? Can my heart hold it? What would that mean? How would that feel to have a "heart as big as the world" as Sharon Salzburg writes about? To open my heart to all of humanity, not just my own little family and loved ones? Could I open my heart to "the Donald," to Isil, to the people who kill little children? I don't know, but I know it's time to try. I know it's time to at least crack open a bit.

In the philosophy that I study, we practice seeing the Soul of each person, understanding that that is where we are connected, not on the level of the personality. I think that's the only way I can "love" those people who are so full of hatred.

The final piece to this story came as the sun entered the sign of Aquarius. When I was researching for the full moon ceremony, I realized that Aquarius has a lot to do with love, and BIG love. It's all about inclusivity, universality, group love, impersonal love. It's soul-centered ruler is Jupiter, the ruler of the second ray of Love Wisdom. So, I believe that these events are not a co-inky-dink. They are leading me to my next step of breaking my heart wide open.

Maybe I'll start with the annoying neighbor next door and work up to "the Donald."

Standing in the shower after I wrote this, an old hymn from my childhood came pouring into my awareness. It goes like this:

Deep and wide, deep and wide, there's a fountain flowing deep and wide. Deep and wide, deep and wide there's a fountain flowing deep and wide.

This is how I want my love to be.

This is how I want to feel love, deep and wide, flowing through me like a fountain.

The Buddhist practice of Lovingkindness is also called Metta.

You begin by sending this prayer to those people you feel closest to. After establishing that practice you start to include whoever you may have negative feelings toward. Finally you use the prayer to include the whole world. Below is just one version of the prayer. You can add the words that most resonate with you.

May you be at peace
May you be free of suffering
May you remember the beauty of your own true nature
May you be healed
May you live your life with ease
May all beings be free

I know I've said it before but it's still true. It's difficult to keep your heart closed to people you are praying for.

March 2018
Unconditional Loving

Sitting outside, bare feet on the earth, I'm contemplating the upcoming Gemini Full Moon.

Michael Robbins' words come to me, "I believe that if one thing is in place, all the rest will follow: that one thing is truly and simply the love of humanity."

Suddenly I see how if I lift my personal love, with all its codependent tendencies, up to a higher level my vision and my heart expand. My fear has been that if I focus too much on loving all of humanity I may feel overwhelmed by the suffering and pain. If I can barely tolerate my own family's pain how can I ever hold the pain of the world? But as I sit in meditation and hold this vision of loving the world, instead of feeling burdened, I begin to notice a feeling of liberation, of lightness. After all I can't just go to the world and say, *I brought you some chicken soup, I hope you feel better, and by the way, I'm always available if you need me.*

Opening my heart fully to all of it I feel only a deep sense of compassion, and the, *let me fix it for you,* thought does not follow. Isn't it interesting how all of these threads of awareness keep weaving into a tapestry of beautiful understandings?

Another gem came to me this week in the form of an astrology newsletter from my friend Pam Younghans (www.northpointastrology.com). She defined unconditional love as "loving in all conditions." So, loving despite the suffering, loving even though meaning may be hard to grasp, and loving the highest in everyone. She went on to say, "When we love unconditionally we pay more attention to our loved one's shining ability to make their lives work than we do to fixing the problem for them and we shift our support from commiserating to holding our thought and energy at as high a vibration as we can, knowing that being in alignment ourselves is the greatest gift we can offer, and that diminishing our light does not help others expand theirs."

If I take this at a more global level, I understand that if I pay more attention to my *faith* in humanity than to commiserating about how awful everything is, I shift my support to a higher vibration and I can see the world from a place of alignment. When I hold this higher perspective, I have a greater capacity to envision the planet in light and I can focus on the potential that is there for transformation.

This doesn't preclude taking action of some sort to assist in the transformation, but when I come from a place of alignment the action feels different than when I am just reacting to old conditioned habits of "trying to fix."

This upcoming full moon is a great opportunity for us to open to the heart of humanity. It is sometimes referred to as the Festival of Humanity. The Great Ones await our invocative appeal and will pour down upon the planet this great love, to all.

Is it possible for us to hold in our imaginations light, love, and power pouring down from the spiritual realms into the heart of every human?

The Great Invocation

From the point of light within the mind of God
Let light stream forth into human minds,
Let light descend on Earth.

From the point of Love within the Heart of God
Let Love stream forth into human hearts
May the Coming One return to Earth.

From the center where the Will of God is known
Let purpose guide all little human wills.
The purpose which the Masters know and serve.

From the center which we call the human race
Let the Plan of Love and Light work out
And may it seal the door where evil dwells

Let light and love and power restore the Plan on Earth.

Om Om Om

The above Invocation or Prayer does not belong to any person or group but to all humanity. The beauty and the strength of this Invocation lies in it simplicity, and in its expression of certain central truths which all men, innately and normally, accept----the truth of the existence of a basic Intelligence to Whom we vaguely give the name of God; the truth that behind all outer seeming, the motivating power of the universe is Love; the truth that great Individuality came to earth, called by Christians, the Christ, and embodied that love so that we could understand; the truth that both love and intelligence are effects of what is called the Will of God; and finally the self-evident truth that only through humanity itself can the Divine Plan work out.

    —Alice Bailey

CHAPTER 17
MAGIC

What is magic anyway? I believe that magic is one way that the universe guides us, supports us, informs us. I believe it is always present. The universe isn't going anywhere, but we have to open our eyes to it, look for it, invoke it.

In the next two entries I share with you some of the ways that magic has worked in my life. I'm inspired by its power, by its ability to present itself to me when I need it most of all how it assists me so profoundly in my own healing.

April 2016
Do You Believe in Magic?

In these confusing and chaotic times do you ever find it difficult to find your clarity, to make decisions, to know what "right action" would look like?

Because of my tendency to want everyone to be happy and to make sure no one is thinking badly of me, I often find it challenging to discern my true, authentic voice from the myriad of conditioned messages that are floating around in my brain.

One of the things I've come to rely on when I can't make sense of things is to invoke magic. By magic, I mean, inviting the Universe to help me out. I ask for signs, then I watch very carefully.

Probably the most dramatic example of this in my own life is when my ex and I decided to separate in the fall of 1993. We decided to let our fifteen-year-old son stay in the family home and we would rotate in and out every two weeks. This meant I needed to find a place to live. I was in anguish trying to think of what I could do to make sure my son could reach me if he needed to. He was too young to drive so it would have to be somewhere within biking distance.

One day on my walk through Woodway, I saw a for sale sign at one of the big estates there. I immediately flashed on a story I read about the amazing woman called SARK. She was an artist and visionary and a magician of the first order. One day as she was walking through the streets of San Francisco she was holding in her mind the picture of the perfect place for her to live. She could see the cottage in her mind, in great detail. On that walk, she actually happened upon the exact little house. By a series of synchronicities (magic, I call it), she actually ended up living there.

Well on my walk this story came into my mind. I wondered if this huge mansion might have a guest house. That's as far as I got because my rational mind gave me every reason that was a stupid idea. But every day on my walk the urge came back. Finally, I garnered my courage and called the realtor to see if there was a guest house. Yes, as a matter of fact there was. I hung up. I knew the house belonged to the family of one of my daughter's school friends, but still I was scared and embarrassed and feeling skeptical.

But one day after several weeks of going back and forth in my mind I screwed up my courage and called their home. The wife answered. I explained the situation and asked her if there was any way they would consider renting out the guest house while it was on the market. She assured me there was no way, but agreed to ask her husband, just as a courtesy, I'm sure.

Imagine my surprise when she called me back a few days later and said her husband would like to meet at the guest house and talk things over. Well, to make a long story short, we met, we liked each other, they agreed to let me stay there, *rent free*, until the house sold. There was only one condition. Oh, Oh, I thought, here it comes. They wondered if I would be willing to walk the trails on the six acres to keep the brush down and the trail clean. Oh, shoot, I really don't think I can do that, I laughingly said to myself. A few weeks later I moved in and had a beautiful, secluded, quiet place to live, rent free for the next six months, and only a half mile from my home.

Now that's magic.

And honestly, it was more than just finding a place to live. I felt like the universe was supporting me in my decision to leave my marriage. I remember writing in my journal, "I'll never doubt again." (Oh, if only that had been true.)

Another realization came from this experience. Magic is always available to us if our eyes are open and our hearts are receptive. We must just attune to that vibration of possibility, and wonder, and expectation, and be willing to act when we receive a nudge.

Of course, it's also important to make clear that we are surrendering to a Higher Will. If it's not for our higher good, do we really want it?

The other part of surrendering has to do with the right timing of things. We must let go of our idea of *how* something is going to manifest and *when* it will happen. We don't always know the larger picture that is involved so to trust that all is unfolding in perfect timing is so important, especially for our peace of mind.

One of the things I've noticed about asking for signs when I'm conflicted or indecisive is that if I pay attention to who I call to ask for feedback I get a clue as to my true feelings. It seems like subconsciously I know what one of my friends will say and so I automatically go to the person who is going to support a certain action. Then I see that what they say is really what I wanted to do, but I wasn't clear until I heard their perspective.

Lately I've had two cases where I have been given signs through a book I was reading or a file that I happened to open on my computer that had been there for a year and I had never looked at it. All of a sudden there was clarity and I could feel it in my body as I read.

The first case was involved a big decision I had to make about whether to help a friend out who was in need. My initial tendency is to always say yes, of course. But this was a large commitment and part of me said, no, I can't. But then I felt guilty and selfish. I was raised in a home where the doors and the arms were open to any stray that happened by. So, unable to decide, I just picked up a book I had been reading and came across a paragraph in which the author was talking about service and sacrifice. One line flashed forth in brilliant light as I read, "Does it exhaust you to even think about saying yes?' Oh yah, I thought, that's it. This act would not be coming from a place of fullness and abundance. It would be coming from a place of obligation and self-sacrifice. Clarity achieved. Thank you, Universe.

The second event had to do with a number I was doing on myself because I didn't yet feel completely back to normal after my injury last year. I started questioning whether I was just in a rut, stuck. Why wasn't I more motivated to get out there and do something? Then completely randomly, with no thought of my inner dilemma, I happened to open a document on my computer that had been sitting there since January. It was an astrological reading for this year and specifically for my rising sign, Capricorn. In it, I heard that I might be experiencing a "lull" in my activities, at this time of the year. That this was not a time to be "pushing" or "efforting" and that things would change within a few months.

My body immediately relaxed, and a feeling of deep gratitude emerged for this small little sign that relieved so much anxiety in my body.

Blessed be.

January 2018
Can it Really Be That Simple? The Magic of Asking

First the backstory:

I'm working on a new project. When completed I will have recorded twelve full moon ceremonies that could be used as an educational tool to learn about the planets and constellations, or it could be used as a way to hold a full moon ceremony without anyone leading it. Just put on the recording. I'm creating this with the help of the SoulBridging website that I write for each month. You can learn more about this project and how to purchase these recordings on my website, theoneheart.org.

I had just returned from a meeting in Portland with my friend, Therese, who is the executive director for SoulBridging. We brainstormed ideas and I came back to Seattle excited to get on with it.

A few days later, I awoke, knowing I had the whole day with no commitments, a rarity, for sure. My plan was to dig right in and begin working on the project, but I woke up lethargic and with a fuzzy brain (not a rarity, by the way). Then, the disappointment set in of the possibility of a wasted day with no progress.

I recognized this state of mind as it happened frequently to me as I was writing my book and creating my card deck. Some days I would wake filled with energy, vitality, and inspiration. The words would just flow with no effort. I would even dream about phrases I could use to describe something I was working on. Other days, I felt empty and dry and so I would postpone my writing until I felt more energetic or excited about it.

I knew I was dealing with some level of resistance, but the noticing didn't seem to make it go away. This back and forth between empty and full is one of the reasons it took me so long to finish my book, five years to be exact. I didn't want to get stuck on that seesaw again.

I realized that I had not yet meditated that morning when lethargy kicked in. The content of my meditation for some time had been the Angel of America meditation. It was my way of believing I could assist in the healing of our country. If you are curious about this meditation you can email me, and I will send you a copy of it. At any rate, this particular morning, for some reason, I was drawn to a meditation recorded by William Meader, my teacher. I hadn't heard this meditation for several months, so I was curious why I was drawn to it this day. It was called The Unfoldment. In it we ponder on some Soul quality that we wish we had more of in our lives. Qualities like compassion, forgiveness, inclusivity, understanding. Well, what popped into my mind was, "Divine inspiration."

What, I thought. *Is that even a Soul quality?* Nevertheless, I went with it.

William asked us to imagine what our thoughts would be if this quality was present in us. My thoughts were, "I can do this. It's not that hard. I know this material. I want to serve, and this is one way I can do that." Then he asked us to imagine how we would feel, if this quality were present. I immediately felt excited and energized. Finally, we were asked to imagine how this quality would work itself out in our daily lives, our physical reality. I saw myself sitting at the computer working diligently and consistently every day on my project. The final suggestion was to imagine the entire personality flooded by the light of the Soulful gift we had invoked.

When I finished the meditation, I noticed that my mind was alert and focused. My body felt energized. I got up, went to my computer and worked for several hours until the first ceremony was completely finished. I was totally inspired.

My first thought was, *Wait, what, is it really that easy? Fifteen minutes ago, I was tired and lethargic, now I'm all charged up.* Divine inspiration completely washed away my resistance. All I had to do was ask for what I needed and allow the energy in me to shift.

I've come to believe more and more strongly, in my "later years," that a co-creative relationship with the unseen realms is a significant part of our evolutionary journey. There is so much help available to us if we just ask. As we strengthen that connection we can work much more effectively and efficiently and with less strain.

Let me give you another example. When I first started doing full moon meditations I was so nervous and anxious. Partly because of performance anxiety but also, I was worried no one would show up and I was sure that would reflect badly on me. (Sidebar: Whenever it is about me, it is ego, not Soul.) Then I remembered, *My job is just to show up, do the best I can and leave the rest to Spirit. It's a partnership, after all, the Spirit's job is to make sure the people who need to be here are here and that they get what they need to receive.*

Whew!!! That was such a relief.

I truly believe that our angels, guides, teachers, and Beings of Light on the other side are there to help us when we need it. So, I ask myself again:

Is it really possible that it can all be this easy?

And I think the answer is yes, but we must ask for what we need and then be *willing* to receive. We must be willing to let go of our resistance and rest in our conviction that we are not alone on this journey.

Addendum:

An additional thought about the writing process. What I've come to realize, but don't always follow through on, is that if I commit to just sitting down each day and begin to write then I usually get into it. Even if I start out feeling uninspired. I think most writers would agree that if we always waited to be inspired it would take forever to get anything finished. This particular day I'm talking about I totally forgot that piece of wisdom and it was sweet to remember that help was there when I asked for it.

CHAPTER 18
SEX, ONLINE DATING, AND PARTNERSHIPS

There is only one entry included in this next chapter because I never wrote about sex on my blog. I realized, however, that this is still somewhat of a taboo subject, especially for elderly women of my generation. Since I am a Scorpio whose energy is related to all things sexual, how could I not write about it?

Be forewarned. I will be explicit. It is my story and to tell it honestly and fully, I need to start from the beginning, so the journey will cover many years. You always have the option, of course, to skip this chapter entirely if this is not of interest to you, but I hope you will override your concerns and continue on, as I'm sure the themes of this journey are common to many of us.

I will talk about my sexual history first, and how it affected my being in intimate relationships and how I related to sex as I aged.

Online dating was a unique experience for me, so I will share how that all came about in my late sixties.

In the blog portion of this chapter I discuss what partnership means to me at this point in my life and how I have made my peace with it.

I labeled my very first orgasm "Mt. Vesuvius" because it was like a volcano erupting within me, hot molten lava filling my cells with their fire. I was left trembling and spent. This was my Lady Chatterley moment. The earth did move.

I was forty-two years old.

But let's start at the beginning.

I was in love, at seventeen, with my future husband. In those days premarital sex was almost considered a sin, so we abstained until we were engaged, three years later. I was on fire with lust, but after several months I wondered what all the fuss was about. Never reaching orgasm, I was mostly left panting and frustrated.

We were both virgins and woefully uneducated about anything sexual. I didn't even know what a clitoris was, and neither did he. We fumbled around, never discovering that beautiful little spot and what it could bring.

In my mind I had this fantasy that once we were married it would be different. He wouldn't have to disengage before his climax to prevent a pregnancy. A few months before our wedding I began taking the pill, so I was convinced that once we could just take our time and not worry about a baby and everything would be okay.

My memory of our wedding night was that I left the bed after our lovemaking, went into the bathroom, and wept.

Things didn't improve for the next year and in desperation I talked to my mother about it. She referred me to the family doctor who told me that once we were finished with school (we were juniors in college) and had some time to relax everything would be okay. So, I waited. This was not a taboo subject between my husband and me. We talked endlessly about it, but neither of us had any idea what to do about it.

We graduated and took a trip to Europe, came home, taught for a year in Bellevue, and then moved to California where teachers made more money.

I decided to take action. Determined to find out how to deal with our "issue" I screwed up my courage and asked my new gynecologist, a male, if he could help me. It was humiliating and so difficult to bring it up, especially to a man. My memory of those years, when I went from doctor to doctor, trying to find answers is that most of them were embarrassed, didn't want to talk about it and never gave me any helpful advice.

I remember one doctor in particular who seemed genuinely interested. He asked me lots of questions about my sexual history. That was a first. Then I lied. I said everything was great. Immediately I was ashamed and horrified at myself. Here was a doctor that was finally paying attention and I was lying. So, I admitted I was lying and broke down in tears and told him my story. He was actually taking notes. Just as I was beginning to feel relaxed and open, he said, "Thank you for sharing this information with me. I am writing a book about this very subject and I'm glad to hear your story." And he ushered me out of the office.

The literature in the early 60s around sexuality was mostly geared toward the woman enticing the man. I remember reading one book where the advice to having great sex was to meet "your man" at the door, when he returned from work, scantily clad, with a martini in your hand. It was assumed, first of all that it would be the man returning from work, and secondly, that of course it was our job to make the effort to turn him on, not the other way around. Many of the books I read spoke of women not having orgasms as "frigid." That was the label they gave it. I began to think of myself that way. That there was something wrong with me, even though I didn't feel frigid. I felt passion and lust, I was just frustrated. But part of me felt like I wasn't a *real* woman.

We soon reached a dead end in our attempts to figure things out and decided that we would make the best of things and just get on with our lives, as unsatisfactory as that particular aspect was. We joked that maybe things would be better in our next lifetime. We both just sort of accepted that this was the way things would be and there was nothing more we could do about it. It was an uneasy alliance.

Sex became something I wanted to avoid since it was such a frustrating experience for me, so I slowly disengaged from any intimate act that might lead to sex. My husband, I'm sure, internalized that rejection and felt inadequate. My mindset in those days was that he was supposed to know what to do and why didn't he? He was supposed to give me orgasms so why didn't he? I began to feel angry and resentful, as unfair as that was. Making love became a no-win situation for both of us. If I acquiesced, I felt used; if I refused, I felt guilty. If he pursued me, he felt afraid of my rejection. If he persisted and I gave in he felt ashamed and inadequate.

I remember deciding, in desperation, that I would try one more thing. Maybe if we decided ahead of time that we would have sex on Wednesdays and Fridays and no other time, that I would relax and just enjoy our connection those other days. And on the days we agreed to have sex I would try to get myself in a romantic mood, so I could enjoy it. All that happened was that I began to dread Wednesdays and Fridays.

It was during this time that all hell was breaking loose around "open marriages" and sexual freedom. We both took a detour and got involved with another couple who were our best friends. I remember specifically thinking, *This guy will know how to give me an orgasm,* because we all thought that they were the perfect couple. They always acted so sexual around each other. It didn't work. I still didn't have orgasms. I felt an even deeper sense of shame as I realized it really must be my fault. At least I wasn't blaming my husband any longer, but it increased my feelings of inadequacy.

As an interesting sidebar, I am still friends with the woman, they ended up divorced, and years later she told me he was a terrible lover. It was all a show. Unfortunately, her husband ended up falling in love with me and he would talk endlessly about his fantasy of being married and having a family with me. I knew I wasn't in love with him and had no plans to divorce my husband, but when he talked about his joy in anticipating having children my own longing came forward. I recognized that I shared that excitement, although not with him. The affairs only lasted a few months but after it was over I had a conversation with my husband and shared with him my feelings about wanting a family.

It was 1973. We had now been married for eleven years and we were in our early thirties. Masters and Johnson had just published their seminal work on human sexual behavior, and I was so excited to see that there was a couple in our area who were doing this type of counseling. At the same time, I went off the pill, as we decided to try for a baby. We went to the counselors and I remember feeling such a sense of relief to finally unload all of my concerns and frustrations onto people who were willing to listen and who I hoped had information that would help us. I was motivated by the thought that I really wanted to get this issue resolved before we had children as I knew that once a child came there would not be a whole lot of energy around sex, at least for a while.

This was the first time I was introduced to the idea of masturbation as a way to have an orgasm. Don't laugh, it's true. That's how naïve I was. I had never masturbated in my life, so this was totally new to me, but at least I learned I had a clitoris and what it was there for.

I faithfully did my homework. Masturbate several times a week and see what happens. Well, I tried, very hard. My hand would give out before any release would come and I would give up in frustration. Then a few months later I was pregnant. Our counselors ended our sessions saying we had tricked them. That we only came to therapy to get pregnant. This was so not true, and we left feeling abandoned and once again, helpless.

Fast forward ten years. My husband was drinking too much and in one conversation we had about this we made a deal. He'd go to AA if I go back to therapy to see if I can get any more help around the sexual issue.

I began with another therapist. One on one, just she and me. I immediately felt at ease with her. She was down to earth, warm hearted and a great listener. She began to educate me about women's sexuality. Part of my homework was to go home, take a mirror and just examine my genitals. Find out what they looked like and then stimulate them to see where my sensitive spots were. I learned about the sexual response cycle and she told me she thought my body had just learned to respond in a certain way because of all the years of no release. She also gave me masturbation homework, but she offered the insight that I needed to slowly work myself up to really wanting sexual release. She asked if there anything that I knew aroused me sexually. I admitted that I liked to read Penthouse magazine where people would write in their stories of their sexual experiences. So that became part of my homework, to buy Penthouse magazine. I remember being so embarrassed to go to the store and ask for that magazine, but I did.

She also suggested I set the scene. What made me feel romantic and turned on. Well, candles, soft music, maybe a fragrance wafting through the room. So, three times a week I would get my husband off to work, get the kids off to school, close and lock my bedroom door and go at it. Naked on my bed. It was a bit intimidating, but I stuck with it. After a few weeks I had made no progress. She suggested a vibrator. Wow, I remembered that several years back I had bought one, thinking that might help. Interestingly, even though we had moved since then, I knew right where that vibrator was. I got it out and began using it, but it was small and was only used to insert itself into my vagina. It didn't touch the clitoris. My therapist gave me a different type and showed me how to use it.

She also, suggested I talk to my mom about her sexual history and see what I could learn from her. So, I did. I am forever grateful to my mother who shared so openly with me, without hesitation. She admitted to me that she had never had a problem having orgasms. When I asked her if she enjoyed oral sex, she looked at me and said, "What's that?" When I explained to her she looked horrified and said, "No, I would never do that." I said to her, "Do you realize how unusual that is? To be so orgasmic without ever having your clitoris stimulated?" Of course, I don't know what positions they were using, but I can only imagine that it must have been "missionary style." So perhaps some clitoral stimulation that way, but still, I was impressed.

That day I went home from our conversation and began my homework. Using the new vibrator this time I reached that same peak that I always did, only this time, at the moment I was there, I distinctly heard my mother's voice say, "KAREN, GO FOR IT." And my Mt. Vesuvius moment arrived.

I remember clearly reaching for my journal and writing, "I just had my first orgasm, but I'm sure I'll never have another one."

And my obsessive period began. Convinced I could never duplicate Vesuvius, I began taking every spare moment I could to masturbate. Climbing out of bed in the middle of the night, grabbing my vibrator and a blanket, and going to sit in front of the gas fireplace, I'd have my little fix. Ten or fifteen minutes before the household came home, I would be in my room having fun. Then I began slipping into my room while everyone was home, locking the door and just getting off. I had to convince myself I could have an orgasm, anytime, anywhere.

At one practice session I was buck naked on the bed going at it when my young son walked in on me. Evidently that lock wasn't as strong as I had thought. He looked at me and said, "What are you doing?" As I very casually covered myself up, he asked, "What is that in your hand?" Calming myself down a bit I said, "Well this is a vibrator and Mommy uses it when her muscles are sore, and she wants to relax. Do you want to try it?" He played with it for a few minutes and then got bored and walked off. I was grateful that I had the presence of mind to not scream and tell him to get out of my room.

Another time, I came out of my room after a "practice session" to find my children had put out a plate with bread and milk right outside the door. I asked them what this was for, and they said I was in there so long they decided I was in jail and they thought they would bring me some food. Out of the mouths of babes.

I finally convinced myself I could have an orgasm anytime I wanted, and it was so empowering to finally take responsibility for my own sexual pleasure. I could give myself the satisfaction I desired. As I began to know my own body in a different way, I was more vocal with my husband about what I wanted. He was finally off the hook.

As I grew more confident my therapist suggested I show my husband how I masturbated. What???? Really???? That felt very scary. Masturbating while someone watched? But I did it and he was very impressed. We began to have a more normal and fulfilling sex life, one in which both of us came away satisfied and feeling that close connection that comes with pleasurable intimacy. He even commented one night as I was hot to trot, "I don't think I'm going to be able to keep up with you." Talk about a shift!!!

I began to notice a difference in him. He became softer and more accommodating. I realized what it had cost us, to be without this closeness for so many years, and I regretted all the lost opportunities to create a stronger connection. But I believe the body has its own timing, and this would prove to be very true in the next few years.

Meanwhile, my therapist suggested I come and share my story with her graduate students studying female sexuality. I will be forever grateful for this wonderful woman who knew just when to invite me out of my comfort zone into my next step. I began speaking every semester that she taught the class. Soon I was speaking at her workshops and even appeared on her television show. I was always adamant that my sexual issues were not a result of being molested or abused, it was just a lack of education and knowledge about my body. I believed that with my whole heart at the time.

Then, one day, the local TV station here in Seattle called and asked if I would be on their afternoon program. By this time it felt like second nature to be talking about orgasms and sex toys and sexuality in general, so I agreed. I found that I enjoyed sharing my story and public speaking, so that was another side benefit.

Meanwhile, back on the home front, I can't remember if it was several months or a few years that this sexual honeymoon with my husband went on, but somewhere during that time, I had a car accident. I was in my mid-forties. Nothing too serious but my doctor prescribed massage and chiropractic care for me.

One day, lying prone on the massage table, completely relaxed and blissed out, the therapist began massaging my right buttock. Suddenly my fists clenched, and I began screaming, loudly, and swearing, "You Goddamn son of a bitch, NO, NO, NO!" I remember being concerned that the people in the next room would call 911, but I couldn't stop myself. After I was spent, the therapist gently asked me to turn over onto my back. The minute I did I saw an image of my grandfather reaching down into my crib and molesting me. I remember the therapist gently processing what she could with me. Another gratitude moment for her gentle presence and for not being afraid of what just happened.

Suddenly so much became clear to me: the memory that I had always carried with me of taking a nap in my bedroom when I was four or five and waking up to realize my grandfather had is hand up my dress, very close to my genitals. It's the only specific memory I had. I did tell my mom, and as I recall she just told me to never be in the same room with him again. I had permission to protect myself, but nothing else was said or done.

Later, my mom told me she had no memory of this conversation. In my own mind I had never connected that incident to being sexually molested, not until the massage. My grandfather did come to me as he was preparing to die and before the revealing massage. He asked me if I remembered what he did to me when I was a little girl. I said, "Yes," thinking he was referring to the incident in my bedroom. He asked me if it had in any way affected my marriage. I reassured him it had not. He then told me that I wasn't the only one. That he had done that to a little girl who was one of my playmates, and he named her. I still didn't connect the dots. He wanted to know if I thought God would forgive him. I didn't even believe in a God at that time, so I told him the only thing I could think of, that if the God he believed in was real then I'm sure he would be forgiven. He did believe in a God of love, after all.

After the revealing massage I suddenly understood why I had had so many sexual difficulties all those years. It wasn't *just* a lack of education or experience. My belief is that my body held onto those traumatic memories and they settled around my pelvic area. That area became frozen and stuck because there was no energy flowing there. No release would be possible until I could inject some energy there. So, those few years or months, as I learned to have orgasms, got the energy flowing again and allowed my body to inform me of what had happened.

I don't think it was an accident how any of it happened. My body also knew, on some level, that I was ready to deal with this issue where perhaps I wouldn't have been any sooner.

The downside of all this remembering was that my body shut down again. Suddenly I couldn't face making love to my husband. I don't remember if I continued masturbating or not, but I know I couldn't tolerate the thought of intimacy. This was a crushing blow to both of us, but I was beyond the point where I could go against the wisdom of my body. My husband was patient and tolerant, but I know it ate away at him. Not just the loss of intimacy, but his anger at my dead grandfather.

It was difficult for me to give my experience legitimacy, even with all the evidence. I felt like I should be able to remember specific times, and places, that I should have a clear memory of those events, but I didn't. I decided to try to track down my little friend from so many years ago that my grandfather had named. It took some time, but I finally reached her by phone. When she picked up the phone I identified myself and asked her if she was alone. She went to a room to be by herself and I told her my story. I asked her if it was true what my grandfather had admitted to me. She broke down in tears and said she had never told anyone about what happened. She then revealed her memories to me. She did have recall about specific incidents. My heart went out to her for what she had suffered, especially in silence. I could no longer doubt the truth.

The first thing I did was inform my siblings and parents. My siblings then talked to their children, and one niece came forward with the story of her molestation by my grandfather. She had held it inside of herself for all those years and never told anyone.

My parents processed it in their own way. My mom didn't believe me, maybe because it was her dad. My dad said, "Well he's dead now so what difference does it make?" I said to him, "Aren't you even angry? If someone had done that to my child I would be furious." But remember this is the man who never got angry. His response was, "Well, if you want me to be angry I will." I could feel in his response his desire to support me, but not knowing how to do that. He wanted to help. He just didn't believe anger would be helpful. I never questioned his pain at hearing the news.

My mom eventually came around. I understood her dilemma. What if you grew up your whole life with an image of your beloved dad and then your daughter tells you he's a pedophile. How do you choose between those two stories? How do you make your peace with that? But finally, she did, and together we healed the wound between us before she died. I know she felt tremendous guilt that she hadn't protected me and that it was her dad that was the abuser.

During this time, I was working on my own healing. It took many years, but I started by working with a process that had been taught to me by my beloved teacher, Laura Fraser, who I mentioned earlier in this book. She trained several of us in a process she called Journey Work. We would sit with a partner, center ourselves, and align with our Soul. Then we would ask that whatever was in need of healing would come to us. For two years I sat with my partners every week and invoked the Soul's guidance for my healing. It was during those sessions that the rest of the body's memories expressed themselves. I would find myself uncontrollably gagging or feeling intense pain all through my pelvic area. This would come on out of the blue, from a totally relaxed state. One time, my sister, who was guiding me through this process, exclaimed, "Oh, Karen, I see this black gooey stuff like tar just pouring out of your genitals." We were working in an altered state of consciousness, so these sensations became easily accessible.

I never did recall specific incidents, but all of these revelations made it hard for me to discount the truth of the abuse. I would get numerous bladder irritations, run to the doctor, but no infections. One day, walking around Green Lake I began to have these feelings in my bladder. Irritation and pain. I didn't think I could make it around the rest of the lake, so I sat down on a bench and I talked to my body. I said, *Okay, listen, I know you are telling me that I have work to do and I do have a session tomorrow at 10:00am, so I promise you I will deal with you at that time. But I need to get around the lake now to my car.* All sensations disappeared. I made it easily to my car. But the other amazing thing was that at a few minutes before 10:00am the next day the pain came back. It was if my body was telling me to be sure and not forget our appointment. We did the session and the pain went away.

For many of those months, every time I would think of my grandfather I would be filled with rage and hatred. I can't remember how many pillows I attacked with a tennis racket to work out that anger. But one day, toward the end of our second year, I saw a vivid image of him in my mind. I immediately connected to the old rage, and with a vengeance I began walking toward him. With no mercy or compassion I began to peel the skin off of him, like peeling a banana. He was screaming in agony and I didn't care. Then I took a really good look at him and I saw a small little flicker of light in his heart. A small candle burning. A wave of understanding hit me. Even this sick, sick man had a light in him. Seeing him as a Being of Light, no matter how dim, I could begin to heal my pain. It took many more years before I could think of him without revulsion, but the hatred and anger lessened.

Unfortunately, by the time my body and my memories were healed enough to resume intimacy with my husband, I found I no longer trusted him. I didn't know why but he just didn't feel safe to me.

Many years before, we had come to a crisis involving his drinking and I had given him an ultimatum. Either quit or we're done. He promised to quit, and for fifteen years I never saw him take another drink. Then one night the kids and I went out to dinner and saw him at the bar with a drink. He finally admitted that he had been drinking all along, but never in my presence. No wonder my body hadn't trusted him. On some level I think I knew I was being betrayed.

We divorced shortly after that. It was 1996 and we had been married for thirty-three years.

I'm sharing all of this for several reasons. First of all, I believe that my story is not unique. Many women have suffered sexual abuse. Many women have difficulty reaching orgasm. Many women end up getting divorced in their fifties, sixties, or seventies. So perhaps my story can give them some degree of permission to commit to their own healing.

Also, I think it's true that many of us have had a hard time valuing ourselves enough to know that we deserve pleasure, whether with a partner or alone. It empowers us when we speak up and ask for what we need, but first we must believe we deserve it.

Secondly, we need to know our bodies well enough to know what to ask for or what to do. Pleasuring ourselves will give us this information. I understand the taboo this is for many of us, especially of my generation. I'm reminded of the joke about the young boy who is in the confessional stall and he confesses to his habit of masturbating. The priest says in no uncertain terms that masturbation will lead to blindness. The young boy responds, "But Father, can't I just keep doing it until I need glasses?"

We are never too old to learn how to use our voices, to courageously take our sexual pleasure into our own hands, and to enjoy our bodies. Even as a seventy-six-year-old single woman I have my vibrator right next to my pillow in my bed, always handy. Let's not deprive ourselves of one of our body's greatest offerings.

A great resource for women who wish to understand more about female sexuality and self-pleasuring is the website of the American Sex Educator goddess, Betty Dodson, www.dodsonandross.com.

I need to acknowledge that all of this sexual history absolutely influenced my later connections to other men and my sexuality as I aged.

After the divorce I swore that was it for me. "Been there, done that. Don't need to do it again," was my motto. I liked living alone and reveled in my freedom. But fate had other ideas and I ended up in two significant relationships in my sixties and early seventies.

I met the first man in a co-ed drumming circle I belonged to. We were friends for a few years before we got together. Looking back on it now, I realize that the draw for me was that he was trustworthy and kind. We were on the same wavelength spiritually, as well.

My husband had been fairly emotionally abusive the last several years of our marriage and often was critical and disparaging of my search for a spiritual path that was mine. I think because he was drinking, when he came home or spent a weekend with us, he was in withdrawals.

This new man was gentle and kind and loving. As I opened my heart in a new way, to someone I truly trusted, and who appreciated me and treated me with respect, I began to enjoy sex again. And I realized that when I felt safe, I could become quite the seductress. I began to see myself differently, as a sexual woman, full and complete, with a loving and responsive partner. There were still moments, however, if I was taken by surprise by his desire for lovemaking, that I would have to remind myself that sex was really fun.

I will say that I never broke the habit of the vibrator. I tell you, there is nothing like an orgasm with a vibrator, sorry guys. I occasionally had orgasms without it, but why bother when it was so easy to just grab it and two minutes later, ka... bam. So, we would make love and give all the pleasuring we could to one another then out would come the vibrator and I would have my Mt. Vesuvius moment. I was always grateful that he accepted this about our lovemaking with no hesitation or feelings of disappointment because, "he hadn't given me an orgasm." I know this was not true of all men.

That partnership lasted about nine years. At some point it felt like the relationship had served its purpose, for me. I realized I could love again. I knew, more clearly, what was important to me in a relationship and what I would and would not settle for. I was stronger in myself and I credit this relationship for a lot of the healing that took place within it.

I stayed single and alone for the next several years, but I began to long for the type of relationship I knew was possible. I read several books on conscious loving, co-creative partnerships, and spiritual soulmates.

Once, within a period of a few weeks, several of my friends suggested dating online. This was a sobering proposition for someone in their late sixties who hadn't dated since they were seventeen. I wasn't sure I even knew how to engage again on that level. The flirting, the courting, starting from scratch with someone. It all seemed like too much. It happened so organically with my other partner that I didn't know how to go about this new way of meeting men. But I went on the website and looked around. I saw one man who really intrigued me, and I began to consider the possibility of joining up.

Then one night I awoke from a dream with my entire profile written out in my head. I knew exactly how I would describe myself and how I would phrase what I was looking for. I got up immediately and went to my computer, wrote it down, edited it a bit over the next few days and joined up. It felt like I had gotten the nudge from the universe. Here is the first profile I submitted.

Okay, so let's get the big stuff out of the way first. It's true, I am in the last third of my life, but only if you are counting in a linear manner. Inwardly I still feel like I'm twenty-five. I am physically fit and energetic, emotionally stable, mentally engaged and spiritually alive. I'm even financially secure. (Imagine that!) My life is filled with everything that I love: great adult children and spouses, meaningful work, wonderful friendships, community, and stimulating studies. I'm not expecting you to fill me up in any way. I already feel full, but could we come together with the expectation that we share the fullness that we each bring to the relationship, rather than with the idea that the relationship will fix our brokenness? I would love to share my fullness with someone who is also passionate about their life. My style is to take things slowly, build a solid friendship and then see how things evolve. I'm old enough to realize that we must really like each other if we are ever to really love each other. Lighthearted, fun loving, laughter, sharing quiet moments, good conversation... does this resonate with you? Are you gentle, but strong in yourself? Are you a person of integrity and compassion? Do you live a congruent life, i.e. does your external life reflect your true values and deeply held beliefs? Do you love to discuss ideas, philosophy, politics? ...Okay, maybe we'll skip that unless you checked 'very liberal' under that category. Do you have a meaningful spiritual life that is inclusive and informs your everyday life? Are you open to new ideas? Do you embrace diversity? I feel like I'm asking for the moon here, but it has just recently come to my attention that the moon is available. Are you ready to go for it?

A favorite quote from Rainer Maria Rilke: 'For one human being to love another: that is perhaps the most difficult task of all, the work for which all other work is but preparation. It is a high inducement to the individual to ripen, a great exacting claim upon us, something that chooses us out and calls us to vast things.' Are you ready to ripen?

I got a lot of responses and dated this way for a few years. It was actually a lot of fun. I met a lot of nice men and enjoyed their company. The fact that most of them were more interested in me than I was in them was a great boon to my confidence.

I made it clear that I was "exploring the possibility" of a relationship, still not at all sure I was interested in a long-term commitment. I figured that joining up online was sort of my way of alerting the universe that I was willing to give it a try.

I became sexual with two of these men. With the first one I surprised myself by agreeing to a "friends with benefits" arrangement. I knew he was not someone I wanted to spend my life with and he knew the same thing, but we enjoyed one another's company and the sex was okay, mostly with the help of my vibrator.

I couldn't believe myself. Experimenting, with no commitment, no love. Was that really okay? I asked my women friends for perspective and they all agreed that especially since I had never had much chance to explore "casual sex" that maybe I needed to feel that freedom. Pleasure with no responsibility. Fun with no commitment. It was immensely freeing. There were no worries about where this would lead, what did this behavior mean? No analyzing, trying to figure it all out, looking for possible red flags.

I realized that I was programmed to feel responsible, burdened and heavy with relationships, mainly because I thought it was my job to make sure we all got along. This level of freedom felt amazing.

The second man wanted more of a commitment than I was willing to make, and I ended it after a few months. The sex with him was okay, also, but I remember writing in my journal. *Just once, before I die, I'd like to have really, really good sex with someone.*

After a few years of dating online I decided to take a break. As exciting and fun as it was, I was sort of burned out with it. Plus, I had now moved into my seventies, and once that age comes up in your profile you don't get nearly as many responses. Very few men sign up for women in their seventies. So, it felt like a good time to give it a rest.

Once again, the universe had different plans. It happened that the state set new requirements for licensing counselors and psychotherapists and I needed to take a test to receive the new license. There was a class that I had to take to prepare for the test. I walked in and took one of the seats up front because I wanted to pay attention and happened to sit next to this really cute guy. During the course of the day we chatted, had lunch and before the day was over, he invited me to go to this restaurant where a band he liked was playing.

There are two funny stories that go along with this encounter. My adult daughter was staying with me for a few months while she looked for a place to live. I called her to let her know I would not be home for dinner and that I was going out with this guy. She immediately became my parent. "Now mom, make sure you take your own car. You don't know this guy from Adam. Don't walk out to the parking lot alone. Don't give him any personal information." On and on she went. I laughed, seeing the role reversal, but appreciating that she was concerned for my safety.

I did take my own car, but after the concert in which we had danced and had a great time, he walked me out to my car. We started kissing and making out, as we old folks call it. I was lit up. Whew, what a kisser. I was still so shocked at how easily I got aroused. Anyway, it got late, and I finally headed home, after we exchanged phone numbers. (Sorry, kiddo.)

On the drive home I got a call on my cell phone. It was 12:30am. "MOM, WHERE ARE YOU? ARE YOU OKAY?" I reassured her I was fine and that I was headed home. When I got there, she told me she had called her brother and said, "Mom's out with a new guy and she hasn't gotten home. What should we do?" My son said, "Let's give her another half hour and if she isn't home by then, call me right back." I was in hysterics, laughing so hard. HA!!! Finally, the tables were turned, and they knew just what it was like to be the parents of teenagers.

Just a little diversion there for your amusement.

Anyway, the man and I went on to have a relationship for the next two years (2011-2013). And I thanked the universe for giving me my wish for really, really good sex. This man treated my body like a temple. There wasn't any part of it that he didn't love. We spent many hours blissed out together. He was only too happy that I could use my vibrator and take care of myself if I needed to. We sometimes even shared it. I reveled in the joy I felt in my body and the confidence that this brought me.

After two years, the psychological issues emerged that we had basically ignored, the ones that you really need to work out if you are to go ahead into a permanent relationship. These turned out to be deep uncrossable barriers for us and the relationship ended. We had seen each other through two years of dealing with our aging parents- the death of my father, and putting his mom in an adult home. I will always be grateful to him for his support and participation in the care of my dad, and for helping me to love my body in a deeper way. The confidence I felt in myself as a beautiful sexual woman was greatly strengthened.

After this breakup I needed time to gather and regroup and decide what I really wanted. The year was 2013.

Here's a brief summary of the years from 2012-2018 just so you get a feel for the sequence of the next several years.

My son and daughter each blessed me with a grandchild. (2012, 2013, Chapter 7)

After the last breakup, my first priority was to complete my book and card deck, called *Full Moon Magic*. (2013, Chapter 1)

I fell and fractured my shoulder in two places. (2015, Chapter 11)

After recovering I began compiling my blogs to make this book. (2018)

The next entry will describe to you where I currently am in the relationship arena. Some of the information is a repeat, but it will bring you up to date.

May 2018
Single on Purpose

This entry originally appeared on lorian.org.

How did I get to this place, from being in committed relationships most of my adult life to contentedly single? Over the past seventy-six years, one of my life lessons has been learning to trust my inner knowing and feel deeply rooted within myself. Nowhere has this lesson been more pronounced than in my significant relationships.

After ending my thirty-three-year-ling marriage in 1996, my *mantram* became, "Been there, done that. Don't care to do it again." Then fate, destiny, and karma intervened, and over the next several years I explored two other serious relationships that both ended at my request.

All of these partnerships taught me valuable lessons and I honor them for the insights I gained. I learned a lot about my own unhealthy patterns. For example, I recognized how deeply I had sunk into codependency and the belief that it was up to me to fix whatever might be wrong. Trying so hard to hold it all together, I hadn't realized yet that my only responsibility was to fix myself. I didn't need to take on my partner's issues. I also saw that I hadn't been very strong about asking for what I needed. After many years it was hard to really know what it was that I needed, so attuned was I to what the other person wanted.

So, I took some time getting to know myself. And I resolved that I would not succumb to those old habitual responses again. Yet at that time, I still longed for a healthy relationship, and for a few years I dated several men. While it helped to strengthen my confidence in myself, I didn't find the partner I was looking for and in 2013 I decided to give it a break.

During these last five years I have concentrated on my spiritual and psychological growth-- just taking care of me. This change in focus also led to a shift in the way I related to my adult children and some of my friends as I tried to rein in my overprotective tendencies and be clearer and more direct in expressing my needs. Additionally, I became more committed to my meditation practice and full moon ceremonies, and I also started a women's group focused on aging as a spiritual practice.

Even with more outward activity, I could feel my energy going inward. I was getting clearer about my focus. But despite all the work I had done I still didn't trust myself completely. A space had been created for me to delve more deeply and consciously into my own life, yet I started questioning whether this was truly an organic inward cycle or if I somehow stuck in inertia.

Last year, in the middle of an insomniac night I succumbed to the lure of Match.com. I had tried Match.com off and on since 2010 but ended my membership after deciding to give dating in general a break. Perhaps it was a moment of loneliness or boredom. Perhaps it was sleep deprivation, but for whatever reason that night I impulsively renewed my membership.

This time I didn't feel the same excitement about it as I had previously, but I decided to give it another try anyway. As emails came in, I realized I felt no draw, no interest in pursuing any of the responses. But I still didn't really trust what I was feeling, so I dated one man twice. I quickly realized I didn't want to pursue anything with him.

Then another man called me, out of the blue, because he had read one of my blogs. We had a few phone conversations and I saw that he was a person of integrity; but I recognized, again, that my heart wasn't really in it.

I think sometimes the universe sends us these signs to either open us up to new possibilities or to help us get clear about the steps we are being asked to take.

After these experiences I got crystal clear. I didn't want to date. I wasn't interested in a committed relationship. My body was telling me no. And I finally decided to trust what I was hearing.

I love my life. I feel fulfilled, congruent, authentic and filled up-- satisfied in every way that is important to me. I want the focus of the rest of my life to be upon deepening, strengthening, and opening more fully to a partnership with my Soul.

Of course, I know it is possible to be committed to your Soul's journey *and* be in a healthy relationship, but I have learned that for now at least, that is not my path. Coming to this level of trust in my inner knowing and the wisdom of my body has helped me to live with considerably more ease in my everyday life. There is a one-pointed focus and a clarity about my life's direction that allows me to see my singleness as a gift.

A few days after writing this I took a quiz from an astrologer's website about what kind of spring goddess I am, this is what I got:

You hold the energy of the ancient and magical Welsh Goddess Blodewedd, created by the great magicians Math and Gwydion.

They formed her from the blossom of nine different trees and plants – oak, meadowsweet, broom, cockle, bean, nettle, chestnut, primrose and hawthorn and breathed her into life.

Her story goes that she was unfaithful to her chosen mate (the mortal she was created for) and was punished by being turned into an Owl.

But in fact, She was a deity who **went her own way, trusting her own instincts about the path her life was meant to take.**

Her rebellion became her self-realization.

Today, Blodewedd symbolizes the **blossoming and expansion that occurs when we practice self-trust and stay true to our purpose.**

Honour Blodewedd by adorning yourself and your living space with flowers.

Find a picture of an owl and put it up. Reflect on the lessons that this magical bird can offer you.

—From numerologist.com/numerology/can-we-guess-which-unusual-spring-goddess-you-are

Update, June 2018:

Since writing that last blog I have had my horoscope read by two people I trust. Both of them said that this is a year when I need to focus on promoting my work in the world. Jupiter sits right next to my sun, which sits right on my career point on the tenth house.

It was such great confirmation that my decision to stay inwardly focused was right. This book has been sitting in my brain for the last couple of years, and with the intuitive understanding I received, plus the astrological readings, I knew that was the reason why this was not a time for relationships. It would be a distraction from what I need to do right now. So, the final piece of the puzzle is in place and I am committed and determined to finish this book as soon as possible.

It's been an interesting experience. Much different from writing my last book. Partly because I feel such a deep commitment that there is not much resistance. My critical voice is not nearly as pronounced. Also, it feels stimulating to write from my own experience, in my own voice rather than just presenting material for someone else to study. I know my first book was a help to many people, so I don't begrudge for a minute, having written it. But it was a much more difficult book to write than this one has been.

I'm also in a much different place. I'm taking it one step at a time, focusing on just this part, the writing. Not getting distracted with thoughts of, "Who's going to publish it," or "How will I market it" Maybe my faith has grown and I'm willing to let that unfold however it needs to.

I like the rhythm of my days with this dedicated focus. Get up, have my tea outside, feet on the ground. Meditate. Pray. Then begin writing. After that, however long I sit, get up and take a walk. Slow, peaceful, dedicated, silent.

I am content.

CHAPTER 19
AGING AND DYING

"Getting old isn't for sissies," the old saying goes. And it's true. It does take courage to age gracefully. I think we have to practice and hold that strong intention.

My practice started when I fractured my shoulder in 2015, at age seventy-three. For the first time in my life I had to rely on other people to help me with the most mundane things, like getting out of a chair. I remember how humbling it felt, to not be able to do for myself. As I contemplated my situation however, I realized I could use this as an opportunity to practice aging gracefully. I wouldn't complain and carry on. I would accept what was. I would "incline my mind toward joy" as the book *Awakening Joy* reminds us. It does take an act of will to look for the light when it feels dark.

Facing our own mortality is a courageous act. It helps if we have a belief system that gives us comfort about an afterlife, but even with that we worry about *how* we are going to die. I remember asking my dad one time when he was in his last year of life, "Dad, do feel ready to go?"

"Go where?" he replied.

"You know," and I pointed up toward the sky.

"Well, like they say, I not afraid of dying, I just don't want to be around when it happens."

So, yes, I feel some trepidation about how it will all play out for me, but when I start getting into a fear about that, I remember my Scorpionic experience of earthquake fears and that the fear subsided as I took control of what I *could* do.

Several years ago, my daughter returned from a month-long meditation retreat in Thailand. She told me that for part of that time they meditated on their own death. A few weeks later we were spending the day together and she suggested we write about our death. How we saw it playing out, any fears or apprehensions we had, or any insights. Then we shared them with one another.

I tuned into myself and really pondered how I wanted to die. I wrote about the ideal situation, at home, who I wanted to be present, the atmosphere I desired, candles, soft music, sandalwood incense, quiet voices, subdued lighting. I just wrote it all out. I realize none of it might be possible, but if it is, at least my children will know my wishes.

My daughter then suggested I keep a death file and add to it as thoughts or wishes came to me. So, I did that. After I read the book *On Being Mortal*, I called both my adult children. We met and had a lengthy conversation about how I saw the end of my life unfolding and how I wished it could be. I shared everything I had become aware of, and I promised to take care of as many of the details as I could, that were in my control. I told them it was more important to me to have a certain quality of life, than it was to just focus on keeping me safe. Of course, none of this may be in our control but just in case, I wanted them to know what I hoped for.

After that conversation I got busy. I organized all the financial information I had into a file. All the insurance data, the bank accounts with numbers and PINs. All my passwords for my computer. Everything I thought they might need to make things go more smoothly. Suze Orman's Blue Box was helpful for this. I wrote out my obituary and a possible memorial service, but only if *they wanted it.* I wasn't going to care.

So, these were things I could control. I wanted to set it up as best I could to make it easier on them when the time came. We all agreed we would need to re-visit this conversation, maybe many times, as the years went by and things changed.

I felt a huge relief, just accomplishing that much, and I'm sure it eased some of their anxiety as well.

In these last few entries you will read a bit more about my dying "ruminations."

June 2017
What's So Funny About Getting Older?

A year or so ago I realized that I want to grow older with a group of women. Maybe it was around the time of my fall when I fractured two bones in my shoulder and was dependent, for a time, on others for my care. What I noticed is that it was *mostly* the women who came to my aid, not exclusively but predominantly. That wasn't a big revelation to me, but I had never been more grateful for my tribe.

Shortly after that I read two books that have to do with examining the way we age and the quality of life that we wish to have as we get older: *Being Mortal*, by Atul Gawande and *When Breath Becomes Air*, by Paul Kalanithi. (More about them in a later blog.)

I began to ponder this question of how I wanted to age. What quality of life was important to me? I realized that I really wanted to have the support and understanding of my women friends as we traveled through these last years. Could we help each other grow old with some degree of grace, as well as drive each other to the doctor's appointments when we fall or get sick?

I decided to start my own group. I chose six women who I knew were all on a spiritual path; that was an important consideration to me. They ranged in age from sixty, to senventy-eight, and most of us are single. We decided to start with a book, called *Aging as_a Spiritual Practice*, by Lewis Richmond. We meet once a month, have a brief ceremony, share what is going on with us and talk a bit about the book. We decided that laughter was important to us as well as movement, so each month we share something that has made us laugh. Dancing is also a part of our time together as well as singing. It is such fun.

Going through my notes today in preparation for our next meeting I came across all of the jokes I have collected and shared during this past year and got tickled all over again. You know, the good thing about not having such a great memory is that you can enjoy the same things countless times. So here are some of the funnier ones.

"Old age is coming at a really bad time."

"I laughed so hard tears ran down my leg."

"I'm so old I remember when water was free, and you had to pay for porn."

"I'm so old I can remember going through a whole day without taking a picture of anything."

"As I've grown older, I've learned that pleasing everyone is impossible but pissing everyone off is a piece of cake."

"The idea is to die young... as late as possible."

Charlie Brown and Snoopy are having a conversation. Charlie Brown says, "Someday we will all die, Snoopy."

Snoopy replies, "True, but on all the other days we will not."

"I don't think outside the box. I don't think inside the box. I don't even know where the damn box is."

"Getting lucky means walking into a room and remembering why I'm there."

"I'm at that delusional age where I think everyone looks wayyyy older than I do."

"A group of your neighbors wish to announce that the 'one way' frosty glass in your bathroom is facing the wrong way."

"Exhaustipated means I'm too tired to give a shit."

And finally,

I no longer ask myself, "What do I want to let go of, and what do I want to hang onto?" Instead I ask, "What do I want to let go of and what do I want to give myself to."

—Parker M. Palmer

November 2015
On Turning Seventy-Four

I'm one of those people who has never paid much attention to my age. In the past, I would have to stop and think about how old I was when someone asked. My birthdays came and went without much fanfare, until I hit sixty. Something about this milestone felt really big.

Not being one to make a big deal about parties, I was surprised when one day as I was walking in the woods an entire ceremony played itself out in my imagination. I could see all the components of a big celebration. It was a bit stunning since I hadn't really thought of sixty as a time to celebrate. In any event, I went with it.

I invited all of my family, my drumming circle, and a few close friends. We drummed and sang and in spite of the incredulous looks of my eighty-nine-year-old father we carried on.

I asked each person who wanted to, to come to where I was sitting and cut off a lock of my hair. As they did this they were to share a memory they had of me. When everyone was finished, my daughter-in-law proceeded to give me a buzz cut. I had decided I needed to shed an old identity and this seemed symbolically meaningful. I have to say it felt totally liberating to not even have to think about hair. I also changed my married name to the original Danish name of my grandparents. I had consulted with a numerologist who helped me with the exact spelling that would call in the energy I most wanted to embody, spontaneity, joy, and freedom.

After the cutting and the drumming, I stood up proudly and said, "my friends and family may I present to you Karen Sophia Johannsen"

It was a big moment for me, claiming my ancestry and shedding an identity that no longer served me. We then went to the local senior center (yikes, that was hard, calling myself a senior) and danced the night away. It was one of the most joyful days of my life.

So, my sixties passed, and I still didn't give it much thought until I hit seventy. Now that sounded really old. It took me some time to make my peace with that. I think the most sobering part was realizing that my time here on earth really was coming to an end. Fifteen, maybe twenty years if I'm lucky, and twenty years goes by in a flash.

I did finally settle in and accept my age even if my body took some time to catch up.

Now I've just turned seventy-four and a friend of mine, Heidi Robbins, recently wrote a blog about her feelings of approaching fifty. It's a beautiful piece about the issues we all face as we age. I reprint it here with her permission.

Dear Friends,

I'm 48. Let's start there.

It's not my birthday and I won't be celebrating until April Fool's Day, but I've been thinking about age and the span of a life and beauty and the Soul.

Forty-eight was old, old, old when I was 10. So old. Typing 48-- here, now-- is like taking my clothes off.

There. Now I'm naked and we can talk.

I celebrated my 40th birthday with no reservation. I invited 40 people. My husband toasted me. I boldly and with enthusiasm entered a new decade. But somewhere early in the journey of my fifth decade on earth, I began to be elusive about just how many years had passed. While I used to announce my age with a kind of relish, I have in recent years been vague about each new number--feeling like I'm moving away from some ideal, juicy, full, fecund time with a kind of crushing and unstoppable linearity.

Though it's a rare woman (may their numbers grow!) who looks in the mirror with glee and approval, I've spent the last few years looking in the mirror and feeling resigned. I see dark circles under my eyes and not so resilient skin and am not kind to myself. I look in the mirror and imagine fantastical creams to take away all the new shades and spots and creases and caverns. Then I remember even if they existed, I probably wouldn't buy them because I don't want to spend the time or the money. Let me say it now. I am easy going. I love who I am and what I do in the world. I know I am worthy. I know I have made and am making a difference. I know I am giving my gift. I have a good life.

Let me say too that I think women are beautiful at every age. I love how we radiate our light. I love how we adorn ourselves. I love how light, wisdom and care dances in and through us. I love being friends with women of all ages and celebrating our beauty. My mother and my mother-in-law are gorgeous. I look at them and think HURRAY! These are lives well lived. They are beautiful and own it.

I even know I am beautiful. I know that I love well and that love pours through and people see light and kindness and not necessarily wrinkles and wretchedness.

Still, I haven't quite slain the dragon of age. Beyond physical beauty, there are 101 inner monologues about what one should have accomplished by a certain age-- about success, about worth, about passion. We can all fill in the blanks. By this age, I should be married. By this age, I should have children. By this age, I should have written a book, spoken to a crowd of thousands, SUCCEEDED. What's your flavor? How old are you? What SHOULD you have done by now?

My own craziness (as part of a larger craziness) only becomes clear when I listen to my friends. I've heard many of my gorgeous, early 30 something pals say, "Oh God, I'm so old. I'm so far behind. Now I'll never..." And I think "What? Are you crazy?"

I can only imagine my dear friends in their 60's, 70's and 80's would ask me the very same question. "Am I crazy?" Frankly, every one of us, no matter our age, should consider ourselves crazy if we judge our growth strictly in linear time or give up because 'it hasn't happened yet.' There is no proper order in which to discover love, express ourselves, embrace our beauty or give our gifts.

We all might respond, "No, we are not crazy. We have just temporarily fallen into a societal blindness where Soul and the beauty of it is much harder to see and value." It's a blindness where quantity will always win over quality, doing is always victorious over being and the celebration of youth and physical beauty trumps wisdom and generosity 9 times out of 10.

The greatest secret which is ours to discover again and again--and really which is not so secret--is that linear age has nothing to do with our beauty, our worth, our inner life. It is irrelevant when it comes to our radiance or giving our gifts. It does not capture our passion, longing and our deep love. Our wrestlings, wrestling with age, are often a conversation about the clay of our bodies. The clay of our bodies changes. So be it. We are sculpted and molded by the lives that we live. What a blessing we have this clay as transportation, as a sacred vessel through which to LOVE.

The beauty living within each of us is revealed in the dance between that clay and the Soul. The Soul is ageless. Every moment we have the choice to dance with timelessness, spaciousness and trust. We can swirl with a boundless life in the confines of a changing body.

It's our conversation with timelessness that keeps us vibrant and young. We are ever dancing with infinite possibility. We just have to wake up to that reality. The vastness of LOVE is forever beckoning. Are you in love? If not, why not? Partner or no, are you IN LOVE? Love frees us from the constraints of ordinary time. We can all fall in love this instant. Wherever you are, open your heart and find something to love. Here, Now. And again.

Even in front of the mirror, if I stop my wretched monologue and say, "That's quite enough now!" and look into my own eyes, I can fall into love with the Soul who has traveled far. Imperfections fade. Failures soften. Light will always win the day. I can even look so deeply I meet my 10, 20, 30, 40-year-old self and say "Hello love. I see you. I honor you. I am grateful for you." I can look ahead to my 50, 60, 70-year-old self and say,

"I will celebrate and greet you with joy. I can only imagine the riches you have to impart."

It's all for me to choose.

Oh friends. I'm 48! I want to have a big party--inside and out-- at 50. What a potent, juicy age full of promise. As I see it from here, I'll be in the thick of a full on wave of Self-Acceptance and celebration, falling in love again and again.

When I finished reading Heidi's blog, I felt compelled to respond.
Here's what I wrote:
Hey Heidi,
Thank you for the wise words on aging. I can tell you from here, I'll be 74 next week, that it gets easier to accept the inevitable march of time and for me it has come with more of a sense of ease about what is. It's okay that I didn't do EVERYTHING I thought I would. It's okay that I made mistakes and could have done some things better. It's really okay that I am just here, right now, in this place.

I don't have the same urgency about what's next or what I should be doing, partly because my body has shown me that it's silly to pretend I'm still 25, but also because I am learning to accept my own comfortable pace... and it's a snail I'll tell you, and I'm learning to rest in that.

There is still passion and commitment and dedication but now I check in with my body before I take any bold actions.

There is a lot of looking back at this stage as the number of years ahead is diminishing. And mostly when I look back I am proud and satisfied. I did okay. I held onto my commitments, my obligations, I did my duty. I let Saturn have its way with me. (The Lord of Time, Responsibilities, and Karma.)

Later in life I learned how to more easily stay true to myself. I feel good that I've helped people, that I've been mostly unselfish, that I've put something into the world that will be part of my legacy, my children, my books. So, all in all, a life well lived, is how I feel and that brings me a sense of joy and comfort.

Just thought I'd share my bird's eye view from here.

Much love and gratitude for all you have put into the world in your short 48 years.

Xoxoxo,

Karen

Older now, you find holiness in anything that continues.
—Naomi Shihab Nye

March 2016
On Being Mortal

As I mentioned earlier, I've recently finished reading two books having to do with death and dying and how it is that we die in this country. The first book, *Being Mortal* by Atul Gawande, poses the idea that our system of caring for the elderly has the wrong focus. Instead of doing everything we can to make sure old people, sick people, dying people are safe and their physical needs are taken care of we should make it a priority to ask them what quality of life they wish to have when they become dependent on care.

Of course, physical safety is important, but this author posits that purpose and quality of life far outweigh the advantages of making safety the number one priority. He asks us to re-think this idea and have these conversations with our loved ones, so we are prepared, when the time comes, to carry out their wishes.

One man who was asked this by his daughter when he became terminally ill just said, "Don't pull the plug unless I can no longer have ice cream or watch football." What if she hadn't understood that and the time came to make a decision? As it was, she was completely relieved to be off the hook and agonizing over what was the best thing to do.

The second book chronicles the life of a neurosurgeon named Paul Kalanithi, only in his mid-thirties, who is diagnosed with an incurable cancer. He journals his struggle in the book, *When Breath Becomes Air*.

> You that seek what life is in death,
> Now find it air that once was breath.
> New names unknown, old names gone;
> Till time end bodies, but souls none.
> Reader!! Then make time, while you be,
> But steps to your eternity.
> (Baron Brooke Fulke Greville, "Caelica83")

He describes his struggle with how much effort to give his recovery when it may further damage his body and only increase his life span by very little. He comes to the decision that what is most important to him is being around for the birth of his first child and fulfilling his lifelong dream of writing, so he writes this book in the last few months of his life. His concluding paragraph is written to his eight-month-old daughter. He tells her not to forget what it has meant to him to be filled with joy at her presence in his life. That he did not wish for more than that. That he will "rest satisfied, in this time, right now." He wants her to know what an enormous gift that was for him.

I have thought of this paragraph many times since finishing the book. Maybe it's because in my seventy-fifth year I realize in a more dramatic way that my time is limited, fifteen, maybe twenty years if I have my father's genes, but the reality is we never know.

I've pondered whether I will go so gracefully into the night, fulfilled and satisfied. As it stands, at this moment I feel content with the life I have lived. I know I have made a difference. My hope is that whether I am in pain, suffering, or mostly unconscious that there will be a deep part of me that will be at peace because I know I have had a glimpse of my life's purpose and have tried my best to live it. I know that I have touched people with my presence. I've counseled people with a loving and compassionate heart. I've taught little children with a joy I didn't know was inside me. I've mothered my own children with love, patience, and guidance. I've given voice to my deepest spiritual beliefs through my writing, my full moon ceremonies, the classes I've taught, and my speaking gigs.

This, I think is the grace of a life fully lived.

That I am able to look back and say to myself, "Well done."

In the end
These things matter most:
How well did you love?
How fully did you live?
How deeply did you let go?

ACKNOWLEDGMENTS

I'd like to thank all the beautiful writers and poets who inspired me, lifted me up and nourished me when I felt empty. I wish I could have quoted you all, but I couldn't get everyone's permission. So, I will just list you here.

Jan Richardson, John O'Donohue, David Whyte, Miriam Dyak, Claire Zimmer, Danielle LaPorte, Derek Walcott, Eckhart Tolle, Ram Dass, Sylvia Boorstein, Pema Chodron, Hafiz, Caroline Casey, Maya Angelou, Tosha Silver, Chani Nicholas, Frank Clark, James Baraz, Marianne Williamson, Byron Katie, Jack Kornfield, Greg Kimura, Matt Kahn, Rev. Safire Rose, Mark Nepo, Eileen Cady, Kimberly Jones, Mark Hack, Teresa Campos, Jeff Foster, Melissa Gayle West, Tara Mohr, Wayne Muller, May Sarton, Tama Kieves, Anne Hillman, Mary Oliver, Hugh Prather, Florence Scovel Shinn, Em Claire, Patricia Monaghan, Baba Hara Dass, Mooji, Astrid Alanda, Pam Younghans, Sam Keen, Naomi Shihab Nye.

And last but certainly not least, Heidi Rose Robbins. You inspire me every day with your words, your presence, and your radiance.

Thank you to all those devoted fans of my blog. Without your feedback, I probably wouldn't have had the courage to put it all together and send it out.

I'd like to thank my family for not laughing at me when I decided I wanted to be a writer at age seventy. Your support means everything.

And to my "Magnificent 7" the women who are my foundation, my support, my laughing and dancing cohorts. May we always be there to laugh and dance together.

Gratitude, also to The Lucis Trust. Permission has been granted to use extracts from the Alice Bailey books by The Lucis Trust who hold copyright.

Many thanks to my wonderful muse, Drena Griffith, whose inspiration uplifted me when I was in my "doubting Thomas" mood.

So much gratitude and appreciation for my gifted son-in-law, Coren Lindfield, whose photograph graces the cover and back of the book. He also designed my beautiful website.

And my deepest gratitude to those unseen Beings whose presence I invoke every day: Joachim, Quan Yin, Master DK, Master KH, Lord Buddha and of course the Master Jesus.

APPENDIX

The Ten Tenets of the Esoteric Philosophy

1. There is only One Life.
2. There is a chain of Life throughout all of cosmos.
3. The One Life expresses itself through Seven Rays.
4. Every human soul is found upon one of the Seven Rays.
5. There are five initiations that lead to enlightenment.
6. Occult meditation accelerates spiritual evolution.
7. There is a hierarchy of Masters overseeing the evolution of humanity.
8. Modern day discipleship is based on the blending of the mind and heart.
9. Spiritual service is the hallmark of the Aquarian Age.
10. Service is founded on the principles of co-creative magic.

These principles are taken from classes and workshops given by William Meader. Reprinted here with permission. (www.meader.org)

THE SEVEN RAYS

Every sign in the zodiac and every planet in the sky is a receiver and transmitter of energy. These energies emanate from the seven rays and descend upon us powerfully at each full moon. These archetypal streams of energy pour through the cosmos and condition all expressions of life.

From the esoteric perspective it is understood that at each incarnation one of these seven rays will characterize the quality of soul energy that we will express. Thus, we are told that there are seven different types of souls, each one expressing a different quality. For more information on how to determine your own soul ray see the online questionnaire entitled the Personality Inventory Profile (www.pip3.com) You will be given a graph that shows you the hypothetical distribution of rays within your makeup.

Every month as the sun moves into a different constellation, we become receivers of different ray energies. It is therefore helpful to note the qualities of these rays so that we can be receptive to their emanations and learn how to more fully integrate them into our systems.

Ray I – The Ray of Will and Purpose

This is a dynamic, fiery, electric energy. It initiates new and powerful ideas that stimulate change. It can be a destructive force as old patterns are destroyed so that beauty, purpose and spiritual will can be revealed.

Ray II – The Ray of Love and Wisdom

This great being radiates pure love in all forms and is the most potent of the seven rays in our solar system. This energy activates the Christ principle within the hearts of all humanity. Its basic qualities are: radiance, divine love, attraction, wisdom, expansion, the power to save, and inclusiveness.

Ray III – The Ray of Active Intelligence

This Lord uses the ray energy to stimulate the mind to materialize the divine idea. This work is closely related to matter and the personality in every human being. The personality was created to express its divinity and under the influence of this ray we learn to create until we become co-creators with Divinity itself.

Ray IV – The Ray of Harmony through Conflict

The keynote of this ray is harmony through the conflicting desires of the personality and the soul. Its purpose is to create beauty through the free interplay of the personality and the soul, to produce balance, unity, beauty and at-one-ment.

Ray V – The Ray of Concrete Knowledge and Science

The keynote of this ray is mental development and the plane of mind is its main sphere of activity. Within this plane we find the lower concrete mind and the higher abstract mind. "The higher mind must be allowed to purify the lower mind in order to make it the powerful and constructive tool it is meant to be." *(Burmester, Helen The Seven Rays Made Visual, p. 35)*

This ray facilitates that process and once the lower mind is purified it becomes a channel for the inflow of higher mind energy (intuition).

Ray VI – The Ray of Devotion and Idealism

The qualities of this Lord are a strong, almost militant focusing upon an ideal, a one-pointed devotion and a divine sincerity. The energy of this ray assists us in transforming our selfish and personal motivations for service into the unselfish, impersonal devotion and service to higher values and for the good of all humanity.

Ray VII – The Ray of Ceremonial Magic and Order

The energy of this ray joins spirit with matter by bringing spiritual love and wisdom into practical expression, (white magic). The forms are built which accommodate the best of the human spirit. First the crystallized forms must be destroyed so that the true values hidden in the forms can be released. These values are law and order and peaceful coexistence.

—Taken from the book, *Full Moon Magic* by Karen Johannsen with permission from Michael Robbins to reprint.

The goal of evolution for humanity is to become consciously and livingly aware of the nature of these energies and begin to know and use them...Even a dim perception of that vast aggregation of intelligent Forces...will serve to bring into clearer light the realization that our solar system and consequently our earth and we ourselves are part of this immense interrelation of energies and forces.

-Helen Burmester, *The Seven Rays Made Visual,* p. 39

Because these forces are, we are; because They persist, we persist; because They move in form and space and time, we do the same.

—Alice Bailey, *Esoteric Astrology,* p. 602

THE ENNEAGRAM

The enneagram is more complex than what is shared with you below. If you are interested, you can google it and find all the data you might need. I include the basics here because I refer so often to being a Two Type on the Enneagram scale. This summary was written by Emile Haddad.

The Enneagram

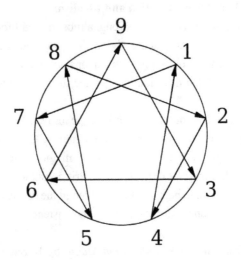

A Brief Tour of the Nine Personality Types

The Enneagram is a model for consciousness development, and hence it is multi-layered and can be complex. To support this development, the model begins by identifying one's personality type in order to understand the obstacles and opportunities available for consciousness development.

The Enneagram identifies nine distinct personality types and thus nine different pathways for consciousness to grow. Each of the nine Enneatypes idealizes and imitates a particular quality of *Being;* these qualities include strength, brilliancy, love, will and joy, among others. This process of idealizing and attempting to imitate these qualities is one of the main reasons we find ourselves continuing to live out the fixated behaviors of our enneatype, even when we'd rather live more from our true potential.

The following is a very brief description of the nine personality types. These summative depictions do not articulate the multiple intricate layers that the Enneagram model reveals for these character structures.

Type-1: The Reformer

Essence: The essential knowing of ONEs is that we and the world are deeply good, and that *Reality* is perfect. ONEs are originally joyfully enthralled with the goodness and perfection of the *Universe*.

The wound: An early experience giving rise to the recognition that the world as they know it doesn't meet the personality's idea of perfection.

Identity/personality role: To become a "Reformer;" an attempt by the personality to bring perfection, order and goodness into their life and the life around them.

Basic Desire: A drive towards doing the right thing, goodness, integrity, excellence.

Passion/emotional vice: Anger arises from their inability to create the perfect order and goodness in the world around them.

Fixation/mental attitude: Resentment and frustration about the condition of the world and their inability to repair it from their ego self; tendency towards controlling and critical behaviors.

Virtue: Serenity arising from a sense of *Being* joyfully enthralled with the goodness and perfection of the *Reality* as it is.

Type-2: The Helper

Essence: The essential knowing of TWOs is that the *Universe* is made of absolute love and that they are the beloved in the *Universe* and so is everyone else.

The wound: An early experience leading them to conclude that the world is not capable of loving them unconditionally or meeting their essential knowing that they are the beloved in the *Universe* and so is everyone else.

Identity/personality role: To become the "Helper;" driven to love, help and serve others, without realizing that their motivation is the need for others to love them. They identify with the need to be needed, whether the need is actually there or not.

Basic Desire: To give and receive love.

Passion/emotional vice: Pride arising from perceiving themselves as indispensable servants and lovers of humanity even when not needed or asked for. The pride feeds a sense of false humility that keeps them from recognizing their own needs.

Fixation/mental attitude: Flattery becomes an expected reward for *Being* helpful; they become dependent on the recognition of others for their good deeds as a way to sustain their sense of identity as *Being* loving and loveable.

Virtue: Humility arising from the recognition of their own limitations of sharing their love unconditionally, and that it is the grace of the *Divine* that brings their true experience of love; love of self as well as of the other.

Type-3: The Achiever

Essence: The essential knowing of THREEs is that everything in the *Universe* is on an evolutionary path of impermanence, lacks constancy and is transitory and that only the *Divine Consciousness* endures and gives us the endurance to withstand the passing nature of all things.

The wound: An experience that convinced THREEs early in life that they are separate from the *Universe* and its Wholeness. This perception leads them to think it's up to them to keep things from falling apart.

Identity/personality role: To be the "Achiever," an extremely pragmatic stance driven to achieve and get results in the world. Driven and highly energetic in the realm of productivity that they forget and lose their sense of self to the work at hand. The role motivates them and protects them from their inner pain.

Basic Desire: To feel valuable and be acknowledged as a positive contributor in the world

Passion/emotional vice: Self-Deceit arising from putting the world and their achievements in it ahead of their personal needs. Driven by the pressure to succeed, they can slip into almost any image mask to please the people around them and generate the success they desire. They act the part to perfection and their self-deceit is partly generated from coming to believe the masks they inhabit.

Fixation/mental attitude: Vanity becomes the mental attitude resulting from consistent and long record of achievements and successes. They are optimistic about positive results, intelligent, dynamic, and productive and can have more energy than anyone in the room, all of which adds to a sense that they have no equal in their arena; their image masks exacerbate the issue.

Virtue: Authenticity arising from resting in the impermanence and fallibility that they deeply know and deeply fear within themselves. They surrender to the recognition that they cannot keep the *Universe* or themselves from the transient nature of change and from the chaos that change can bring into their life.

Type-4: The Individualist

Essence: The essential knowing of FOURs is the recognition that our true identity is a mystery that is oceanic, unfathomable and mysterious. This sense of mystery about themselves, the *Universe* and their place in it drives them to appreciate the beauty of creation, the intimacy with the other and the depth of experience that is possible, drawing them to constantly seek a more complete union with the *Divine*

The wound: An experience in which the serene union with a larger, essential and beautiful *Reality* was severed early in life. They desperately try to create an outer world of unity, balance, beauty and symmetry to make up for the separation they feel.

Identity/personality role: As an "Individualist," they seek to recreate the original lost blessing of knowing themselves and everyone else as unique creations of the *Divine*, with beauty, mystery and in harmony with their surroundings. Their contributions often have a twist of creativity and non-dual abstract thinking.

Basic Desire: To be uniquely themselves as the *Universe* meant them to be and to see the uniqueness in everyone else.

Passion/emotional vice: Envy is the outcome of a desire to connect to the *Original Source* through their attempts to be unique. They know they belong in it though they have lost their contact with it, and this shapes a sense of life long longing. The longing for contact with the *Origin*, the beauty inherent in it and the harmony that holds the whole in a coherent one-ness causes them pain and deep loss and grief.

Fixation/mental attitude: Melancholy arises from a sense of despair that they can't experience their wholeness. The loss of contact with their *Essential Self* leaves bereft that they are missing something essential within them.

Virtue: Equanimity for this type is found when they are in the deepest experience of contact with themselves and the other. A sense of inner equilibrium is felt that reflects the balance of the *Universe*. The longing for something outside of them ceases.

Type-5: The Investigator

Essence: The essential knowing of FIVEs is their soul's capacity to be illuminated and to illuminate and to make things clear. They are inherently aware of the majesty, genius and power of a creation that can hold all the parts in one *Whole* and recognize that they are their own unique form and flavor within it.

The wound: An experience of early separation from their essential connection to the *Divine* leads to a loss of ability to discern *Reality* from illusion leaving them feeling terrified and unsafe in the world.

Identity/personality role: As the "Investigator " FIVEs turn to their minds to try to re-experience the lost illumination from the *Divine,* but since they are already disconnected from the source, no matter how hard they try to acquire knowledge, they are left empty and feeling that they don't know enough thus opening the way to reliance on false beliefs and ideas.

Basic Desire: To acquire mastery and understanding of the depth of *Reality*

Passion/emotional vice: Avarice for knowledge and for personal privacy becomes the driving force behind their way of life. They can't get enough knowledge to satiate the anxiety born out of the disconnection from the *Illuminating Source.* Their isolation increases as they strive to gain more and more knowledge to no avail.

Fixation/mental attitude: An attitude of Stinginess takes over their way of being as they become pre-occupied with hording knowledge and saving all the time they have for their studies, further keeping them from connecting with the larger *Reality* around them.

Virtue: Non-Attachment liberates the heart of the FIVE from having to cling and hold to the need to be illuminated through the effort of acquiring more and more knowledge. It restores their sense of real knowing once they leave their books behind and begin making contact with themselves and their *Essential Beingness.*

Type-6: The Loyalist

Essence: The essential knowing of SIXs is a sense of resting in the full *Presence* of the *Divine* and trustfully being held by *Being.*

The wound: An experience of early betrayal leads to a lost sense of *Presence* in their life and creates a defensive posture and an attempt to bend *Reality* to a manufactured experience of being held by the *Universe.* "I will make it happen; I will prove it and I will maintain it."

Identity/personality role: As the "Loyalist", SIX's put their trust of being held in external authorities, groups, laws and structures of certitude rather than trusting their own guidance.

Basic Desire: To have support and guidance; to be held by a safe and benevolent *Universe.*

Passion/emotional vice: Fear arises for SIXs when they lose their sense of holding and disconnect from *Presence.* Their anxiety begins to grow and their awake-ness shifts to vigilance, then to watchfulness, hyper-vigilance, suspicions, and finally paranoia. In essence their anxiety leads to a sense of awake-ness without *Presence.*

Fixation/mental attitude: an attitude of Cowardice is the result of their emotional hyper-vigilance. Out of their suspicion they project and re-define their experience through a distrustful lens. They stay keyed up out of a false sense of wakefulness from being on guard all the time.

Virtue: Courage arises when SIXs learn to work with their fear, ultimately moving them to find their true inner authority which allows them to trust in the benevolent *Universe* and perfect *Presence* they once knew. A quality of wakefulness arises, in which true *Presence* arises around them and within them, and through which an unshakable courage emerges for one to walk their path in life without trepidation.

Type-7: The Enthusiast

Essence: The essential knowing of SEVENs is that *Reality* is utterly satisfying. They sensed the *Universe* as a place of absolute freedom with no limits and abundant resources, all of which gave them great joy and radiant optimism.

The wound: Early experiences that produced pain and lack of freedom they could not process lead to a desire to ignore and repress the negative. Instead they learn to fantasize and plan for a future that has as little pain as possible.

Identity/personality role: As the Enthusiast, SEVENs learn to internalize their optimism to the point that they have difficulty seeing or acknowledging the shadow side, the dark and painful aspects of their experience.

Basic Desire: To be satisfied and content and to experience the joyful adventure of living.

Passion/emotional vice: Gluttony arises in their over indulgent enthusiastic approach to life in order to satisfy an insatiable quest for new experiences, options and joy in an attempt to be filled up by life's promise of absolute freedom.

Fixation/mental attitude: Planning becomes a fixated solution to satisfy an attitude of "more is better" leading to an inability to commit and stay with any pathway they encounter. This leads to constant movement to the next thing in order to keep the enthusiasm alive and the pain away.

Virtue: Sobriety arises when they realize that it is not in the *content* of experience that they will find happiness, but rather it is in the *quality* of their attention and *Presence* to experience that they will discover the promise of utter satisfaction, contentment and freedom of *Reality*.

Type-8: The Challenger

Essence: The essential knowing that *Reality* was in itself warmth, nurturance, protection, empathy, connection, and clear recognition of how weak, needy, and hungry we all are. It holds our vulnerability gently in its protective arms.

The wound: Early experience that leaves them vulnerable, raw, unprotected and un-nurtured leads to a stance that denies and rejects neediness with a stiff upper lip. They deny their vulnerability and close their access to their heart's pain.

Identity/personality role: The attitude of the Challenger arises from the stiff upper lip stance, which is accompanied by anger, intensity and a decision to protect themselves and those around from any such injustices in the future.

Basic Desire: Self-protection and a desire for the *Universe* to treat them and others justly.

Passion/emotional vice: a Lust for intensity driven by anger and power to promote justice and protect the innocent in the way that they were not protected in their own early life.

Fixation/mental attitude: Vengeance becomes their driver to equal the scales, protect the innocent and find purpose behind the pain they endured alone.

Virtue: Innocence is discovered when EIGHTs are willing to face their human vulnerability and acknowledge the mercy required to accept their pain. It is in the recognition that real strength and power resides in the acceptance of their tenderness that the heart is restored.

Type-9: The Peacemaker

Essence: The essential knowing that the *Universe* is an expression of an all loving *Divine Presence*, made from love and of love. They recognize that we are *Being* itself as a manifestation of *Divine Love* and sense that love changes everything and resolves everything.

The wound: Early experience that leaves NINEs with a sense of loss from oneness with the *Universe*, leaving them feeling disconnected, insignificant, peripheral and not real. "I don't exist, I'm nothing, I don't matter."

Identity/personality role: As "Peacemakers" they want to avoid conflict at the cost of their own needs and wants. They allow themselves to be overlooked and are happy to be in the background out of a false sense of humility.

Basic Desire: Wholeness, peace and harmony drive their actions and the way they present themselves.

Passion/emotional vice: Sloth is a condition that emerges from their loss of oneness, leading to a lack of focused energy and a pattern of 'checking out' emerges. Because they feel they are insignificant and don't matter, they tend to withdraw from engaging with life directly by staying busy on the periphery.

Fixation/mental attitude: Indolence is a mindset that keeps NINEs from facing life directly with all its challenges and opportunities; they prefer to look at the bright side of life so that their peace of mind is not shaken by the realities in front of them. This distorted approach to life set them up to escape into "premature Buddhahood."

Virtue: Decisive Action becomes the beacon for a mature NINE. By discovering and developing their feelings of self-worth, their inner focus and drive grow into clear decision making and action, the trepidation to engage life directly begins to dissolve. They develop the gift of accepting others without prejudice and become unbiased arbitrators; they see the positive in both sides of a conflict. They become harmonizers that seek a sense of fairness, making them effective promoters of peace and justice.

An Introduction to the Structure of the Enneagram of Personality Types

The Centers: The Enneagram identifies three Centers of energy/consciousness that govern the basic orientation of any personality, the **Head Center**, the **Heart Center** and the **Body Center**. Each Center is associated with three specific personalities which are more aligned with that center than the other two Centers, creating a total of nine personality types within the Enneagram model. This means that there are **Three Head Types, Three Heart**

Types and **Three Body Types**.

The Types: Each of the nine personality types has its own emotional patterns (called **Passions**), mental habits (called **Fixations**) and physical relationship to the body. Each type's emotional pattern is associated with a **Virtue** that the personality is trying to reach for and live by. Each type's mental habits are associated with a **Holy Idea** (I call it Ascendant Quality) that the personality is trying to reach for and live by. These character structures are fluid and open to be impacted and changed by multiple influences articulated in the model and represented in the diagram.

The Subtypes: These are **Instinctual Drives** that arise from *Being* in a physical body and are associated with the **Body Center**. Each type has access to all three drives at various levels and they are often not very well balanced, with one of the drives *Being* more predominant or active than the other two. These drives are called the **One-To-One Instinct**, the **Social Instinct** and the **Self-Preservation Instinct**.

The Wings: The nine types are organized around a circle (sometimes called the rim) in a specific order that relates to their association with the Energy Center they belong to, as well as a number of other relationships; these relationships are illustrated by the line of the circle as well as the inner lines within the circle that connect certain types to each other in specific ways. There are mystical roots to all this that are too involved for this brief narrative. The Wings are the two numbers (types) found on either side of any type as seen on the outer rim; for example the wings for type four are type three and type five. The wings for type nine are type eight and type one, etc. Those wings impact that type in specific ways and at certain periods in one's life, thus allowing for "movement" in which that personality has freedom to expand and grow or contract and devolve;

illustrates another way in which each personality is a dynamic system and not a static structure.

Dynamic Lines: These are the inner lines that connect the types within the circle. Again, they indicate a different kind of relationship between the types that are connected, and therefore illustrate another type of movement that is available to each type for purposes of growth and expansion or for potential contraction and devolution of the personality.

A Brief History of the Enneagram

The Enneagram of Personality Types is a modern synthesis of a number of ancient wisdom traditions; its origins can be traced to the third century

BC and the Alexandria Library. The symbol of the Enneagram has roots in antiquity and can be traced back at least as far as the works of Pythagoras. The philosophy behind the Enneagram contains components from mystical Judaism, Christianity, Islam, Taoism, Buddhism, and ancient Greek philosophy (particularly Socrates, Plato, and the Neo-Platonists), all traditions that stretch back into antiquity.

The model was almost lost to history had it not been re-discovered by George Gurdjieff a Greek-Armenian mystic in the early 1900s. His understanding of its basic philosophical principles was acquired from a two-year monastic stay with monks in the Egyptian desert west of Alexandria.

In the 1950s Oscar Ichazo, a Bolivian born philosopher, drew on his knowledge of a number of these mystical traditions to synthesize the basic principles of the model and develop a deeper, more current psychological understanding of the personality types associated with it. His work became the foundation of the current Enneagram model used today. The psychological depth of the Enneagram was further developed and clarified by the work of Claudio Naranjo in the 1970s

Emile Haddad
Awareness coaching and spiritual guidance
206-954-0241
Emile@catalystbcc.com
catalystBCC.com

BIBLIOGRAPHY

Angelou, Maya, poem, *The Human Family*

Bailey, Alice, *Esoteric Astrology*. New York, Lucis Publishing Co. 1951

_____*Esoteric Healing*: A Treatise on the Seven Rays, Vol. IV, New York: Lucis Publishing Co. 1953

_____*Discipleship in the New Age*, Vol. I, II. New York: Lucis Publishing Co. 1972

_____*Glamour A World Problem,* New York: Lucis Publishing Co. 1950

_____Externalization of the Hierarchy, New York: Lucis Publishing Co. 1957

Balyoz, Harold. *Signs of Christ*, Flagstaff, Arizona: Altai Publishers, 1979

Baraz, James and Shoshana Alexander, *Awakening Joy*, Bantam Books, 2010 awakeningjoy.info

Cady, Eileen. guidance@findhorn.org

Casey, Caroline. *Making the Gods Work for You: The Astrological Language of the Psyche.* New York: Three Rivers Press. 1998

Claire, Em, poem, *What is it You Were Given?*

Dass, Ram, *Polishing the Mirror. How to Live from your Spiritual Heart.* Sounds True, 2013

Das, Krishna. Sri Argala Stostram, You Tube

_____Jesus on the Main Line, You Tube

Dyak, Miriam, poem, Spring Cleaning. voicedialogueworld.com miriam@ miriamdyak.com

Foster, Jeff, poem, *Resting in Each Step.* lifewithoutacenter.com

Gawande, Atul, *Being Mortal: Medicine and What Matters in the End.* Metropolitan Books, 2014

Gibran, Kahil, poem, *On Children*

Hillman, Anne, *The Dancing Animal Woman* .annehillman.net

Kahn, Matt, *Whatever Arises, Love That. A Love Revolution That Begins with You.* Sounds True, 2016. mattkahn.org

Kalanithi, Paul, *When Breath Becomes Air*. Random House, 2016

Keen, Sam, *Hymns to an Unknown God*, Penguin Random House, 1994

Kieves, Tama. tamakieves.com

LaPorte, Danielle. Blogs: *Refuse to Worry (and how to be more useful to your friends)* and *The Lie of Inadequacy.* daniellelaporte.com
_____Book: *The Desire Map, A Guide to Creating Goals with Soul,* Sounds True, 2013

Marquez, Gabriel Garcia, *Love in the Time of Cholera.* Penguin Random House, 1985

Meader, William, *Shine Forth. The Soul's Magical Destiny.* Source Publications, 2004

Mohr, Tara, poem, The Rhythm, *Your Other Names.* Self-Published. taramohr.com

Moorjani, Anita. *Dying to Be Me. My Journey from Cancer to Near Death to Healing.* Hay House, 2012

O'Donohue, John. Poem, For a New Beginning, *To Bless the Space Between Us.* Doubleday, 2008

Oliver, Mary, poem When I am Among the Trees, *Thirst,* Beacon Press, 2003

Prather, Hugh. *The Little Book of Letting Go,* Canari Press, 2000

Richmond, Lewis, *Aging as a Spiritual Practice: A Contemplative Guide to Growing Older and Wiser.* Gotham Books, 2012

Richardson, Jan, poem, Lazarus Blessing, *Circle of Grace,* Gospeller Press, Orlando Florida, 2015. Used by permission. janrichardson.com
_____ poem, Blessing in the Chaos, *Book of Sorrow, A Book of Blessings for Times of Grief,* Wanton Gospeller Press, Orlando, Florida, 2016. Used by permission, janrichardson.com
_____poem, Insomnia Blessing, *Book of Sorrow. A Book of Blessings for Times of Grief,* by Jan Richardson, Wanton Gospeller Press, Orlando, Florida, 2016. Used by permission, janrichardson. com

Riso, Don, *The Wisdom of the Enneagram.* Penguin Random House, 1999

Rumi, Jellaludin, poem, The Guest House. Translated by Coleman Barks.

Sarton, May, poem, Now I've Become Myself, *Collected Poems 1930-1993.* © W.W. Norton, 1993

Shinn, Florence Scovel, *The Game of Life and How to Play It.* Dover Publications, 2010

Silver, Tosha, *Outrageous Openness,* Atria Books, 2014

_____Change Me Prayers, Atria Books, 2015

Singer, Michael, *The Surrender Experiment: My Journey into Life's Perfection*, Harmony, 2015

Spangler, David, *Starheart*. Lorian Press, 2013

Walcott, Derek, poem, Love After Love, *Sea Grapes*. Macmillian, 1976

West, Melissa Gayle, *Silver Linings*: *The Power of Trauma to Transform Your Life*. Fairwind Publishers, 2003. melissagaylewest.com

Williamson, Marianne, *A Return to Love,* Harper Collins, 1992

Whyte, David, *The House of Belonging*, Many Rivers Co. 1997

Wright, Machaelle Small, *Map: Medical Assistance Program*, Warrenton, Virginia, Perelandra, Ltd. Publisher, 1990

RESOURCES

Below is a list of practitioners and teachers that I have been personally involved with and can highly recommend. Most of them are local, in the Seattle area with the exception of William Meader who lives in Portland, Heidi Rose Robbins who lives in California, and Michael and Tuija Robbins who live in Finland.

—N'Shama Sterling, teacher and facilitator of the Enneagram Personality Types. nshama.sterling@gmail.com

—William Meader, my personal teacher for the last sixteen years on the Ancient Wisdom teachings. This esoteric philosophy is the one I reference often in the book. William teaches all over the world and has a depth of understanding about this philosophy that is rare. He brings abstract ideas down into practical everyday life and makes them understandable. You can see him talk about Esoteric Astrology, Revealing the Soul's Intention, and many other topics on his YouTube channel or check out his website for many free talks and articles. www.meader.org/

—Karin Granstrom, MD, CRS. Karin is an amazing healer who I turn to whenever I am stuck. She helps professional women deeply relax and tune into their body wisdom, replacing stress and pain with clarity, confidence and new possibilities. She uses body awareness, imagery, gentle touch, dialogue and tapping (EFT, Emotional Freedom Technique). www.karingranstrom.com

—David Martin, MD. David is more than an MD. He is a skilled acupuncturist that I have been using for many years. He practices Five Element acupuncture which focuses on balancing all the elements in your body: water, fire, air, metal and wood. He is also a skilled counselor and dream interpreter. I use him for all of those things. He is a jewel. www.davidrmartinmd.com

—Heidi Rose Robbins. Heidi is a master astrologer as well as a published poet. I quote many of her poems in this book. I have used her as an astrologer for many years. She was one of my original teachers of astrology. She is perceptive, intuitive, and always sees the highest possibilities present when she reads your chart. Don't miss out on a reading with her. heidirose4@aol.com

—Tom Kenyon. Tom is an internationally known sound healer. He has an amazing voice and range, and channels tones from other dimensions. I know, it sounds "woo woo", but until you've sat in a room with 300-400 other people and listened to his voice transport you, you cannot pass judgment. It's truly a transcendent experience. He has much free downloadable music that he has recorded as well as channeled writings that you can read from the groups he works with, mainly the Hathors, on his website: tomkenyon.com

—Laura Bailey. Laura uses her healing hands to offer amazing skin care and wonderful facials. Here's how her website describes her services:

—Samara Skincare is a personal urban sanctuary dedicated to the fusion of esthetics and energy medicine. A destination to restore energy balance in the body and revitalize with a therapeutic facial, or a relaxing hand and foot treatment. Each guest is treated individually and holistically. As a technical artisan and proprietress of Samara Skincare, Laura Bailey delights in this work and wants you to be informed of how to receive and experience your own beauty. www.samaraskincare.com

—Marianne Streich. Marianne is a long time Reiki Master with extraordinary healing abilities. She has given me sessions that completely shifted my perceptions and helped stabilize my emotions. https://reikiforliving. org

—Katlaina Rayne. Katlaina has been my "go to" person for intuitive readings since I first met her in graduate school in 1985. She really hones in on relationships, underlying psychological issues, and current challenges you might be facing.

I have found her wisdom invaluable and very accurate as I've asked her everything from how my kids are doing to deeper questions about my spiritual path. Mostly, I come away from a reading with her with reassurance that what I intuitively felt was confirmed, but sometimes the information is unexpected and presents an entirely different perspective than what I had thought before.

She is also a psychotherapist who specializes in helping people connect with their own inner wisdom and let go of obstacles to transformation. Some of her modalities include EMDR, Interpersonal Psychotherapy, dream work, the Enneagram, and art therapy. You can email her at katlaina.rayne@whidbey. net. She lives on Whidbey Island. Her phone number is 360-524-4157

—Pam Younghans. Pam is a person whose weekly *Northpoint Journal* always treasure. She has a beautiful, clear way of talking about astrology that anyone can understand. I often use her material to help me prepare for my full moon ceremonies and also forward her weekly posts to many of my friends who read her as well. You can sign up for her free newsletter at www. northpointastrology.com

—David Spangler. David is a spiritual philosopher and self-described "practical mystic." He helped transform the Findhorn Foundation in northern Scotland into a center of residential spiritual education. He now resides in Issaquah, WA.

He has been instrumental in my life in reminding me that the subtle realms are real. Through his books, teachings, and webinars I have developed a much closer relationship to this dimension of reality. He is a wizard with a jolly twinkle in his eyes that conveys the joy and lightness with which he walks through the world. He holds a depth of wisdom about the unseen realms, due in part to his long-time association with his "allies" from these worlds.

The organization he helped to establish in 1974 is called The Lorian Association based in Issaquah, WA. It is an educational non-profit and spiritual resource center. David's current public work is mostly through online education, newsletters and a quarterly publication called *Views from the Borderland*. A separate publishing company, Lorian Press LLC, publishes much of his material and both my books. David can be reached through www.lorian.org

—Michael and Tuija Robbins. They have a spiritual center in Finland. Every Wednesday through Sunday they hold a worldwide meditation with a different focus each day. For example, one day they have a meditation on the reappearance of the Christ. Another day they pick a country that they can direct their energies to in order to invoke healing and light into that country. I've participated whenever I can for the last several months and have found this a wonderful practice. It has deepened my own practice as I connect to the world-wide community and feel the power in a united intention. It's called the ASK program and can be found at www.makara.us/portal/?page_id=211

—Joan Jerman. Joan is a gifted intuitive healer that I have known for many years. I attend her workshops whenever I am able. She offers a transformational opportunity to meditate with others, align with truth and receive healing frequencies and guidance. I always come away feeling deeply blessed and aligned with my higher knowing. She also offers a mentoring program in which she guides you in ways to connect more deeply with your own inner wisdom. You can contact her at 206-755-9109 or at her email address: joanjerman@hotmail.com

OTHER OFFERINGS BY KAREN JOHANNSEN

FULL MOON MAGIC BOOK AND CARD DECK

The book, *Full Moon Magic*, educates us about the astrological and spiritual significance of each full moon period. All of the signs, planets, and houses are discussed as well as how to create your own full moon ceremony

The card deck consists of 76 cards, 6 for each astrological sign. The first card explains the qualities of that sign as understood from an esoteric and exoteric perspective. The remaining 5 cards contain keynotes, meditations, and mantrams that help you focus on the specific intention for the 5-day full moon period. Purchase and learn more about this set – www.theoneheart.org/book

AUDIO SET OF 12 FULL MOON CEREMONIES WITH GUIDED MEDITATIONS FOR EACH ASTROLOGICAL MONTH.

This thirteen-part audio series is designed to support you in learning about and using the energies of the full moon. Use the recordings on your own or develop ceremony around the full moon to share with others. Each recorded meditation includes the qualities of the astrological sign as well as the energy that the full moon offers. Meditations are general enough to be used each year during the astrological sign. This program will assist you in maximizing the energy of the full moon and creating your own ceremony. Complete Program Includes:

- The value and benefits of full moon meditation – Introductory audio
- Audio recordings include one recorded full moon ceremony for each astrological sign (12)
- Creating A Full Moon Meditation Ceremony – Downloadable guide
- Downloadable E-book: *Full Moon Meditation and Ceremony*
- Written script for each astrological sign's meditation
- A downloadable "Full Moon Mediation Journal" containing pre-written questions focused on each astrological sign's energy.

Purchase this set at www.theoneheart.org.

Monthly full moon ceremonies and audio meditations posted on the website: www.soulbridging.com. Click on link, *Life Practices*.

Radio interview with CUTV news and podcast with Heidi Robbins, Astrologer, at www.theoneheart.org.

CPSIA information can be obtained
at www.ICGtesting.com
Printed in the USA
FFHW012345030319
50770928-56197FF